AF779273

RXpert SERIES
Student's Companion

INDIAN SYSTEMS OF MEDICINE

RXpert SERIES

M. PHARMACY

INDIAN SYSTEMS OF MEDICINE

Soumya Bhattacharya
Assistant Professor
Guru Nanak Institute of Pharmaceutical Science and Technology
Kolkata, West Bengal

Mithun Rudrapal
Associate Professor
Department of Pharmaceutical Sciences
School of Biotechnology and Pharmaceutical Sciences Vignan's
Foundation for Science, Technology and Research Vadlamudi,
Guntur, India

PharmaMed Press

An imprint of BSP Books Pvt. Ltd.
4-4-309/316, Giriraj Lane,
Sultan Bazar, Hyderabad - 500 001.

Indian Systems of Medicine
***by* Soumya Bhattacharya and Mithun Rudrapal**

© 2025 *by Publisher,* All rights reserved.

No part of this book or parts thereof may be reproduced, stored in a retrieval system or transmitted in any language or by any means, electronic, mechanical, photocopying, recording or otherwise without the prior written permission of the publishers.

Disclaimer: The authors and publishers have taken due care to provide authentic, reliable and up-to-date information related to the subject. However, neither the authors nor the publisher shall be responsible for any liability for any damage caused because of the use of this book. The respective users must check the accuracy from other sources too.

Published by:

PharmaMed Press™

An imprint of BSP Books Pvt. Ltd.
4-4-309/316, Giriraj Lane, Sultan Bazar, Hyderabad - 500 001.
Phone: 040-23445688
E-mail: info@pharmamedpress.net
www.bspbooks.net/www.pharmamedpress.net

ISBN: 978-93-48734-87-7 (Hardback)

PREFACE

हिताहितं सुखं दुःखमायुस्तस्य हिताहितम्। मानं च तच्च यत्रोक्तमायुर्वेदः स उच्यते॥

"Hita hitam sukham dukham ayustasya hita hitam manam cha taccha yatroktam Ayurveda cha uchyate."

– Ayurveda defines life as a balance between what is beneficial and harmful, happiness and sorrow, health and illness, and the measures for leading a meaningful and healthy life.

India's traditional systems of medicine - Ayurveda, Yoga, Siddha, Unani along with Homoeopathy - represent an invaluable repository of healing knowledge rooted in the profound connection between humanity and nature. These time-tested systems, collectively known as Indian Systems of Medicine (ISM), have evolved over centuries and continue to hold relevance in modern healthcare. Their emphasis on balance, prevention, and natural remedies provides unique insights into addressing contemporary health challenges.

This book, "**Indian Systems of Medicine**", is designed as a comprehensive resource for students of **M. Pharm.** in **Pharmacognosy (second semester)**, adhering to the Pharmacy Council of India (PCI) syllabus. It serves as a guide for students to delve into the principles, formulations, and therapeutic applications of Indian systems of medicine while emphasizing their integration with modern scientific standards and research methodologies.

The book covers foundational concepts of Ayurveda, Siddha, Unani, and Homoeopathy alongside insights into **Naturopathy, Yoga, and Aromatherapy**. It explores formulation development, standardization techniques, and Good Manufacturing Practices (GMP) for ISM formulations, as outlined in **Schedule T**. Moreover, it addresses contemporary challenges in quality assurance, safety monitoring, and regulatory frameworks, ensuring students are equipped to meet global standards for herbal and traditional medicines.

The importance of this book extends beyond academics. It provides **AYUSH practitioners** with a robust reference to deepen their understanding of traditional practices while aligning with modern regulatory and quality standards. It also highlights the role of initiatives such as the **Traditional Knowledge Digital Library (TKDL)**, Geographical Indication Bills, and the contributions of institutions like **AYUSH, CCRAS, CCRS,**

CCRH, and CCRU, which are pivotal in preserving, standardizing, and advancing ISM.

As a resource for **Indian Systems of Medicine** and **Indian Knowledge Systems (IKS)**, this book also emphasizes the need to preserve and document the invaluable wisdom of traditional medicine. By doing so, it not only bridges the gap between ancient practices and modern research but also aligns with India's efforts to position IKS on the global healthcare map.

The integration of clinical research, quality control measures, and contemporary challenges in this book ensures its relevance for students, practitioners, researchers, and academicians. It aspires to inspire innovation and exploration while fostering a deeper appreciation for the principles that underpin traditional medicine.

We express our heartfelt gratitude to the entire team of **PharmaMed Press** and **BSP Book Pvt. Ltd. Hyderabad** for their unwavering support in publishing this book. Their dedication to academic excellence has been instrumental in transforming this vision into reality.

We also acknowledge the pivotal roles played by organizations like the **WHO, AYUSH, Indian Pharmacopoeia Commission, ICMR** in crafting guidelines for standardization, safety, and quality assurance of traditional medicines. Their contributions have been integral to ensuring that ISM practices meet global standards while preserving their authenticity.

Lastly, we honor the all of **ISM practitioners and healers** whose wisdom forms the bedrock of Indian systems of medicine.

It is our sincere hope that this book not only meets the academic needs for students of **M. Pharm** in **Pharmacognosy** but also serves as a valuable resource for **AYUSH practitioners** and all stakeholders committed to advancing **Indian Systems of Medicine** as a part of Indian Knowledge Systems while preserving their rich heritage.

- ***Authors***

- It is hard to accurately describe the unique action of a medicine in terms of Rasa, Guna, Virya, and Vipaka.

Although not inexplicable in absolute terms, it requires explanation that goes beyond the Rasa Panchaka.

Some of the behaviors attributed to Prabhava have already been clarified in terms of either modern or traditional Ayurvedic concepts.

As a result, efforts should be made to continue proving a cause-and-effect connection between the medication activities related to prabhava.

Panchakarma (DETOXIFICATION PROCESS)

- Panchakarma refers 5 procedure of Detoxification and cleansing of human body which includes:

Snehan: Snehan refers oil massage. The entire body is massaged with medicated oil in a certain way that encourages the toxins to migrate toward the digestive system.

Additionally, oil massage helps to nourish the nervous system and reduce tension by making the surface and deep tissues soft and supple.

Swedan: Every day, shortly after the snehan, svedana, or sudation, is given. To further loosen the person's toxins, a herbal concoction may be added to the steam. Svedana enhances the flow of toxins into the digestive tract by liquifying them.

Vaman: Vaman is emesis or vomiting induced by Emetics. This procedure helps in cleansing of GIT and helps in eliminating excess mucous and toxins from the body.

Virechan: Virechan is the procedure of removal of toxin through purgation . Natural purgatives are used for this purpose

Basti: Basti is done by delivering medication using enema through rectal route. The therapy offers significant benefits, especially for complex and chronic disorders. Homemade decoction with oils, ghee, or milk are administered to the rectum depending on the type of sickness, and this produces incredibly beneficial results. This therapy is extremely effective against vata-dominant disorders like piles, arthritis, and constipation.

1.2.2 DIAGNOSIS

- In Ayuveda diagnosis is always done of the patient as a whole. The physician diagnose the patients internal physiological characteristics and mental status.

Contents

CHAPTER 1

Fundamental Concepts of Ayurveda, Siddha, Unani and Homeopathy Systems of Medicine

1.1 AYUSH/INDIAN SYSTEMS OF MEDICINE

The Ministry of AYUSH was founded on 9th November 2014 to promote the optimal development and propagation of AYUSH systems of health care. Previously, it was known as the Department of Indian System of Medicine and Homeopathy (ISM&H) and was established in March 1995 and further renamed as Department of Ayurveda, Yoga and Naturopathy, Unani, Siddha and Homoeopathy (AYUSH) in November 2003.

AYUSH department and ministry was created for development of Education, Practice, clinical trial and Research in Ayurveda, Yoga and Naturopathy, Unani, Siddha and Homoeopathy.

1.2 FUNDAMENTAL CONCEPT OF AYURVEDA

Ayurveda is considered as one of the oldest system of medicine in the world. In India it is now considered as one of the recognized system of medicine under Ministry of AYUSH (Ayurveda, Yoga, Unani, Siddha and Homoeopathy). Ayurveda is recognized globally as one the well-organized traditional system of medicine which focuses on holistic approaches of curative as well as preventive medicine.

***The term Ayurveda is derived from two Sanskrit words*:**

Ayu/Ayur means Life

Veda means Sacred Knowledge.

Thus, Ayurveda is considered as Knowledge of Life. As per the Indian Knowledge system, Ayurveda is considered as Fifth veda or additional part of 4th veda Atharva veda.

Basic concept of Ayurveda was expressed in several Sanskrit verses as follows:

"Sarve bhavantu sukhinah, sarve santu niramayah, Sarve bhadrani pashyantu, ma kashchid dukhabhagbhavet."

means: May all be happy, may all be free from diseases, may all see goodness, and may none suffer from sorrow.

"Svasthasya svasthya rakshanam, aturasya vikar prashamanam."

means: The aim of Ayurveda is to protect the health of the healthy person and alleviate the suffering of the diseased.

"Ayur vedah swasthyamaayushyam, aarogyam, abhivridhischa."

means: Ayurveda is the science of life, promoting health, longevity, and well-being of individual.

"Shariramadyam khalu dharma sadhanam."

Translation: The body is the prime means for achieving righteousness and fulfillment of duties. "Samadosha samagnishcha samadhatumala kriyah, Prasannatmendriya manah, svasthya ityabhidhiyate."

means: The balanced state of doshas (bioenergies), agni (digestive fire), and malakriya (excretory functions), along with a cheerful mind and senses, is called good health.

1.2.1 BASIC PRINCIPLES

Three basic theories are associated with human anatomy, physiology, pathophysiology and pharmacology which are considered as pillars of Ayurvedic System of Medicines:

i. Panchamahabhuta Siddhanta

ii. Tridosha

iii. Rasa, Guna, Virya, Vipaka and Prabhava

(i) Panchamahabhuta Siddhanta

According to Ayurveda, Human or every living and non-living entity is composed of 5 (Pancha) maha Bhuta (great element) of this universe. These are:

Prithvi /Earth: which symbolically represent form and shape of the body. This element symbolizes everything that is firm and stable within our body. It refers the skeleto-muscular system of our body.

Apa/Water: maintains moisture in our body, It refers diverse fluids or liquid components present in our body, including saliva, gastric juice, lymph, blood, and particularly water. Water, being a fundamental and essential element, plays a vital role in sustaining human life.

Agni/Fire: represents energy and heat. Agni refers transformation and metabolism of different matters including diet in our body. It also refers our digestion, metabolism, net energy metabolism

Vayu/Air: vital force control respiration; It encompasses the energy generated by various internal movements such as the heartbeat, inhalation, and exhalation. This element sustains the body's internal fire and keeps it burning.

Akasha/Space: It represents hollow spaces of our body including vacuoles or pores responsible for transportation.

Panchamahabhuta is basically represents human anatomy and physiology. It represents skeleto-muscular system, circulatory system, Digestive system and metabolism, respiratory system, vacuoles, cavities, synapses, joints.

(ii) Tridosha

In Ayurveda Tridosha concept highlights human physiology and pathophysiology. Tridosha include 3 humours, Vata, Pitta and Kapha. As per this concept our body is composed three humours and which are in a balanced ratio in individual. Combined effort of these three govern primary vital forces of body. The balanced state of these 3 (which is in definite ratio and varying person to person) is responsible for health and wellness of individual and imbalance lead to disease.

Each dosha is further a combination different element of Panchamahabhuta.

Dosha	Quality	Elements	Function
Vata	Light, Dry and Cool	Air and space	Regulates vital force, different tissues of the body, perception and control mind
Pitta	Hot, Moist and Light	Fire and Water	Digestion, absorption, distribution and excretion of food; regulate body temperature
Kapha	Heavy, Cold and Moist	Water and Earth	Act as coolant and buffer system, regulate excessive heat and dryness

- Tridosha → dhatus= good health

- Tridosha ↘ =disease

dhatus

Health or sickness depends on the presence or absence of a balanced state of the total body matrix including the balance between its different constituents.

Dhatu-mala-siddhanta

A living person is made up of the seven basic tissues known as Dhatu (Rasa, Rakta, Mansa, Meda, Asthi, Majja & Shukra) as well as the body's mala waste products, such as feces (purisha), urine (mutra), and perspiration (sweda). This concept signifies the presence of different tissues:

Rasa: Lymph

Rakta: Blood

Mansa: Muscular tissue

Meda: Adipose tissue

Asthi: Bones

Majja: Bone marrow

Shukra: Reproductive system.

(iii) Rasa, Guna, Virya, Vipaka, and Prabhava

In Ayurveda, pharmacodynamics of medicine is explained by five essential concepts known as Rasapancaka or Panchasheel: Rasa, Guna, Virya, Vipaka, and Prabhava.

- **Rasa:** refers to a therapeutic agent's characteristics, mode of operation, and flavor. Rasas exist in Dravya /Drug because of the "panchabhootas" that it contains.

The six rasas are made up of different Panchamahabhuta elements:

Madhura: Due to the higher amounts of "pruthvi" and "jala,"

Amla: because of the higher amount of "agni"

Lavana: Due to the high levels of "jala" and "agni,"

Thikta: Due to the increased presence of "akasa" and "vayu,"

Katu - because of the enhanced 'agni' and 'vayu' presence.

Kashaya: due to an increase in "pruthvi" and "vayu"

- **Guna:** The Guna refers the quality of medicines and affects the tridoshas, effect of Guna of drug supersedes its Rasa. There are twenty gunas as given below.

- guru (heavy) - laghu (light)
- mandam (slow) - theekshanam (fast)
- seetham (cold)- ushanam (hot)
- snigdha (oily)- rooksha (rough)
- sleshmam - gharam
- sandram - dravam
- sookshmam (micro)- sthoolam (macro)
- visadam - pichilam
- sthiram (static)- chalam (mobile)
- mrudu (soft)- katinam (hard)

- **Virya:** The potency by which a drug acts are known as *Virya* which refers the ultra chemical action of the drugs. It may be of two types-
    - ***Ushna*** (hot)
    - ***Shita*** (cold)

  Virya influences the balance of tridosha. Shita virya indicates kapha and ushna virya indicates pitta.

- **Vipaka**

Vipaka refers the formation of end product after digestion and metabolic transformation.

***It is of three types*:**

- Madhura/Sweet (affects Kapha)
- Amla/Sour (affects Pitta)
- Katu / astringent (affects vata)
- Prabava
- Prabhava is an attribute of a substance that leads to behaviours distinct from and in opposition to those attributed to rasa, guna, virya, and vipaka. Prabhava stands for the distinctive and unique behaviors of substances that are not explicable in terms of the pharmacological behaviours of their many independent constituent principles. This idea explains why the entire medicine is safer and more effective than its individual parts.

The diagnosis also involves the following examinations:

- General physical examination
- Pulse examination (essential for the examination and determination of Prakruti of Tridosha, determined with the help of 3 fingers)
- Urine examination
- Examination of the faeces
- Examination of tongue and eyes
- Examination of skin and ear including tactile and auditory functions.

However, in modern days pathological and other diagnostic tools are used for the diagnosis.

1.2.3 TREATMENT BRANCHES

Types of Treatment

The treatment of disease can broadly be classified as

- Kayachikitsa (Medicine)
- Salyayantra (surgery)
- Salakya chikitsa (ENT)
- Kaumāra-bhṛtya /balyachikitsa(paediatrics)
- Vishagara-vairodh Tantra (Toxicology)
- Bhūtavidyā(Mental ilness)
- Rasāyantantra(Promotional health/rejuvination)
- Vājīkaraṇatantra(aphrodisiac)

1.3 UNANI SYSTEM OF MEDICINE

Legendary Scholar Avicenna/*Ibn e Sina* defines Unani System of Medicine as "It is the science in which we learn various states of body in health and when not in health and the means by which health is likely to be lost and when lost, is likely to be restored"

Genesis of Unani Medicine

- The origins of Unani medicine are based on the doctrines of the ancient Greek (Unan) physicians Hippocrates and Galen.
- Further it was later developed and modified through systematic experiment by the Arabs, especially by Islamic scholar-physician Ibn e Sina or Avicenna.

- In time of Caliphate (the political-religious Muslim state which was initiated in 632 CE), the large number of Greek knowledge was translated into Arabic language. Along with different discipline, knowledge on principles of medicine was translated in Arabic. With additional contributions of medical knowledge from different parts of the Middle East and South Asia, Unani medicine is also represented as Arabian, or Islamic, medicine.
- Arabic scholars and physicians enriched the system of medicine with their own contributions and expertise.
- Unani Medicines was further enriched by incorporating the best practices available in the contemporary systems of traditional medicines practiced in Iraq, Persia, Egypt, Syria, India, China and other Middle East countries.
- It was further evolved into a more descriptive medical system in middle age era by Persian and Arabian physicians, like Rhazes (al-Razi), Avicenna (Ibn-e- Sina), Al-Zahrawi, and Ibn Nafis.

1.3.1 UNANI IN INDIA

- Unani system of medicine was introduced in India with the patronage of The Delhi Sultans (rulers). They employed and supported the scholars and physicians of Unani System. During 13th and 17th century A.D. Unani Medicine was its peak in India.
- However, the system faced severe challenge during the British rule in India.
- During British rule, it was mainly Sharifi family in Delhi, the Azizi family in Lucknow and the Nizam of Hyderabad due supported Unani System and also employed as a Royal medicine.
- The Unani system of the Medicine was further revived during the struggle of Indian freedom movement.
- Hakim Ajmal Khan, was also one of the foremost freedom fighters and renowned physician in the country who established an Ayurvedic and Unani Tibbia College (inaugurate in February 13, 1921 by Mahatma Gandhi) and Hindustani Dawakhana a pharmaceutical company for manufacturing of Ayurvedic and Unani medicine in Delhi in 1916.

- After independence the Unani System was officially integrated as Indian systems of medicine under the patronage of the Central Government.
- Today the Unani system of medicine has recognized practitioners, hospitals and educational and research institutions and considered as one of the AYUSH medicine.
- The Central Council for Research in Unani Medicine (CCRUM) is an autonomous organization under the Ministry of AYUSH, Government of India was established in 1978. The CCRUM as the apex government organization for research in Unani Medicine has been involved in research and clinical trials of Unani system of medicine.

Mohammad Ajmal Khan (11 February 1868 – 29 December 1927).

1.3.2 PRINCIPLE OF UNANI MEDICINE

Unani medicine was originated in Greece almost 2500 years back and evolved as herbo- animo- mineral medicne (Approximately 90% herbal, 4-5% animal and 5-6 % mineral). With a deep philosophy and scientific concept this medicine was developed as a holistic medicine.

***Unani system of medicine was evolved on the basis of four humors of Hippocratic medicine*:**

The four humors of Hippocratic medicine are:

- **black bile (Greek: μέλαινα χολή, *melaina chole*):** The word "melancholy" evolved from Greek μέλαινα χολή (*melaina kholé*) meaning 'black bile'. Excessive or unnatural black bile secreted by the spleen may results Depression.
- **yellow bile (Greek: ξανθη χολή, *xanthe chole*):** Excessive release of yellow bile causes aggression, and reciprocally excess anger leads to liver disorders and imbalances in the humours.
- **phlegm (Greek: φλέγμα, *phlegma*):** Phlegm is related to apathetic behaviour, as preserved in the word "phlegmatic'.
- **blood (Greek: αἷμα, *haima*)** The blood was believed to be produced exclusively by the liver. It was associated with a sanguine nature (enthusiastic, active, and social)

Different psychological expression due to predominance of 4 humours

The well-known Hippocratic four-humor theory serves as the basis for the Unani system's main principle. This assumes that the body is made up of four humors blood, phlegm, yellow bile, and black bile.

Basic physiological principles *of Unani (Al-Umoor al-tabiyah)*:

According to these, human health is maintained by the harmonious arrangement of *al-umoor al-tabiyah*, or the seven basic physiological principles.

- Arkan (Elements)
- Mizaj (Temperament)
- Akhlat (Humors)
- Aaza (Organs)
- Arwah (Spirits)
- Quwa (Faculties)
- Afaal (Functions)
- these seven natural components maintain the balance of human health in the natural constitution by interacting with each other,
- Every individual constitution has a self-controlling capacity or power, called *tabiyat* (or *mudabbira-e-badan*; *vis medicatrix naturae* in Latin), or to maintain the seven components in equilibrium.

Arkan and *mizaj*: elements and temperament

Arz (earth), maa (water), nar (fire), and hawa (air) are the basic four simple, indivisible entities that create Arkan, which also makes up all other creatures in the universe.

The four arkan's activities and interactions (imtizaj) have predictable results.

Due to ulfat-e-keemiyah (the body's acceptance of a medicine) and nafarat-e-keemiyah (the body's rejection of a medicine), these elements regularly transform into different states of creation and degradation.

Expert Unani physicians/hakims assert that they are able to perceive, identify, and understand such states.

- The essential *mizaj* (temperaments) are of 4 types including hot, cold, moist, and dry.
- These are further compounded of those single temperaments like, hot and dry, hot and moist, cold and dry, and cold and moist.
- The and *mizaj* is equilibrium of the individual's elemental combination, as regulated by *tabiyat*, provides a stable constitution or health.
- Therefore, *mizaj* plays an essential role in Unani to characterize a person's normal state (physical, mental, and social), as well as the nature of a disease.

Each of the four elements/Arkan has its own temperament/Mizaj as follows:

Element	Temperament
Air	Hot and Moist
Earth	Cold and Dry
Fire	Hot and Dry
Water	Cold and Moist

Principle of Akhlat/Humours:

As previously mentioned that, Unani Medicine was evolved on the doctrine of Hippocrates 4 humours and which was further refined by Galen and Avicenna.

Principle of Akhlat represented by:

dam (blood),

balgham (phlegm),

safra (yellow bile),

sauda (black bile).

- These humours represent human dispositions respectively, sanguine, phlegmatic, choleric, and melancholic. Each person has a specific humoral makeup, determined by the predominance of a given humour. The quality and quantity of the humours in an individual is fixed and affected by environmental factors.
- The theory of humours (*nazaria-e-akhlat*), which is the pillar of practice of Unani medicine. Their continuous action and reaction causes the breakdown

of complex macromolecules into simpler compounds, which are further incorporated into the body as a fluid.

- Aaza (Organs)

  Aaza refers various organs of the human body. The health or disease of individual human being's organ regulates state of health of the entire body.

- Arwah (Spirits)

  Ruh (Spirit) is a volatile substance, produced from the inspired air, it regulates all the metabolic activities of the body. It burns the akhlat latifah to produce quwa (powers) and hararat ghariziyah, which is considered as a source of vitality for all the organs of the body. These are essential in the diagnosis and treatment of disease.

- Quwa (Faculties)

  Quwa / Faculties are of 3 types including:

- Quwa Tabiyah (Natural power): refers the metabolism and reproduction. Liver mainly regulates the metabolism which control the cellular metabolism in other tissues and finally regulates the growth and development.
- Quwa Nafsaniyah (Psychic power): indicates nervous and psychic power and regulated by brain. This power helps in perception and helps in response to external stimuli.
- Quwa Haywaniyah (Vital power) enables all the organs to accept the effect of psychic power/ Quwa Nafsaniyah. This power is situated in the heart.

Afaal (Functions)

- This component indicates the functions and movements of all the organs of the body. In healthy individual, the various organs are not only in proper shape but also in their respective functions.
- This is essential to have full knowledge of the functions of the human body in full detail.

Prevention of Disease in Unani

Unani medicine emphasized on environmental influence in disease prevention. Six essentials pre-requisites (Asbab Sitta e Zaroriayah) have been mentioned for the promotion of health and prevention of disease which are

- Air (Hawa)
- Food and drinks (Makool wo Mashroob)
- Bodily movement and repose (*Harkat-wo-sakoon-e-jismiah)*
- Psychic movement and repose (*Harkat-o-sakoon nafsaniah)*
- Sleep and wakefulness (*Naum-o-yaqzah*)
- Evacuation and retention (*Ihtebas* and *istifragh*)

1.3.3 TREATMENT IN UNANI

Unani Medicine has mainly 4 categories of treatment strategies /therapy which are as follows:

Regimental therapy (Ilaj-bil-Tadbir): This is a special technique/physical methods of treatment to enhance the constitution of body by detoxification and elimination of waste materials and enhancing body's immunity to protect health. It includes:

- Venesectio (Fasd)
- Cupping (Al-hijama)
- Sweating (Tareeq)
- Diuresis (Idrar-e-baul)
- Turkish bath (Hamam)
- Massage (Dalk, Malish)
- Counter irritation
- Cauterization (Amal-e-Kae)
- Purging (Ishal)
- Vomiting (Qai)
- Exercise (Riyazat)
- Leeching (Taleeq-e-Alaq)

- **Dieto therapy (Ilaj-bil-Ghiza):** In Unani, by regulating the quality and quantity of food several diseases are treated successfully. Certain foods are considered as laxative, diuretic and diaphoretic.

Pharmacotherapy (Ilaj-bil-Dawa)

This type of treatment involves the utilization of herbal, animal or mineral drugs which also has their own temperament and comparing them with the **patient's** temperament.

- Drugs are used in the form of powders, decoctions, infusion, Jawarish, Majoon, Khamira, Syrup and tablets etc. The system has set rules for prescribing alternative drugs.

Surgery (Ilaj-bil-Yad):

Even though the Unani system is credited with being a pioneer in surgery and having created its own tools and processes, this therapy has relatively little practical use. Only some minor surgery is currently performed with the technology.

1.3.4 VARIOUS UNANI FORMS OF DRUG

Preparation	Drug character
Saffof	Powder crude drug
Sharbat	Aqueous concentrate with sugar
Mazoom	Powder drug with honey
Jawarish	Concentrated mazoon
Araq	Distilled aromatic water
Kohal	Ophthalmic formulation
Marham	Drug in ointment bases
Joshanda	Decoction
Khaishanda	Infusion
Shiaf and battis	Suppositories and Pessaries

1.4 HOMOEOPATHIC SYSTEM OF MEDICINES

Homoeopathy is a recognized medical system in India through the **Homeopathy Central Council Act, 1973.** Homoepathic system has blended well into the ethos and traditions of Indian holistic system that it has been recognized as one of the national systems of medicine.

Homoeopathy is derived from two Greek words:

Homoios (Like) and pathos(suffering);

Homeopathy can be defined as a "dynamic, holistic and vitalistic system of individualistic drug therapeutics, based on the law of similars, potentially capable to cure diseases that are curable and relieves symptoms of incurable nature".

1.4.1 GENESIS OF HOMOEOPATHY

Homoeopathy was initiated by **Christian Friedrich Samuel Hahnemann(**10 April 1755 – 2 July 1843). Dr. Hahnemann was a qualified allopathic physician.

Christian Friedrich Samuel Hahnemann (10 April 1755 – 2 July 1843)

similia similibus curantur

In 1790, Hahnemann applied and evaluated the effect of antimalarial drug Cinchona in his own healthy body.

- Surprisingly, After taking the cinchona bark, symptoms of intermittent fever(malaria) were developed in his healthy body and also observed that disappeared on dicontinuation.
- This observation leads Hahnemann to an idea that was published in 1796 as "Essay on a New Principle for Ascertaining the Curative Power of Drugs", which was followed in 1810 by his famous work The Organon of the Healing Art/medicine.
- Further sequences of experiments lead to development of different principles of Homoeopathy

1.4.2 HOMOEPATHY IN INDIA

- India was exposed to homoeopathy by early 19th Century. John Martin Honigberger (1795-1869), Royal physician of the Punjab in the time Maharaja Ranjit Singhji published his book entitled, 'Thirty five years in the East, Adventures, Discoveries, Experiments and Historical Sketches relating to Punjab and Kashmir, in connection with Medicine, Botany, Pharmacy etc., together with an original Materia Medica and a Medical Vocabulary in four European and five Eastern Languages' in 1852,
- Honigberger introduced homoeopathic system of Medicine in India in 1839
- After which, In the middle of 19th century when homoeopathy was gaining popularity gradually, a landlord, Babu Rajendra Lal Dutta (1818-89) in the supported and established Native Homoeopathic Hospital and Free Dispensary. [Ghosh'18]
- In, 16th Feb, in 1867, Mahendra Lal Sircar (1833-1904), the great allopathic physician of Calcutta and patron of Indian science declared publicly about his belief on homoeopathic system of medicine.
- Within one year, he published the first homoeopathic journal of Asia, 'The Calcutta Journal of Medicine' in Jan. 1868. In 1867, the first homoeopathic hospital in Benaras was established by Mr. Ironside.
- In 1881, Pratap Chandra Majumdar associated with M M Bose and D N Roy established 'The Calcutta School of Homoeopathy' on the 14th February in 1881 which was further renamed as 'Calcutta Homoeopathic Medical College'.
- In 1973, Homeopathy Central Council Act was enacted and recognized as one of the national system of medicine in India.
- On the 10th December 1975, National Institute of Homoeopathy was established for the purpose of research and clinical trials in Homoepathy.

1.4.3 BASIC PRINCIPLES OF HOMOEOPATHY

Homoeopathy is based on following principles:

- principle of individualization
- Principle of similia
- Principle of simplex
- Principle of minimum
- Law of proving
- Law of dynamization/potentization
- Vital force

Principle of individualization

According to Homoeopathy, no 2 individuals are same (considering the physical /genetic makeup), so that the same disease affecting 2 different persons cannot be similar. Responses against same disease by 2 different individuals are different. So, two different individuals may received different medicine/remedy although suffering from same disease.

Principle of similia

This law explained that the selected treatment by medicine can cause a variety of symptoms in healthy people that are similar to those seen in patients.

- The Similia Similibus Curentur principle, states that likes should be treated similarly, supports this rule. According to the Law of Similar, every homoeopathic remedy has been scientifically proven to have the ability to cause a specific set of symptoms in healthy people. When these symptoms match those of a natural disease, the remedy acts as a therapeutic agent and aids the body in treating the disorder.

Principle of simplex

This principle governs that only one homeopathic medicine should be prescribed at a time from Homoeopathic Materia Medica and directs to choose and administer such a single remedy, which is most similar to the sick person's symptoms. Here drug profile is matched with patient's symptoms profile.

Principle of minimum

- Minimum dose should be administered, so that when administered, there is no toxic effect will be observed on the body.

Law of proving

- Drug Proving *is the systematic process of getting knowledge of the substances intended for the cure of diseases.*

- It is the process of finding the pathogenetic power of medicine by administering it in to the healthy individuals volunteer of different age and both the sex. It is also considered as Homeopathic Pathogenetic Trial (HPT).
- **Law of dynamisation/potentization**
- Main fundamental of Homoeopathy is based on the concept of potentization of medicine / Drugs by which they retain maximum medicinal powers without producing any toxic action on the body.
- It was found experimentally by Dr. Hahnemann that when he diluted drugs are powerfully succussed (a specified process in homoeopathy), they achieved strong and long medicinal powers.

this technique of producing drugs can acheive:

(1) - The toxicity of drug used in crude dosage have sequentially reduced

(2) – enhance the hidden (dynamic potency) medicinal properties of the drug.

Method of Potentization

- ➢ Serial dilution
- ➢ Succussion
- ➢ Trituration

Serial Dilution: In serial dilution, mother tincture (extract of crude drugs) is serially diluted with the help of vehicle (alcohol/lactose etc.) Centesimal dilutions, frequently referred to as "C" dilutions, are the most typical form. One part of the Mother Tincture and nine parts of ethanol are combined in a brand-new vial to create the 1C, which is then vigorously shaken (succussed). As opposed to the Mother Tincture, which is a 1/10 dilution of the plant itself, the end result is a 1/100 dilution of the plant. By combining 1 part of the 1C with 99 parts of ethanol in a fresh vial and successing, the 2C is produced. Frequently, the 3C is produced by successing a mixture of 1 part of the 2C and 99 parts of ethanol in a fresh vial.

Similarly, 1/10 dilution is known as X or decimal dilution.

- ➢ **Succussion:** It is the essential step of enhancing potency of drug by continuous shaking and striking of the tincture with vehicle against a solid support.

plant material/crude drug → soaking in alcohol → mother tincture → 1 part MT+99part inert vehicle+10 succusion → 1C

Homeopathy's unique idea of a vital force recognizes the presence of a spirit-like energy that powers living things both in health and disease. This idea, which has nothing to do with religion, contends that a living cell's cytoplasm, mitochondria, nucleus, DNA, and RNA are not all that constitutes life, just as the components of blood, bone, and muscles are not all that constitute a living being. Homeopathy holds that every living thing possesses an inherent force that keeps its functions in balance and distinguishes between the living and the dead. The vital force defines the level of mental, bodily, and spiritual wellness in that living being.

1.4.4 DIAGNOSIS

- Homoeopath generally collect extreme details of case history
- Major symptoms location, sensation, modality and concomitant is investigated
- The study of detailed case history helps to build up a 'symptoms picture' of patient; this matched with 'drug picture'

1.4.5 MEDICINE IN HOMOEOPATHY

Sources of Homoeopathic Medicine

Source	Example
Plant origin	Aconitum napellus, Strychnos nuxvomica, Allium cepa
Animal origin	Blatta orientalis, Tarentula hispanica, Apis mellifica
Mineral and chemical origin	Mag Phos, Natrum Muriaticum
Sarcodes	Adrenalin (secretion of medulla of supra-renal gland) Pancreatinum (extract from pancreas of beef)

Table contd....

Nosodes	Influenzinum, Anthracinum- lysate obtained without addition of antiseptic from the liver of rabbit suffering from Anthrax. Tuberculinum avis
Imponderabilia	Xray, Magnet, Moonlight

Sarcodes: Homeopathic medicines made from healthy animal tissues or secretions. In Greek, sarcode means fleshly.

Nosodes: Homeopathic medicines prepared from disease products from humans or animals; from pathogenic organisms or their metabolic products; or from decomposition products of animal organs.

Imponderabilia: Homeopathic medicines prepared from energy, emanating from natural and physical reactions. It means "not weighable", i.e. which have no perceptible weights. They are energy forms such as sunlight (Sol), magnetic fields (Magnetis Polus Australis), radiation (X-ray).

1.5 SIDDHA SYSTEM OF MEDICINE

One of the earliest known medical systems is Siddha. This medical approach has its origin in Tamil traditional medicine from south India. Ancient India had a very strong following for this system. (Estimated age: greater than 10,000 years). The Siddha system of medicine is regarded as one of the oldest types of conventional medicine.

It was believed that Maharshi Agasthya introduced this system in Southern part of India.

The Siddha system, which has Thamizh antecedents and is related to that language, is the final example of an Indian classical language still in use today.

According to recent archeological findings, the Siddha system dates back to around 10000 BC. The Thamizh civilization, the only prehistoric civilization still in existence, is what makes up the Siddha system.

1.5.1 BASIC PRINCIPLES

The Siddha system of medicine considers the universe as a macrocosm and the human race as a microcosm. Man is, in other words, a tiny cosmos all by himself. According to this theory, man is made up of the same five fundamental elements that make up the universe: Earth, Water, Fire, Air, and Space. The genesis and formation of these fundamental components, as well as their involvement in the formation of every substance in the world and in people, are all explained by the Pancheekaranam theory (Five Fold Combination) of Siddha science.

Each of these five elements is considered to have two qualities, namely subtle and gross, according to Pancheekaranam doctrine. These factors can never function separately; they always coordinate their actions. Different chemicals can be created by combining them in different ratios. As a result, this theory asserts the existence of 96 fundamental components, which is the fundamental idea driving this holistic medical science.

- These 96 fundamental elements that make up the human body are primarily conditioned by:

Vaatham, Pitham, and Kabham are the three humours that make up Uyir Thathukkal (also known as Trithodam or Mukkutram). Udal Thathukkal, or the seven tissues that make up Saaram, Senneer, Oon, Konzhuppu, Enbu, Moolai, and Sukkilam, are the physical constituents. The 96 elements cover every human's physical, physiological, psychological, and intellectual characteristics.

Relationship between the basic elements (*Panchabhootam*), five sense organs (*Pori*) and functions of these sense organs (*Pulan*)

Panchabhootam	Sense organs	Functions of sense organs
Earth (*Nilam*)	Nose	Smell
Water (*Neer*)	Mouth	Taste
Fire (*Thee*)	Eyes	Vision
Air (*Kaatru*)	Skin	Touch
Space (*Aagayam*)	Ears	Hearing

The term "life force" is also known as "Uyir Thathukkal" (Three Humours). The three humours, or Vaatham, Pitham, and Kabham in Siddha, are in charge of creating, maintaining, and destroying the human body and health. Our body remains healthy while they are in the state of balance (4:2:1—the ratio in which they exist) but becomes ill or dies when this ratio is disturbed.

Vatam: 'Air' and 'Space' are represented by Vaatham. All mental and physical movements are controlled by it. Vaatham controls sensory and motor functions. **Vaatham** is distributed throughout the body, however it is most prominent below the navel.

Pitham: Pitham is in charge of maintaining health and represents the element "fire" (thee) in our body. It controls the chest and abdominal regions and keeps the body at the proper temperature for appropriate physiology. Within our body, it manifests itself in five different ways.

Kavam: Earth and water combine to form the compound Kavam. It is in charge of endurance, body build, strength, and joint movements. It controls the area around the head and neck. There are five variations of Kavam.

1.5.2 DIAGNOSIS

In order to make a diagnosis, an examination of eight items—known as "enn vakaith thervu" is necessary. Which are:

1. **Na (tongue):** White in kapha, ulcerated in anemia, yellow or crimson in pitha, black in vatha.
2. **Varna (color):** Vatha is dark, pitha is yellow or red, and kapha is pale.
3. **Svara (voice):** Low-pitched in kapha, slurred in drunkenness, high-pitched in pitha.
4. **Kan (eyes):** Muddy conjunctiva; pitta-related yellowish or red; kapha-related pale.
5. **Sparisam (touch):** Vata is dry, pitha is warm, kapha is cool, and different areas of the body perspire differently.
6. **Mala (stool):** Vatha is represented by black stools, pitha by yellow, kapha by pale, and raja by dark red.
7. **Neer (urine):** Early morning urine is examined; straw colour indicates indigestion, reddish-yellow colour in excessive heat, rose in blood pressure, saffron colour in jaundice, and looks like meat washed water in renal disease.
8. **Nadi (pulse):** The confirmatory method recorded by radial artery.

1.5.3 SIDDHA SYSTEM DRUG

The Siddhars used three types of drugs: Thavara (herbal goods), Dhathu (inorganic substances), and Jangamam (animal products). Dhathu medicines are further classed as follows: a) Uppu - (Water-soluble inorganic substances or drugs that give out vapour when put into fire), b) Pashanam - (Drugs not dissolved in water but emit vapour when fired), c) Uparasam - (Similar to pashanam but differ in action), d) Loham - (Not dissolved in water but melt when fired), e) Rasam - (Drugs which are soft) , and f) Ghandhagam - (Drugs which are insoluble in water, like sulphur).

- The medications employed in siddha medicine were categorised according to five characteristics: Suvai (taste) Guna (persona). Veerya (strength) Mahimai (activity) and Pirivu (class).

CHAPTER 2

Naturopathy, Yoga and Aromatherapy Practices

2.1 NATUROPATHY

Naturopathy is one of the popular holistic system of medicine which integrates modern scientific knowhows with ancient philosophy of healing based on natural selfcare. According to World Naturopathic Federation (2021), Naturopathy is defined as, "A system of healthcare with a deep history of traditional philosophies and practices and with medically trained practitioners who utilize a breadth of natural treatment modalities and practices in the provision of person-centered healthcare. The term naturopathy includes both naturopathy and naturopathic medicine."

According to the manifesto of the British Naturopathic Association, "Naturopathy is a system of treatment which lays emphasis on the existence of the vital curative force within the body."

Naturopathy relies on self-healing power of nature and uses natural therapies like dietetics, botanical medicines, fasting, exercise, natural powers, lifestyle management in holistic way to cure and prevent diseases. Naturopathic medicine can improve the **vitalism** (**"**An inherent capacity to live, grow, develop, and heal") in individual.

Naturopathy, a unique form of traditional and complementary medicine, is widely practiced globally and has deep historical and cultural ties to Europe. It draws heavily from traditional nature-based healing methods predating the 18th century, rooted in the observation of natural interactions between plants, animals, and their environment.

2.1.1 HISTORY AND DEVELOPMENT OF NATUROPATHY

Naturopathy was introduced to the United States during the 1800s, originating from Germany. The term "Naturopathy" was introduced by John Scheel in 1895 and gained prominence through the efforts of Benedict Lust, regarded as the Father of modern Naturopathy. Lust played a crucial role in popularizing Naturopathy in the US in the early 20th century. The Naturopathy movement, which began in Germany and spread to other Western nations, initially focused on water-based therapies, also known as hydrotherapy. Vincent Priessnitz played a significant role in popularizing water cure therapy globally, followed by contributions from other notable figures. Louis Kuhne is noteworthy for introducing the concept of the Unity of Diseases and Treatment, providing a theoretical foundation for this approach.

2.1.2 NATUROPATHY AS INDIAN SYSTEMS OF MEDICINE

Indian sub-continent is pioneer of holistic medicine and well acquainted with self-healing concepts of nature from Ayurveda and Upanishads from dawn of the civilization. It is expected that, Indian population should accept the power of natural healing and principles of naturopathy.

The beginning of modern of Naturopathy in India began with the translation of Louis Kuhne's book "New Science of Healing" from Germany. This translation into the Telugu language was undertaken by Shri D. Venkat Chelapati Sharma in 1894, followed by translations into Hindi and Urdu in 1904 by Shri Shroti Kishan Swaroop. These efforts significantly enhanced the widespread dissemination of Naturopathy.

Adolf Just's book "Return to Nature" deeply influenced Mahatma Gandhi, leading him to become a staunch advocate of Naturopathy. Gandhi wrote numerous articles promoting Naturopathy in his newspaper Harijan and conducted experiments on himself, his family, and members of his ashram. Gandhi also frequented Dr. Dinshaw Mehta's Nature Cure Clinic in Pune from 1934 to 1944. In honor of Gandhi's influence, the Government of India established the **National Institute of Naturopathy** in 1986. Gandhi's advocacy attracted support from many Gandhian leaders, including former Prime Minister Shri Morarji Desai, Ex-President Shri V.V. Giri, Acharya Vinoba Bhave, Ex-Governor of Gujarat Shri Shrimannarayanji, and Shri Balkova Bhave, who all played pivotal roles in advancing this health movement.

The National Institute of Naturopathy (NIN), located at "Bapu Bhavan" on Tadiwala Road behind Pune Railway Station in Pune, is an autonomous organization under the Ministry of AYUSH, Government of India. This historical site, named after Mahatma Gandhi, who spent a total of 156 days here whenever he visited Pune since 1944, holds significant importance. Previously known as the "Nature Cure Clinic and Sanatorium," it was operated by the late Dr. Dinshaw K. Mehta. The All India Nature Cure Foundation Trust was established within this facility, with Mahatma Gandhi serving as its lifelong

Chairman. Many national and international activities were conducted by Gandhiji from this location.

Presently, In India, naturopathy is part of the Indian Systems of Medicine referred to as AYUSH (Ayurveda, Yoga and Naturopathy, Unani, Siddha, Sowa-Rigpa and Homeopathy). Several renowned physician and naturopath like Dr. Mahavir Prasad Poddar, Dr. Janaki Sharan Varma, Shri Sharan Prasad, Dr. Vitthal Das Modi, Dr. Kulranjan Mukherjee, Dr. Khushi Ram Dilkash, Dr. S.J. Singh, Dr. Hiralal, Dr. Sukhram Das, Dr. J. M. Jussawala, Dr. Sukhbir Singh Rawat, Acharya K. Laxman Sharma, Dr. B. Vijaya Laxmi, Dr. Ganga Prasad Gaur Nahar, Dr. M.M. Bhamgara, Dr. VegiRaju Krishnam Raju, etc. have taken significant role to promote the naturopathy in India.

In India, a five and half year's degree course of Bachelor of Naturopathy & Yogic Sciences (BNYS) is offered in different colleges.

2.1.3 PRINCIPLES AND PHILOSOPHIES OF NATUROPATHY

Naturopathy is based on holistic and cultural ethos of early Western Medicines. The fusion of naturopathic philosophies and principles into a biomedical comprehension of health and illness, which characterizes the naturopathic profession.

Naturopathy is based on the following philosophies:

Vitalism: Vitalism believes that living organism contains a force or energy distinct from non-living in addition to physical and chemical elements of life and which is inherent capacity to live, grow, develop, and heal.

This philosophy suggests the existence of an inherent self-organizing force within all living beings, acknowledging life's inherent order and intelligence. This innate intelligence, which energizes every individual, extends beyond mere physical or chemical aspects to regulate life, health, and the healing process. Naturopathic methods enhance and assist this natural process by identifying and eliminating barriers to health and recovery, and also promote an internal and external conditions.

Holism: The philosophy of holiness in naturopathic treatment believes on consideration entire person or body instead of considering a particular part or organ which is suffering from ailment ("The body is a complex adaptive system that exists as a unified whole").

This principle believes that the spiritual, psychological, functional, and structural aspects of a person are interconnected and interdependent. When treating an individual, the holistic approach treats intrapersonal and interpersonal dynamics, along with that interaction of each person with their environment, external influences, and social interactions.

Naturopathy is based on following 7 principles:

I. **First, Do No Harm (primum non nocere):** Naturopathy emphasizes on safe and non-invasive approach of treatment without any adverse effect which never suppress or destruct natural self-healing power of individual.

II. **Healing Power of Nature (vis medicatrix naturae):** Naturopath or naturopathic doctors support, facilitate and enhance the natural power of healing. They identify the root cause of disease and address the obstacles for natural healing powers. Naturopathy treatments such as herbal medicines, optimal nutrition, adequate hydration, exercise and bodywork, the vis medicatrix naturae stimulate the innate healing process.

There are various instances of the vis medicatrix naturae in human health, such as:

- When a finger is injured, the body initiates a natural healing process through the innate inflammatory cascade, releasing chemicals that stem bleeding and kickstart tissue repair.
- Fever serves as a natural defense mechanism against infections, with the benefits of experiencing a febrile state generally outweighing any negative effects.
- Vomiting or diarrhea occurs as the body's response to food poisoning.
- Aligned fractures often undergo spontaneous healing.

III. **Treat the Cause (tolle causam):** Instead of merely addressing the symptoms, naturopaths identify the root cause of disease and normal healthy condition. Using a multi-dimensional approach, naturopaths explore a wide range of factors which may influence the imbalance in health and cause diseases. These factors may include genetic predisposition, social, environmental influence, medical interventions encompass both past and present utilization of prescribed medications for medical and cosmetic purposes, surgical procedures, and other medical treatments.

IV. **Treat the Whole Person (tolle totum):** The naturopathic approach to healthcare prioritizes the individual, adhering to a "person-centered" philosophy. By embracing the principle of "Treat the Whole Person", naturopathy adopts a holistic care model, acknowledging that the entirety of an individual surpasses the mere sum of their parts. Naturopathic medicine emphasizes the importance of harmonious functioning across all aspects of an individual for achieving quality of life as well as optimal health. Recognizing the complex interplay of factors in health and disease, naturopathy advocates for comprehensive and personalized approaches to assessment, diagnosis, and treatment.

V. **Doctor as Teacher (docere):** Naturopath doctors serve as an educator to sensitize, empower patients to more accountable to maintain their own health. Here doctors act as a lifestyle coach for patient and provide proper social, physical and mental support to an individual who can take proper decision on their healthy life style

VI. **Health Promotion and Disease Prevention:** Preventing disease and achieving optimal health are central goals of naturopathic practice. Naturopathic care emphasizes collaborating with individuals and communities to sustain health and enhance wellness across all life stages. This holistic approach to healthcare and prevention entails applying naturopathic principles concurrently, identifying and addressing the underlying causes of symptoms and diseases, devising comprehensive treatment strategies that leverage the healing potential of nature, educating patients about recommended lifestyle changes to attain complete health, and empowering patients to actively participate in their journey toward wellness. Community Education is one of important approaches of naturopath to aware community people about promotion of health, quality of life and preventing diseases.

VII. **Wellness and Wellbeing:** Naturopaths support the wellbeing of individual wellness rather than simply just avoiding or addressing illness. These wellness include mental, physical, social and spiritual wellness and supporting body's natural balance and innate healing powers.

2.1.4 SALIENT FEATURES OF THE NATUROPATHY TREATMENT

Naturopathy embodies a holistic approach to human well-being and serves as a platform for promoting healthy living. Its core principles emphasize the significance of a nutritious diet, clean water, physical activity, fasting, exposure to sunlight, and effective stress management. The key features of Naturopathy include:

- All diseases, barring traumatic and environmental conditions, share a common origin and treatment approach. They stem from the accumulation of unhealthy substances within the body, and their treatment involves eliminating these toxins.
- Naturopathy posits that the primary cause of diseases is the buildup of harmful substances in the body, with bacteria and viruses acting as secondary triggers. These pathogens infiltrate the body only when it harbors accumulated toxins.
- Acute illnesses are viewed as the body's innate efforts to self-heal, while chronic diseases arise from incorrect treatments or the suppression of acute ailments.
- Naturopathy relies on the inherent healing power of nature, affirming that the human body possesses innate mechanisms to ward off diseases and restore health.

- Healing in Naturopathy targets the entire body system, addressing ailments comprehensively.
- Naturopathy is known for its effectiveness in managing and treating chronic conditions within a relatively shorter timeframe.
- Treatment in Naturopathy aims to bring suppressed diseases to the surface and eliminate them permanently.
- Naturopathy addresses all dimensions of human health, including mental, physical, social, and spiritual aspects.
- Viewing the body as a unified entity, Naturopathy considers "food as medicine" and avoids reliance on external medications.
- Spiritual practices, such as prayer, are deemed integral to Naturopathic treatment, respecting individual faith traditions.

2.1.5 TYPES AND DIFFERENT MODALITIES OF NATUROPATHY

2.1.5.A DIET THERAPY

Diet therapy is one of the important part of naturopathy and naturopathic foods are categorized on the basis of their alkaline acidic residue component in body Following 3 types of diets are considered under naturopathic diet therapy.

Eliminative Diet	Soothing Diet	Constructive Diet
•The Eliminative diet prioritizes detoxifying the body, incorporating foods that promote rejuvenation. •Typically serving as the initial phase in dietary therapy, it lays the groundwork for overall health restoration. • This diet comprises items such as lemon water, citrus juices, green tea, and similar options aimed at purifying the system.	•The Soothing Diet follows the detoxification phase and represents the second stage of dietary treatment. • During this stage, patients are provided with foods containing higher carbohydrates and calories compared to the initial phase. •This diet aims to acclimate the body to a non-toxic eating pattern, facilitating improved digestion of solid foods. •Foods included in this stage of diet therapy typically consist of steamed vegetables, vegetable soups, salads, and similar options	•The Constructive diet marks the final stage of dietary therapy, characterized by enhanced bodily function and reduced severity of ailments. •During this stage, the body is provided with whole grains and carbohydrates to support ongoing improvement. • Foods included in this therapeutic regimen typically consist of sprouts, pulses, unpolished rice, and similar options.

2.1.5.B FASTING THERAPY

Naturopathy embodies a systematic approach to healing, grounded in the belief that the accumulation of toxins in the digestive system underlies the majority of diseases. Fasting is considered as a prominent technique within naturopathy which promotes natural healing without the use of chemicals. Fasting therapy involves voluntarily abstaining from food, drink, or both for a specified period.

In Naturopathic therapy, fasting serves to initiate the body's cleansing process and alleviate the burden on the digestive system. Emphasizing the importance of resting the digestive organs, fasting therapy aims to restore their efficiency, which may have been reduced by toxic dietary habits. Unhealthy food choices weaken the immune system, fasting therapy acts as a natural detoxification method, enhancing immunity, and fostering physical, psychological, and sensory well-being in the long term.

Duration of Fasting:

The duration of fasting therapy varies based on factors such as:

- the patient's age,
- the condition of the disease, and
- previous medication usage.

Patients are advised to commence with short fasts of two or three days and gradually extend the duration with each subsequent fast. Prolonged fasting should only be undertaken under the supervision of a specialized naturopath to ensure patient safety. During fasting therapy, patients should refrain from engaging in strenuous mental activities, such as official or business-related work.

Modalities of Fasting Therapy

- Fasting therapy commonly involves water, juices, or raw vegetable juices, with lime juice fasting considered particularly effective.
- Freshly prepared juices are essential for fasting therapy, while canned or frozen juices are not suitable.
- A critical precaution in fasting therapy is ensuring complete emptying of the bowels at the start of the fast through enema administration to prevent discomfort from gas or decomposing matter.
- Enemas should be administered every alternate day during fasting, with a recommended liquid intake of six to eight glasses daily. The primary objective of fasting is to maximize physical rest and mental relaxation.

Benefits of Fasting therapy

- Fasting is beneficial for the restriction of calory intake.
- Reduces the oxidative stress and which is indicated by decreased oxidative damage to proteins, lipids, and DNA during fasting.
- Fasting promotes autophagy [Autophagy is the cellular recycling mechanism within your body. It enables cells to break down and repurpose

their unused or damaged components, transforming salvageable materials into fresh, functional cell parts] and forcing it to repurpose cell components to function.

- Enhance resistance to several oxidative and metabolic stress.
- Enhance immune function.
- Calorie restriction (CR) or intermittent fasting regimens have a profound impact on both overall and cellular physiology. It helps in decrease in body fat and mass, leading to reduced occurrences of myocardial infarction and promoting cardiovascular health. The body's alternative energy reserves, such as ketone bodies like β-hydroxybutyrate, help humans cope with life's additional stressors. In addition to addressing disorders such as obesity, asthma, indigestion, and gas formation, fasting also provides rest to various organs in the body.

2.1.5.C MUD THERAPY

Mud or moistened earth is beneficial to treat different health problems. The Earth comprises various minerals and compounds that contribute significantly to increase the body's immune system. Among these beneficial minerals, clay stands out as a noteworthy element associated with numerous religious beliefs due to its therapeutic properties.

Clay possesses the ability to penetrate the body and address imbalances within. In naturopathy, Mud Therapy involves the systematic application of moistened earth to promote internal benefits. Mud has the capacity to absorb toxins from the body, thus aiding in disease prevention.

Mud therapy is beneficial for the following:

- Retention of the moisture and inducing cooling effects
- Easily adjustable shape and consistency by adding water.
- Accessibility and affordability.
- Absorption of sunlight colours, which are then transmitted to the body.

A mud pack is prepared by wrapping soaked mud in a thin, wet muslin cloth and shaping it into a flat brick according to the patient's abdomen size. The pack is applied for 20 to 30 minutes, and during cold weather, it's recommended to cover both the mud pack and the body with a blanket.

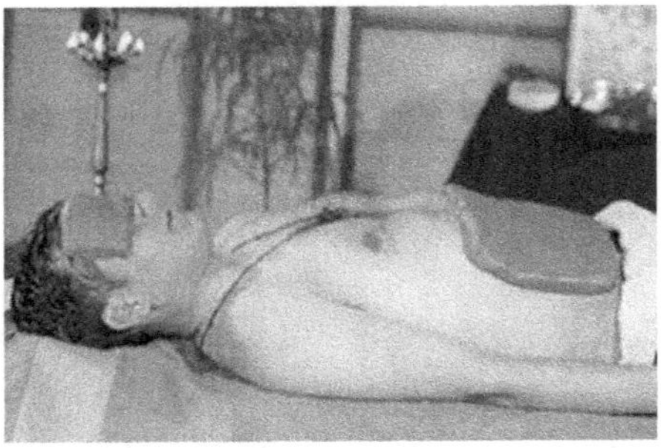

Benefits

- When applied to the abdomen, the mud pack alleviates various indigestion and promotes peristalsis while reducing intestinal heat.
- A generous application of mud pack on the head provides quick relief from congestive headaches.
- Applying mud over the eyes is beneficial for conditions such as conjunctivitis, hemorrhages in the eyeball, itching, and refractive errors, particularly effective in managing glaucoma by reducing eyeball tension.

Mud Bath

During Mud Bath therapy, patients are either seated or lying down while mud, enriched with minerals and natural salts, is applied to their body. This treatment is beneficial for Psoriasis, Leprosy, Urticaria, leucoderma, and various other skin allergies. Careful attention must be paid to prevent patients from catching a cold during the bath. Subsequently, the patient is thoroughly rinsed with a cold water jet spray, although warm water can be used if the patient feels cold. Following the bath, the patient should be placed in a warm bed to prevent any potential illness. The recommended duration for a mud bath is 45 to 60 minutes.

Benefits

- Mud baths impart a refreshing, revitalizing, and invigorating effect on the body.
- They induce a cooling sensation throughout the body.
- Mud therapy is beneficial for conditions such as tension headaches, high blood pressure, skin issues, and constipation.
- The therapy assists in diluting and absorbing toxic substances within the body, facilitating their elimination.

2.1.5.D HYDROTHERAPY

Hydrotherapy is one of the form of naturopathy in which the patients are treated with medium of water in different temperature or other conditions like dissolved salts and pressures.

It harnesses the healing properties of water in various ways and plays a specific role in the treatment plans of patients. It can be incorporated into therapeutic regimens for a wide range of conditions, including:

- Insomnia, stress, and headaches
- Pain management
- Treatment of colds, flu, and other infections
- Disorders of the immune system
- Detoxification and elimination of toxins
- Management of injuries and inflammatory conditions
- Promotion of circulatory and respiratory health

Hydrotherapy employs temperature-based techniques such as hot and cold baths, saunas, and utilizes different forms such as vapor, steam, ice, and fluids, proving effective across its spectrum. Water has long been recognized as one of the most ancient and beneficial remedies for various ailments. Hydriatic applications are administered at different temperatures as part of the treatment protocol.

Benefits:

- Hydrotherapy opens up the pores of skin and make the body fresh and light.
- Altering temperature of water can stimulate blood circulation and joint movement
- As a universal solvent, water's internal use, such as through enemas, colonic irrigation, or consumption, significantly aids in eliminating uric acid, urea, salts, excessive sugar, and other toxins from the body.
- Moreover, it accelerates the healing process by enhancing both catabolic and anabolic reactions necessary for breaking down and removing metabolic by-products of tissue damage, thereby providing a medium for tissue repair.

The various treatment modalities of hydrotherapy include:

Compresses and Fomentation:

Cold Compresses: Such as Abdominal Cold Compress.

Heating Compresses: Including Chest pack, abdominal pack, wet girdle pack, throat pack, Knee pack, and full wet sheet pack.

Hot and Cold Compresses: Applied to areas like the Head, Lungs, Kidneys, Gastro-Hepatic region, pelvis, and abdomen.

Fomentation

Baths: Including options like

Hip Bath (Cold, Neutral, Hot, Stiz Bath, and alternative hip bath),

Spinal Bath & Spinal Spray (Cold, Neutral, Hot),

Foot and Arm Bath (Cold, Hot Foot Bath, Arm Bath, Hot Foot and Arm bath Combined, Contrast Arm Bath, and Contrast Foot Bath),

Steam Inhalation & Steam Bath, Sauna Bath, Sponge Bath, and

Jetspray massages (Cold, Neutral, Hot, Alternate, Circular jet Spray massage).

Affusion Baths: Options such as Cold Affusions, Neutral Affusions, Hot Affusions, and Hot and Cold Affusions.

Cold Shower

Trauma

Immersion Baths

Including Cold Immersion Bath, Cold Immersion with Friction, Neutral Immersion Bath, Hot Immersion, Neutral Half Bath, Graduated Immersion Bath with Epsom Salt, Asthma Bath, and Whirlpool Bath, under water massage.

Enema

Varieties like Graduated Enema, Vaginal Irrigation, Cold Irrigation, Neutral Irrigation, and Hot Irrigation.

Colon Hydrotherapy

This procedure involves cleansing and flushing out the colon or large intestine. It is similar to an enema but more extensive, using clean filtered water under gentle pressure to detoxify the colon of stagnant fecal materials. The number of sessions required varies per individual, with most people needing a series of 3-6 treatments for thorough cleansing.

2.1.5.E MASSO THERAPY

Masso Therapy (The word 'Massage' is derived from the Greek word 'massier' which means to knead) is one of the naturopathic therapies in which body's self-healing power is improved through the massage. It is one of ancient therapies which includes manual manipulation of soft tissues through tapping, shaking, stroking, kneading, pressing, and others.

Different forms of massages improve blood circulation and organ functions in holistic ways. Evidences of mass therapy was observed in almost all ancient civilization.

Modes of Masso Therapy

Masso therapy is done by following modes in which fixed oil (coconut oil, sesame oil, olive oil, mustard oil) along with aromatic volatile oil is used as lubricant and relaxing agent:

Touch,

effleurage (stroking),

friction (rubbing),

vibration (shaking or trembling),

tapotement (percussion),

petrissage (kneading), and

joint movement.

Some types of massage therapy are helpful in most disorders are Vibratory massage, Water massage, and Dry massage

Benefits of Masso Therapy

Physiological impacts of massage therapy can be categorized into reflex and mechanical effects:

Reflex Effects:

- Alterations in muscle tone, either increasing or decreasing it.
- Dilation of arteries, facilitating improved blood flow.
- Muscles may experience a soothing or invigorating sensation.
- Enhanced activity of abdominal organs.
- Boost in immune system efficiency.
- Induction of the relaxation response.
- Stimulation of the heart, enhancing its contraction strength and rate.
- Promotion of peristalsis, aiding digestion.

Mechanical Effects:

- Enhanced lymphatic flow and drainage.
- Breaking down fibrosis and adhesions.
- Stretching muscles that are shortened, thereby loosening muscle fibers.
- Expansion of range of motion.
- Improvement in venous return and circulatory efficiency.
- Restoring proper joint mechanics and biomechanics.
- Elevating muscle temperature.
- Stretching scar tissue.

- Balancing muscle imbalances.
- Strengthening weakened muscles.
- Alteration of muscle tone, either reducing or increasing it.
- Loosening of respiratory mucous.

Masso therapy encompasses all parts of the body and offers numerous benefits. Beyond regulating the nervous system, it also impacts the respiratory system and aids in the detoxification process through organs like the lungs, kidneys, and bowels. Additionally, it increases blood circulation and metabolic functions. Massage contributes to reducing facial wrinkles, filling out hollow areas such as cheeks and neck, and alleviating stiffness.

Evidence based research has highlighted several advantages of masso therapy, including pain and depression relief, lowering blood pressure and heart rate, and reducing anxiety. The theory behind masso therapy involves activating the parasympathetic nervous system via the gate control theory, leading to the release of feel good hormones and chemicals like endorphins and serotonin, preventing fibrosis or scar tissue formation, promoting lymph flow, and improving sleep quality. It's worth noting that these effects are substantiated by well-designed clinical studies.

Whether it's Deep Tissue Massage, which targets deeper myofascial restrictions, or Sports Massage, which employs specific techniques to reduce injury risk and inflammation, various massage modalities effectively address specific areas of the body.

2.1.5.F ACUPRESSURE

Acupressure is one of the important naturopathic medicines originated in ancient China. It is a holistic medicine based on the principal of acupoints activation across the meridians which correct the imbalance between Qi or vital energy. These energy points present on skin surface and rhythmically strengthen the body's natural self-curative abilities.

In acupressure, tension in muscles is alleviated by applying pressure with the hands at precise acupoints, using the thumbs on designated areas, or exerting pressure to balance the flow of physiological energy through these acupoints.

According to traditional Chinese medicine, human body is a cluster of pressure points (Acu Points). An acupoint is the point nearest to the skin's surface, and activating it is the initial and crucial step in acupressure. Acupoint is basically 2 types including local points and distal points. Stimulation of acupoints generates functional response which can be utilize to rectify imbalance of vital force (Qi), self-healing properties and treat ailments and regain healthy state. Application of acupressure on only local points stimulates the therapeutic response on autonomic nervous system. In acupressure, acupoints can be stimulated using elbows, fingers, feet, knuckles, palms, thumbs, or specialized tools. Historically, in ancient China, stones called Bian Stones were utilized to activate acupoints. Nowadays, there is a wide range of tools available for acupressure, including elastic bands with plastic buttons designed to target specific points.

According to Traditional Chinese Medicine, invisible energy flow pathways are present within the body which are refeed as Meridian. There are 14 meridians exist and which resemble to different vital organs or part of the body. If any time, the flow of vital energy or Qi is blocked at any point of meridian pathways may cause the disease. There are 361 pressure points exists on 14 meridians.

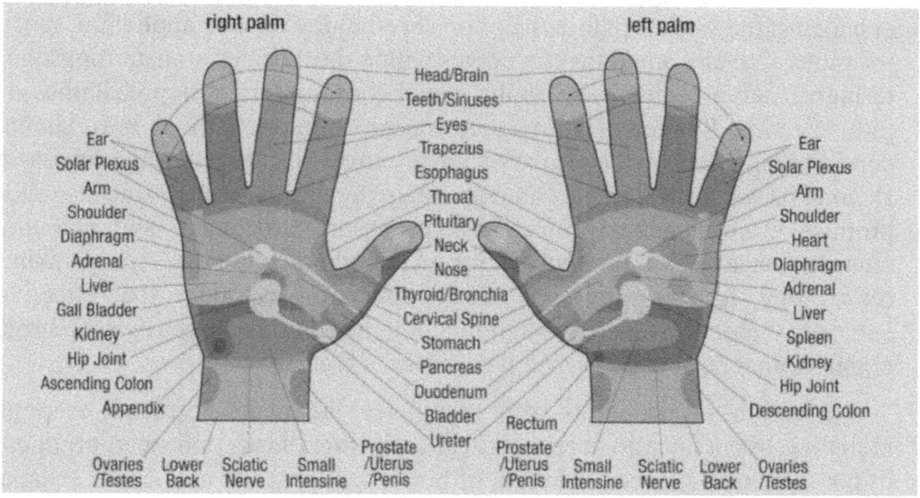

Pressure points on palm

For instance, the pressure point Neiguan (P-6) is primarily employed to alleviate symptoms of nausea and vomiting. To locate it, turn your hand so that the palm faces upward. Position your thumb at the midpoint where the hand meets the wrist, then shift your thumb two finger-widths in the direction of the elbow. This point lies between two prominent tendons, which should be perceptible as you apply pressure.

***Several other commonly utilized pressure points are*:**

Lie Que (LU-7), situated on the thumb side of the wrist, can help boost the immune system.

Qu Chi (LI-11), located on the elbow, is utilized for conditions such as fever, vomiting, diarrhea, and abdominal pain.

Zu San Li (ST-36), positioned below the knee, is beneficial for addressing issues like loss of appetite, acid reflux, and constipation.

He Gu (LI-4), found in the hand, may mitigate side effects of chemotherapy, menstrual pain, and headaches.

Shen Shu (UB-23), located on the lower back, is utilized for relieving lower back pain.

Liang Qiu (ST-34), situated above the knee, may provide relief for osteoarthritis-related knee pain.

In acupressure, gentle but firm pressure with a blunted object or hands is used to activate the pressure points.

According to Gate Control Theory by Melzack and Wall, acupressure at specific point passes pleasurable impulses to the brain which is four times faster than painful stimuli. Continuous stimulation closes the neural "GATES," effectively blocking the transmission of slower pain signals to the brain and enhancing the body's pain perception threshold. Pressure applied at specific locations activates small myelin nerves within the muscles, transmitting signals to higher nerve centres such as the spinal cord, midbrain, hypothalamus, and pituitary axis. Studies using magnetoencephalography (MEG) have shown a conditioning effect on the primary somatosensory response during acupressure. Beyond its subcortical impact on innate pain regulation, acupressure also shows promise in influencing primary somatosensory processing and potentially altering maladaptive neuroplasticity. Auricular acupressure (AA), akin to reflexology, is a non-invasive microacupuncture technique that effectively enhances endocrine function by stimulating the central nervous system through cranial/spinal nerves located on the auricle of the ear.

Activation of acupoints also stimulates the neuro-hormonal responses including hypothalamic-adrenocortical axis which leads enhanced production of cortisol and enhance relaxation of body. Acupressure also cause enhanced production of feel good chemicals like endorphin, serotonin. Acupressure facilitates the nitric oxide (NO) signal, recognized for its role in enhancing local microcirculation through cyclic guanosine monophosphate (cGMP). This process aids in boosting physical performance by inhibiting molecules in the blood that induce fatigue.

Acupressure devices: There is a diverse array of portable acupressure tools on the market, including elastic or non-elastic bands and mats equipped with plastic points. These devices are meticulously designed with patient comfort and ease of use in mind. Additionally, to cater to various patient needs, numerous devices generating electrical impulses and vibrational energy are available to fulfil specific therapeutic requirements.

An **acupressure foot board** comprises multiple upward-extending pressure rods strategically positioned at reflex points corresponding to average foot sizes. These rods are crafted from materials such as plastic, wood, jade, ocher, or metallic magnetic substances and can also be electrically activated.

A **device designed for acupressure on fingers** features a multitude of projections on its inner surface, exerting pressure on the fingertip to enhance blood circulation and create negative ions for therapeutic benefit.

A **clamp** designed for acupressure and reflexology allows for adjustable and reproducible pressure application to specific body areas, maximizing relief and incorporating interchangeable pressure delivery tips.

A **device intended for treating insomnia** applies pressure to rectify ionic imbalances in the treatment area, promoting a calming effect.

An **automatically modulating** acupressure device is specifically engineered to adjust pressure automatically over the wrist (at the P6 acupoint) for the treatment of nausea and vomiting.

An **adjustable foot acupressure** and pain relief platform utilizes massage grains to stimulate acupressure points on the soles of the feet, offering significant analgesic effects.

An **electrical pulse** acupressure system delivers both physical pressure and electrical pulses to acupuncture points, particularly on the outer ear, for therapeutic purposes.

A **finger acupressure** apparatus consists of upper and lower pressing plates with adjustable distance settings, facilitating pressure application to fingers or palm muscles for physical therapy.

A **handheld acupressure device** features a semi-rigid ball attached to a rigid tube via an elastic cord, allowing for targeted pressure application on various acupressure points to address muscle spasms effectively.

Massage footwear incorporates inner sole projections to massage the underside of the foot for therapeutic benefits.

An **opto-mechatronic** acupressure pen provides non-intrusive stimulation for therapeutic treatments without piercing the skin.

A **quantitative acupressure** device offers precise and repeatable therapeutic pressure to the skin and underlying tissue, with a digital controller monitoring the applied pressure.

A **spinal acupressure** device comprises a fabric panel belt with elastic panels, equipped with projections to apply pressure to specific acupressure points associated with the lower spine.

An **acupressure instrument for applying rolling pressure** to the human body delivers rolling pressure on various acupoints for therapeutic purposes.

An **acupressure device for the ear** exerts pressure on external ear acupoints to treat various disorders.

A **detachable acupressure device** in the form of a wristband with projections provides acupressure against joint regions.

An **acupressure ring features inward-extending projections** on its inner surface, along with a visual indicator to assess its function.

An **acupressure apparatus** for treating soft tissue injuries comprises multiple pins to relax and re-energize the body and address soft tissue injuries.

An **acupressure apparatus** with foot control applies pressure to LI4 acupressure points on both hands.

A **point pressure** therapy device utilizes a spherical mounted ball to provide drag across the skin, rather than rolling, for therapeutic benefits.

Acupressure gloves facilitate self-application of acupressure, with nodules fitted on the glove's interior.

Acupoints are now commonly treated by using laser light from laser or **LED diodes or transcutaneous electric nerve stimulation (aka TENS)** in specific wavelengths.

Benefits of Acupressure

Acupressure proves effective in alleviating a range of issues including:

- sinus problems,
- eyestrain,
- neck pain,
- headaches,
- muscle aches,
- arthritis,
- stress-related tension,
- ulcer pain,
- menstrual cramps,
- constipation,
- lower backaches,
- anxiety,
- insomnia,
- and indigestion.

Its holistic approach aims to restore balance to the body and promote overall well-being. Through its healing touch, acupressure reduces stress, enhances circulation, and induces relaxation, thereby bolstering the body's ability to resist disease and fostering a state of wellness.

2.1.5.G ACUPUNCTURE

Acupuncture derived from 2 words Latin acus, "needle", and pungere, "to prick" and it involves the process to manipulate and insert fine filiform needles into particular (specified) points of the body (acupoints) which leads activation across the meridians and correct the imbalance between Qi or vital energy.

into particular (specified) points of the body (acupoints) which leads activation across the meridians and correct the imbalance between Qi or vital energy.

The tradition of acupuncture in China dates back to the Stone Age, where sharpened stones known as Bian shi were used. The exact origins of acupuncture in China remain uncertain. However, the earliest recorded mention of acupuncture can be found in the Yellow Emperor's Classic of Internal Medicine (Huangdi Neijing), which dates back to around 305–204 B.C. Some hieroglyphics discovered from as early as 1000 B.C. suggest the initial use of acupuncture. According to legend, acupuncture originated in China when soldiers wounded by arrows during battles experienced pain relief in various parts of their bodies. This led people to experiment with arrows initially and later with needles, ultimately evolving into a therapeutic practice. Acupuncture later spread from China to Korea, Japan, Vietnam, and other parts of East Asia. The first reports of acupuncture in the West were brought by Portuguese missionaries in the 16th century.

Basic principle and theory of Acupuncture is same as acupressure. Acupuncture is beneficial for the following ailments:

- Rheumatoid arthritis
- Allergic rhinitis
- Headache
- Depression
- Primary dysmenorrhea
- Sciatica
- Nausea and vomiting including morning sickness
- Insomnia
- Bronchial Asthma
- Cervical and Lumbar Spondylosis
- Pain in the epigastrium, neck, face, elbow, tennis, knee, lower back, during dentistry and after operations

2.1.5.H CHROMOTHERAPY

Chromotherapy is a type of naturopathy in which visible range of electro magnetic radiation is used to cure diseases.

Since 2,000 B.C., color has been recognized as a potent therapeutic tool for treating illnesses. With profound effects on mood, colors possess the ability to calm, soothe, stimulate, and harmonize our inner selves, making them one of the most effective modes of therapy. Chromotherapy, an ancient healing practice, utilizes the visible spectrum of electromagnetic radiation to alleviate ailments. This centuries-old theory has been successfully employed worldwide to treat a variety of conditions.

The sun's rays consist of seven colors: Violet, Indigo, Blue, Green, Yellow, Orange, and Red. Each color is believed to be highly effective in addressing different health issues. The process typically involves exposing water and oil to sunlight for specific durations in colored bottles, making colored glasses a practical method for treating various disorders. Colors generate electric impulses and magnetic currents that serve as primary stimulants for biochemical and hormonal activity within the body, thereby restoring balance to the entire system and its organs.

Significance

- Chromotherapy aims to achieve balance in the body's energy centers, known as chakras, by utilizing different colors to either stimulate or calm specific energy points. This approach helps to restore equilibrium and enhance overall well-being.
- Each colour is associated with distinct healing attributes. For instance, blue is commonly employed to induce relaxation and tranquillity, while red may be utilized to boost energy levels and circulation. Through leveraging these therapeutic qualities of colors, chromotherapy seeks to address a variety of health concerns and facilitate healing.
- Colours have psychological impacts on individuals, influencing their emotions, moods, and behaviours. Chromotherapy leverages these effects to foster positive mental and emotional well-being. Warm hues such as orange and yellow may evoke feelings of joy and optimism, whereas cooler tones like green and blue may instil a sense of calmness and serenity.
- Chromotherapy offers a non-invasive and natural approach to treatment that can be used independently or in conjunction with other therapies.

2.1.5.I AIR THERAPY

Air is indispensable for our survival, making Air Therapy a crucial aspect of overall well-being. Engaging in an air bath for approximately 20 minutes daily while wearing lightweight clothing can have a positive impact on our bodies. This therapy plays a pivotal role in replenishing positive energy and restoring natural strength. Combining air baths with exercise and cold rubs enhances their effectiveness, while breathing exercises further augment the benefits. Although deep breathing revitalizes the body and boosts resistance, walking in polluted areas may not yield optimal results. Therefore, it is advisable to avoid polluted environments for maximum efficacy.

Mechanism

During air therapy, nerve centers regulating circulation send blood to the surface in large volumes, facilitating the elimination of toxins from the body.

2.1.5. J MAGNET THERAPY

Magnetic therapy is a naturopathic therapeutic approach that utilizes magnets to treat various ailments. In this method, magnets are affixed to the body using adhesives or worn as jewelry. The duration of attachment varies, ranging from a few minutes to days or weeks, depending on the prescribed regimen. Advocates of magnetic therapy assert that the interaction between the body, the Earth, and other electromagnetic fields induces physical and emotional changes in individuals. They believe that using magnets can address bodily disruptions and effectively alleviate conditions such as headaches, arthritis, migraines, and stress-related pain.

Benefits of Magnetic Therapy:

- Enhances overall well-being
- Alleviates pain symptoms
- Reduces swelling
- Helps alleviate certain symptoms of osteoarthritis
- Facilitates post-operative recovery

Application of Magnetic Therapy:

Magnetic therapy involves the application of electromagnetic devices to harness the healing properties and health benefits of magnetic fields. It has shown promising results in treating various conditions including asthma, heart issues, respiratory ailments, joint pain, spinal problems, digestive discomfort, lower back pain, chest pain, acidity, spondylitis, migraines, blood pressure issues, and weakness.

2.2 YOGA - INTRODUCTION AND STREAMS OF YOGA: ASANAS, PRANAYAMA, MEDITATIONS AND RELAXATION TECHNIQUES

Yoga is one of the important Indian systems of Medicine which is basically a holistic concept that focuses on bringing harmony between body and mind. The word Yoga derived from Sanskrit word ‘Yuj’, meaning ‘to join’ or ‘to yoke’ or ‘to unite’. So, Yoga directly focuses on union of individual consciousness spirit with the universal consciousness and intrinsic environment of human body and mind with external environment.

According to contemporary scientists, everything in the cosmos is an expression of the same underlying quantum reality. When an individual perceives this interconnectedness of existence, they are said to be in a state of yoga and are referred to as a yogi. Achieving this state of unity leads to freedom, known as mukti, nirvana, or moksha. Therefore, the ultimate goal of Yoga is Self-realization, aiming to transcend all forms of suffering and attain liberation or freedom. Living a life imbued with freedom across all aspects, including physical, mental, and spiritual realms, is the primary objective of Yoga practice. Additionally, "Yoga" encompasses an inner science comprising various techniques through which individuals can realize this unity and gain mastery over their lives. Dating back to 2700 B.C., Yoga is often considered an enduring cultural legacy of the Indus Saraswati Valley civilization, serving both the material and spiritual well-being of humanity. Fundamental human values are integral to the practice of Yoga.

The presence of Yoga in ancient India is evident from various seals and fossil remains discovered from the Indus Saraswati Valley Civilization, depicting motifs and figures engaged in Yoga practices. Additionally, the representation of mother Goddess in seals and idols suggests the influence of Tantra Yoga. References to Yoga can also be found in folk traditions, Vedic and Upanishadic texts, Buddhist and Jain traditions, as well as in various philosophical systems, epics like Mahabharata and Ramayana, and theistic traditions such as Shaivism, Vaishnavism, and Tantric practices.

Although Yoga was practiced even before the Vedic period, the sage Maharishi Patanjali played a significant role in systematizing and codifying existing Yogic practices, their meanings, and related knowledge through his Yoga Sutras. Following Patanjali, numerous sages and Yoga masters contributed significantly to the preservation and advancement of Yoga through well-documented practices and literature. The teachings of eminent Yoga masters have spread Yoga across the globe, from ancient times to the present day.

Today, there is widespread belief in the efficacy of Yoga practices for disease prevention, health maintenance, and promotion. Millions of people worldwide have benefited from the practice of Yoga, and its popularity continues to grow steadily, with more individuals embracing its teachings each day.

Contemporary Yoga was developed by the by the teachings of great personalities like Swami Shivananda, Shri T. Krishnamacharya, Swami Kuvalayananda, Shri Yogendara, Swami Rama, Sri Aurobindo, Maharshi Mahesh Yogi, Acharya Rajanish, Pattabhijois, BKS. Iyengar, Swami Satyananda Sarasvati etc.

2.2.1 YOGA BASIC PHILOSOPHY

Yoga is a subtle approach of holistic philosophy to unite the physical state of body with mental health embracing the external alteration of environment. It involves physical exercise, breathing techniques, meditation, relaxation techniques to achieve the vital force, mental health and spiritual growth.

2.2.2 TYPES OF YOGA

It is difficult to categorize streams and schools of Yoga in different categories as different streams of Yoga are interdisciplinary. Broad streams of Yoga are:

Hatha Yoga: Hatha Yog is the most popular form of Yoga which focuses on physical postures (asanas) and breathing techniques (pranayama). It includes several forms including Iyengar Yoga, Ashtanga Yoga, and Bikram Yoga.

However, Yoga is not only associated with breathing techniques and physical exercise. Swami Vivekananda explained 4 forms of Yoga and mentioned the following significance of Yoga:

"Each soul is potentially divine. The goal is to manifest this Divinity within by controlling nature, external and internal. Do this either by work, or worship, or psychic control, or philosophy by one, or more, or all of these and be free. This is the whole of religion. Doctrines, or dogmas, or rituals, or books, or temples, or forms, are but secondary details."

Raja Yoga

Raja Yoga, also referred to as the "royal path," prioritizes the practice of meditation and self-discipline as means to attain spiritual enlightenment. It encompasses techniques such as meditation (dhyana), concentration (dharana), and adherence to ethical principles (yamas and niyamas). Raja Yoga places emphasis on mastering the mind and fostering inner peace and self-awareness.

Karma Yoga

Karma Yoga is the path of selfless action and service. Practitioners engage in their duties and responsibilities without attachment to the outcomes, fostering a sense of detachment and inner tranquillity. Karma Yoga underscores the significance of acting with compassion and altruism, contributing to the welfare of others and society at large.

Bhakti Yoga

Bhakti Yoga, known as the path of devotion and love for the divine, entails surrendering oneself to a higher power through practices such as prayer, chanting, and worship. Practitioners cultivate a deep spiritual connection by expressing devotion and gratitude towards the divine. Bhakti Yoga highlights the importance of nurturing a loving relationship with the divine and acknowledging the significance of devotion and reverence.

Jnana Yoga

Jnana Yoga, the path of knowledge and wisdom, involves seeking self-realization through the pursuit of knowledge, self-inquiry, and contemplation of philosophical truths. Practitioners strive to discern between the eternal and the transient, gaining insight into the nature of reality and the self. Jnana Yoga underscores the importance of acquiring profound understanding and insight into the fundamental truths of existence.

2.2.3 YOGIC PRACTICES FOR HEALTH AND WELLNESS

According to an ancient text of yoga, the Pantanjali yoga sutras, practice of yoga is said to be consisting of eight limbs or Asthanga Yoga (Part of Raja Yoga). The word Ashtanga is developed from two Sanskrit words, "Ashta" and "Anga." "Ashta" means the number eight, while "Anga" refers limb or body part. Therefore, Ashtanga is the union of the eight limbs/organ of yoga, into one complete, holistic system. These eight-limbs of yoga represent the various branches of the philosophy of the yoga sutras. which include:

- ✓ Yama (moral codes),
- ✓ Niyama (self-discipline),
- ✓ Asana (posture),
- ✓ Pranayama (breath control),
- ✓ Pratyahara (sense withdrawal),
- ✓ Dharana (concentration),
- ✓ Dhyana (meditation), and
- ✓ Samadhi (oneness with the self).

The hatha yoga practitioners developed additional techniques like cleansing procedures (kriya), gestures (mudra) and locks (bandhas).

2.2.4 MOSTLY PRACTISED YOGA PRACTICES ARE AS FOLLOWS

Asanas (Yoga Postures):

Asanas are physical postures assigned to promote flexibility, strength, and balance in the body. Each asana has specific benefits for different body parts, organs and systems, including improving posture, enhancing blood circulation, and relieving stress.

Examples of asanas include Tadasana (Mountain Pose), Adho Mukha Svanasana (Downward-Facing Dog), and Padmasana (Lotus Pose).

Pranayama (Breathing Techniques):

Pranayama involves various breathing exercises to improve the controlling and regulating the breath to enhance vital and mental force of body.

Breathing techniques like Ujjayi Pranayama (Victorious Breath), Nadi Shodhana (Alternate Nostril Breathing), and Kapalabhati (Skull-Shining Breath) are commonly exercised.

Meditation

Meditation is associated with the focusing the mind on a single point of concentration or awareness, through the breath, a mantra, music or a visual object.

Meditation helps calm the mind, reduce stress, and developed inner peace and self-awareness.

Different meditation techniques include mindfulness meditation, loving-kindness meditation, and transcendental meditation.

Relaxation Techniques

Relaxation techniques helps to release physical and mental tension by promoting deep relaxation and rejuvenation.

Relaxation Practices like Yoga Nidra (Yogic Sleep), progressive muscle relaxation, and guided imagery are helpful to induce a state of deep relaxation and promote overall well-being.

2.2.5 STEPS OF PRACTICE OF YOGA

A. Invocation

The practice of yoga should commence with a prayer or a prayerful mindset to enhance its benefits.

B. Sadilaja/Chalana Kriyās/Loosening Practices

This step enhances microcirculation. These practices can be done in both standing and sitting posture.

Neck Movements (Development of Neck Strength)

Position: Stand in Samasthiti (Alert Posture)

Procedure

Stage I: (Forward and Backward Bending/Stretching)

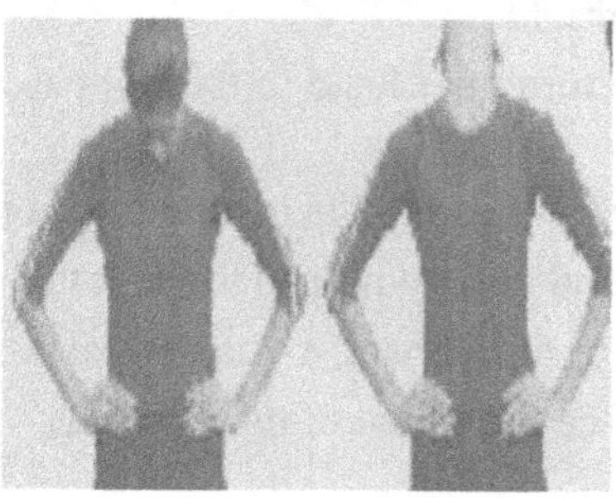

- ✓ Stand with your feet positioned 2-3 inches apart.
- ✓ Keep your hands straight beside your body.
- ✓ This position is Samasthiti, also known as Tāḍāsana.
- ✓ Place your palms on your waist.
- ✓ Exhale and slowly move your head forward, attempting to touch your chin to your chest.
- ✓ Inhale and lift your head up, comfortably arching your neck backward.
- ✓ Repeat this sequence for a total of three rounds.

Stage II: (Right and Left Bending/Stretching)

- ✓ While exhaling, slowly tilt your head to the right, bringing your ear as close to your shoulder as possible without raising the shoulder.
- ✓ Inhale and return your head to the neutral position.
- ✓ Similarly, while exhaling, tilt your head to the left side.
- ✓ Inhale and bring your head back to the neutral position.
- ✓ Repeat this sequence for a total of three rounds.

Stage III: (Right and Left Twisting)

- ✓ Keep your head upright.
- ✓ Exhale and gently turn your head to the right so that your chin aligns with your shoulder.
- ✓ Inhale and return your head to the neutral position.
- ✓ Similarly, exhale and turn your head to the left.
- ✓ Inhale and bring your head back to the neutral position.
- ✓ Repeat this sequence for a total of three rounds.

Stage IV: Neck Rotation

- ✓ Exhale and bend your head forward, attempting to touch your chin to your chest.
- ✓ Inhale and slowly rotate your head clockwise in a circular motion, exhaling as you come down.
- ✓ Complete one full rotation.
- ✓ Then rotate your head in a counterclockwise direction.
- ✓ Inhale and return to the starting position, exhaling as you come down.
- ✓ Repeat this sequence for a total of three rounds.

Notes:

Move your head as far as comfortable, avoiding overstraining.

Keep your shoulders relaxed and steady.

Notice the stretch around the neck and the loosening up of the neck joints and muscles.

This practice can also be done while sitting on a chair.

Individuals with neck pain should perform the practice gently, especially when extending the head backward to a comfortable extent.

Elderly individuals and those with chronic cervical spondylitis may consider avoiding these practices.

Stage II: Shoulder Movement

Posture: Alert Posture (Samasthiti)

Stage I: Shoulder Stretch

Technique:

- ✓ Stand with your feet together, maintaining a straight body posture, and keeping your arms by your sides.
- ✓ Inhale and raise both arms sideways above your head, with your palms facing outward.
- ✓ Exhale and lower the arms in the same manner. Ensure that your palms are open with fingers together.

Stage II: Shoulder Rotation

- ✓ Stand upright.
- ✓ Place the fingers of your left hand on your left shoulder and the fingers of your right hand on your right shoulder.
- ✓ Rotate both elbows in a circular motion.
- ✓ Inhale as you raise your elbows, and exhale as you bring them back.
- ✓ Try to touch your elbows in front of your chest during the forward movement, stretch them back during the backward movement, and touch the sides of your trunk as you lower them.
- ✓ Repeat this movement twice, rotating from front to back.
- ✓ Perform the same movement in reverse. Inhale as you raise your elbows and exhale as you lower them.

Benefits:

Practicing this Yogic kriya helps to maintain the health of the bones, muscles, and nerves of the neck and shoulders.

These practices are beneficial for conditions such as cervical spondylosis and frozen shoulder.

Stage III: Trunk Movement (Kaṭiśakti Vikāsaka)

Posture: Alert Posture (Samasthiti)

Technique:

- ✓ Stand with your legs about 2-3 feet apart.
- ✓ Raise both arms up to shoulder level with palms facing each other and keep them parallel.
- ✓ While exhaling, twist your body towards the left side so that the right palm touches the left shoulder, and return to the center as you inhale.
- ✓ While exhaling, twist your body towards the right side so that the left palm touches the right shoulder, and return to the center as you inhale.
- ✓ Repeat this sequence two more times to complete one round.
- ✓ Relax in the Alert Posture (Samasthiti).

Stage IV: Knee Movement

Posture: Alert Posture (Samasthiti)

Technique:

- ✓ Inhale and lift your arms up to shoulder level, palms facing downwards.
- ✓ Exhale and bend the knees, lowering the body into a semi-squatting position.
- ✓ In the final position, ensure that both the arms and thighs are parallel to the ground.
- ✓ Inhale and straighten the body.
- ✓ Exhale while bringing the hands down.
- ✓ Repeat this sequence two more times.

Notes:

This exercise helps to strengthen the knees and hip joints.

Avoid practicing this asana in case of acute arthritis conditions.

C. Yogasana

Standing Position Asanas		
Name and Technique of the Asana	**Benefits**	
Tadasana (Palm Tree Posture) Tadasana, derived from the Sanskrit words "tada" meaning palm tree or mountain, emphasizes stability and firmness, serving as the foundation for various standing asanas. Technique: ✓ Begin by standing with your feet approximately 2 inches apart. ✓ Inhale deeply as you raise your arms up to shoulder level in front of you. ✓ Interlock your fingers and turn your wrists outward. ✓ Continuing to inhale, extend your arms upward above your head. ✓ Lift your heels off the floor, balancing on your toes as you raise your arms. ✓ Maintain this position for 10-30 seconds, focusing on your breath and stability. ✓ Lower your heels back down to the floor. ✓ Exhale as you release the interlock of your fingers and bring your arms down, returning to the standing posture.	✓ Develops stability in the body, ✓ helps to remove congestion of ✓ the spinal nerves and rectifies faulty posture.	

Table *contd....*

Name and Technique of the Asana	Benefits	
Ardha Cakrāsana (The Half Wheel Posture) Ardha, meaning half, and cakra, meaning wheel, describe Ardha Cakrāsana, where the body resembles half of a wheel. ✓ Stand straight with your feet approximately 2 inches apart. ✓ Support your back at the sides of the waist with your fingers. ✓ Keep your elbows parallel. ✓ Drop your head backward, stretching the neck muscles. ✓ Inhale and bend backward from the lumbar region; exhale and relax. ✓ Hold this position for 10-30 seconds while breathing normally. ✓ Inhale and slowly come back up to the starting position.	Increases spinal flexibility and strengthens spinal nerves and muscles. Aids in the management of cervical spondylosis.	
Sitting Posture		
Bhadrāsana (The Firm/Auspicious Posture) Bhadra signifies firmness or auspiciousness. Sthiti: Long sitting posture (Viśrāmāsana) Sit erect with both legs stretched forward. Support your back with your hands, ensuring total relaxation. This is Viśrāmāsana. Technique: ✓ Sit straight with your legs extended in front of you. ✓ Keep your hands beside your hips, palms resting on the floor. This position is called Daṇḍāsana. ✓ Now bring the soles of your feet together. ✓ Exhale and clasp your hands together over your toes. ✓ Inhale as you pull your heels as close as possible up to the perineum region. ✓ If your thighs do not touch the floor or are not close to it, place a soft cushion underneath the knees for support. ✓ This is the final position. ✓ Stay in this position for some time, breathing normally.	✓ Helps maintain firmness in the body and stabilizes the mind. ✓ Beneficial during pregnancy and relieves abdominal pain often experienced during menstruation.	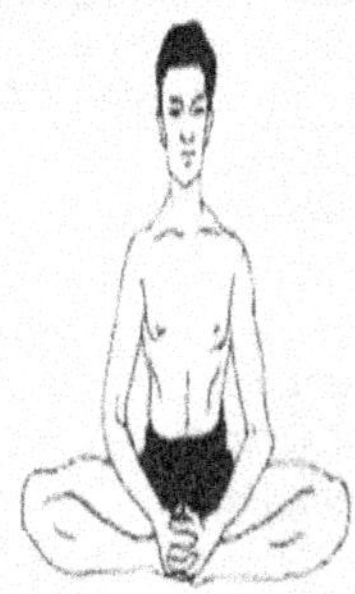

Table *contd....*

Name and technique of the asana	Benefits	
Uṣṭrāsana (Camel Posture) Uṣṭra means camel. The body's position in this pose resembles that of a camel, hence its name. **Sthiti: Vajrāsana** **Technique:** ✓ Begin by sitting in Vajrāsana. ✓ Separate the knees and feet by a few inches and stand on your knees. ✓ While inhaling, bend backward and place the right palm on the right heel and the left palm on the left heel. Exhale during this movement. ✓ Be cautious not to strain the neck while bending backward. ✓ In the final position, the thighs should be vertical to the floor and the head tilted backward. ✓ Ensure the weight of the body is evenly distributed on the arms and legs. ✓ Maintain the posture for 10-30 seconds while breathing normally. ✓ Return to the starting position with inhalation and sit in Vajrāsana. ✓ Relax in Viśrāmāsana.	✓ beneficial for improving defective eyesight. ✓ It helps alleviate back and neck pain. ✓ This posture aids in reducing fat around the abdomen and hips. ✓ Useful for digestive problems and cardio-respiratory disorders.	
Prone Position		
Makarāsana (The Crocodile Posture) Makara, which translates to crocodile in Sanskrit, derives its name from the resemblance the body takes to a crocodile in this āsana. Sthiti: Prone relaxation posture **Technique:** ✓ Lie down on your stomach with your feet wide apart and toes pointing outward. ✓ Bend both arms and place the right palm on the left palm. ✓ Rest your head either left or right on your hands. ✓ Close your eyes and relax your entire body. This posture is Makarāsana. ✓ Makarāsana is used for relaxation in all prone postures.	✓ Promotes relaxation of the whole body. ✓ Aids in the recovery of back problems. ✓ Useful for countering stress and anxiety.	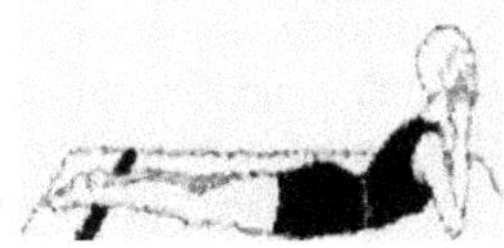

Table ***contd....***

Name and technique of the asana	Benefits	
Supine Position		
✓ Pavana Muktāsana (The Wind Releasing Posture) ✓ The term Pavana translates to wind, and mukta means to release or make free. As the name suggests, this āsana is beneficial for relieving wind or flatulence from the stomach and intestines. ✓ Sthiti: Śavāsana ✓ Technique: ✓ Lie down flat on your back. ✓ Bend both knees. ✓ Exhale and bring both knees toward the chest. ✓ Inhale, interlock the fingers, and clasp the shins below the knees. ✓ Exhale, raise the head until your chin touches the knees and relax. ✓ This posture is Pavanamuktāsana. ✓ Lower the head back to the ground. ✓ While exhaling, lower the legs back to the floor. ✓ Rest in Śavāsana.	✓ Alleviates constipation and provides relief from flatulence, reducing the bloating sensation in the abdomen and aiding digestion. ✓ Generates deep internal pressure, improving stretching of the complex network of muscles, ligaments, and tendons in the pelvis and waist region. ✓ Tones up the back muscles and spinal nerves.	
Uttāna Pādāsana (Raised feet posture) Uttāna signifies raised-upward, and Pāda refers to the leg. In this āsana, the legs are lifted upward while lying in a supine position, hence the name. **Technique:** ✓ Lie comfortably on the ground with your legs stretched out. ✓ Place your hands by your sides. ✓ Inhale slowly and raise both legs without bending the knees, bringing them to a 30-degree angle with the ground. ✓ Maintain this position for 10-30 seconds while breathing normally. ✓ Exhale and slowly lower both legs back down to the ground. ✓ Relax in Śavāsana.	✓ Helps balance the navel center (Nābhi, Maṇipuracakra). ✓ Provides relief from abdominal pain, flatulence, indigestion, and diarrhea. ✓ Strengthens the abdominal and pelvic floor muscles. ✓ Effective in alleviating depression and anxiety.	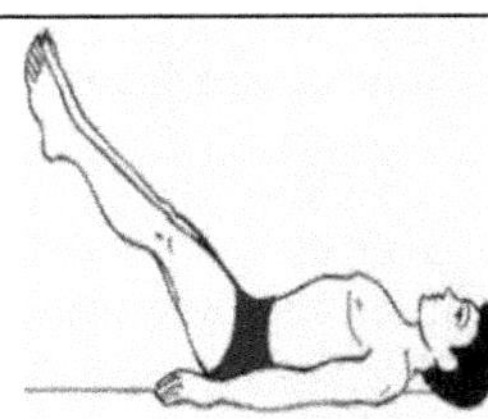

Table *contd....*

Name and Technique of the Asana	Benefits	
Śavāsana (The Corpse/Dead Body Posture) Śava means a dead body. The final position in this āsana resembles a corpse or a dead body. Sthiti: Supine Relaxation Posture Technique: ✓ Lie down on your back with your arms and legs comfortably apart. ✓ Palms should be facing upward, and eyes should be closed. ✓ Consciously relax the entire body. ✓ Become aware of your natural breath and allow it to become slow and shallow. ✓ Remain in this position until you feel refreshed and relaxed.	✓ Helps relieve all kinds of tensions and provides rest to both the body and mind. ✓ Relaxes the entire psycho-physiological system. ✓ The mind, which is usually drawn to the outer world, turns inward, gradually becoming absorbed. As the mind becomes quiet and absorbed, the practitioner remains undisturbed by the external environment. ✓ Found to be very effective in achieving deep relaxation and rejuvenation.	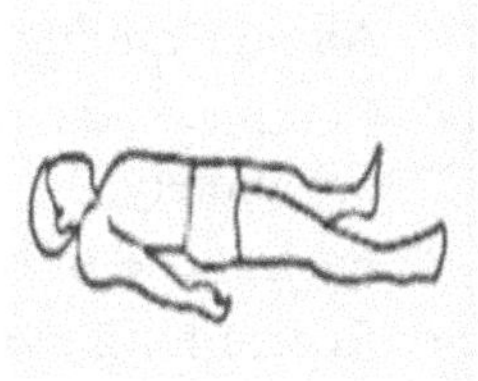

D. Kapalbhati

Sthiti: Any comfortable or meditative posture such as Sukhāsana, Padmāsana, or Vajrāsana.

Technique:

✓ Sit in any comfortable posture.

✓ Close your eyes and relax your whole body.

✓ Inhale deeply through both nostrils, expanding the chest.

- ✓ Exhale forcefully by contracting the pelvic and abdominal muscles, and inhale passively.
- ✓ Avoid straining and continue forceful exhalation and passive inhalation.
- ✓ Complete 30 rapid breaths, then take a deep breath, exhale slowly, and relax completely.
- ✓ Each round of Kapālabhāti should be followed by stillness for a while.
- ✓ Repeat for 2 more rounds.

Breathing:

- ✓ Forceful exhalation is done by contracting the abdominal muscles, with no undue movements in the chest and shoulder region.
- ✓ Inhalation should be passive throughout the practice.

Number of rounds:

- ✓ Beginners can practice up to 3 rounds of 20 rapid breaths each, gradually increasing the count and rounds over time.

Benefits:

- ✓ Kapālabhāti purifies the frontal air sinuses and helps overcome cough disorders.
- ✓ Useful in treating conditions like cold, rhinitis, sinusitis, asthma, and bronchial infections.
- ✓ Rejuvenates the body, keeping the face glowing and vibrant.
- ✓ Strengthens the nervous system and tones up the digestive organs.

Caution:

- ✓ Avoid practicing Kapālabhāti in case of cardiac conditions, giddiness, high blood pressure, vertigo, chronic nosebleeds, epilepsy, migraine, stroke, hernia, gastric ulcer, pregnancy, and during menstruation.

E. Prāṇāyāma - Nāḍīśodhana or Anuloma Viloma Prāṇāyāma (Alternate Nostril Breathing)

The key feature of this prāṇāyāma is alternate breathing through the left and right nostrils with or without breath retention (kumbhaka).

Sthiti: Any comfortable posture.

Technique:

- ✓ Sit comfortably with a straight spine and closed eyes.
- ✓ Relax the body with a few deep breaths.
- ✓ Place the left palm on the left knee in Jnāna mudra and the right palm in Nāsāgra mudra.
- ✓ Use the right thumb to close the right nostril and the ring and small fingers to close the left nostril.

- ✓ Inhale through the left nostril, close it, exhale through the right nostril, then inhale through the right nostril, close it, and exhale through the left nostril.
- ✓ Repeat for 4 more rounds.

Ratio and timing:

For beginners, the duration of inhalation and exhalation should be equal.

Gradually transition to a ratio of 1:2 for inhalation and exhalation, respectively.

Breathing:

Breathing should be slow, steady, and controlled, without force or restriction.

Benefits:

Induces tranquility and improves concentration.

Increases vitality and reduces stress and anxiety.

Alleviates cough disorders.

F. Dhyāna (Meditation)

Dhyāna, or meditation, is a continuous act of contemplation.

Sthiti: Any comfortable posture.

Technique:

- ✓ Sit comfortably with a straight spine.
- ✓ Adopt Jñāna mudra or Dhyana mudra.
- ✓ Touch the tip of the thumb to the tip of the index finger, forming a circle, while keeping the other three fingers straight and relaxed.
- ✓ Keep the palms facing upwards on the thighs.
- ✓ Close your eyes with a slightly upturned face.
- ✓ Maintain a mild focus between the eyebrows and be conscious of your breath.
- ✓ Dissolve your thoughts and aim for a single, pure thought.

Benefits:

- ✓ Meditation is integral to yoga practice, helping eliminate negative emotions and fostering positive ones.
- ✓ Calms the mind, increases concentration, memory, clarity of thought, and willpower.
- ✓ Rejuvenates the body and mind, providing proper rest.
- ✓ Leads to self-realization.

2.2.6 INTERNATIONAL YOGA DAY

Today, yoga is practiced in diverse forms worldwide and continues to gain popularity. Recognizing its widespread appeal, the United Nations designated June 21 as the International Day of Yoga on December 11, 2014, through resolution 69/131.

The International Day of Yoga aims to promote awareness globally about the numerous benefits of practicing yoga. The resolution proposing this day was initiated by India and received support from a record 175 member states. Prime Minister Narendra Modi introduced the proposal during the opening of the 69th session of the General Assembly, emphasizing yoga's significance as a holistic approach for health and well-being. He highlighted yoga's role in fostering unity of mind, body, and action, beyond mere physical exercise.

The resolution underscores the importance of individuals and communities adopting healthier lifestyle choices to promote good health, echoing calls from the World Health Organization to address physical inactivity, a significant contributor to non-communicable diseases.

Yet, yoga transcends physical activity. Renowned yoga practitioner B. K. S. Iyengar emphasized its broader impact, stating that yoga fosters a balanced outlook in daily life and enhances skilfulness in one's actions.

2.3 AROMATHERAPY

The term Aromatherapy derives from 2 words, aroma means good odour and therapy implies treatment. Aromatherapy is one of the popular Complementary and Alternative Medicine which uses essential or scented oils to cure ailments and manage symptoms, stimulates well-being.

2.3.1 HISTORY AND DEVELOPMENT OF AROMATHERAPY

Ancient Civilizations: The application of aromatic plants and their essences for therapeutic purposes dates back to all ancient civilizations including Egypt, China, India, Greece, and Rome. Healing properties of aromatic substances and incorporated them into their medical and religious practices were well recognized by those civilization. For example, ancient Egyptians used essential oils for embalming, medicinal purposes, and rituals of preservation of dead bodies, while in India, Ayurvedic medicine used aromatic herbs and oils for treating various ailments.

Middle Ages: During the Middle Ages in Europe, the knowledge of aromatherapy continued to flourish, albeit often intertwined with spiritual rituals and folklore. Monks and physicians in medieval Europe utilized aromatic herbs and oils for treating ailments, as well as for masking unpleasant odors during the time of the Black Death.

Renaissance and Enlightenment: The Renaissance period saw a revival of interest in natural holistic remedies and botanical medicine. Scholars and physicians, including Paracelsus, explored the therapeutic significances of plants and essential oils. However, it wasn't until the 19th century that modern aromatherapy began to take shape.

Modern Aromatherapy: The term "aromatherapy" was coined by the French chemist **René-Maurice Gattefossé** in the early 20th century. Gattefossé accidentally observed the healing properties of lavender oil when he used it to treat burns he sustained in a laboratory accident. His research and subsequent book, "**Aromathérapie: Les Huiles Essentielles Hormones Végétales**," laid the foundation for modern aromatherapy.

20th Century Developments: Aromatherapy gained popularity throughout the 20th century, particularly in France and Europe, where it was integrated into mainstream medicine. Influential figures such as Jean Valnet, Marguerite Maury, and Robert Tisserand further developed and promoted the use of essential oils for therapeutic purposes.

Contemporary Practice: In recent decades, aromatherapy has become increasingly popular globally, with a growing body of scientific research supporting its efficacy for various health conditions. Today, aromatherapy is practised in diverse settings, including spas, hospitals, clinics, and homes, for promoting health and well-being, reducing stress, managing pain, improving sleep, and enhancing mood.

It is observed clinically that application of aromatherapy in different ways beneficial to reduce stress, anxiety and mental illness along with that several studies exhibits the benefits of Aromatherapy in different physiological condition.

2.3.2 BASIC PRINCIPLE

Odoriferous substances present in essential oils used in aromatherapy stimulates nervous systems through inhalation and with a chain reaction of signals induce chemical response throughout the body.

The molecules of essential oils may reach the brain and exert an effect through 2 different pathways, including the olfactory system and the respiratory system. After inhalation, the molecules would either act directly on the olfactory mucosa or pass into the respiratory tract. These two delivery pathways suggest different mechanisms of action associated with Aromatherapy.

Odoriferous substances binds with Odorant receptors. Olfactory sensory neurons (OSNs) situated in the olfactory epithelium (OE) express odorant receptors (ORs) individually at the ciliary surface. ORs represent the most extensive group within the G-protein coupled receptor (GPCR) superfamily, comprising around 400 and 1200 distinct OR genes in humans and mice, respectively. Activation of odorant receptors by odoriferous substances lead to enhanced intracellular cAMP levels via the sequential activation of olfactory G-protein (Golf) and type III adenylyl cyclase (ACIII). Enhanced level of intracellular cAMP act as a second messenger, which opens the nucleotide gated channel on the cell surface, triggering influx of cations including Ca^{2+} and action potentials, and ultimately initiating neuro-potential transmission and olfactory perception.

In addition to transmitting olfactory signals, essential oils (EOs) can also influence mood through intra and extracellular transport mechanisms. When inhaled into the nasal cavity, the small volatile compounds can traverse the neuronal network of the olfactory system and directly access the brain. Intracellular transport begins when these inhaled molecular compounds bind to surface receptors on target neurons, leading to receptor-mediated endocytosis and internalization. The molecules are then transported to the olfactory cortex via anterograde transport, where they interact with the hippocampus and amygdala. The olfactory nerve and trigeminal nerve are responsible for anterograde transport, with molecules traveling along axons to the olfactory bulb in the case of the olfactory nerve, and connecting to the pons in the case of trigeminal sensory neurons. The pons, part of the hindbrain, relays information to the cerebellum and may regulate breathing rate by projecting to the medulla.

Extracellular transport involves the passage of molecular compounds through the paracellular cleft between supporting cells and OSNs into the lamina propria via fluid movement. Once in the lamina propria, the molecules are further transported externally along axons in the perineural space and ultimately reach the brain parenchyma. They then cross the blood-brain barrier (BBB) and blood-cerebrospinal fluid barrier to access different brain regions.

Moreover, EO molecules can interact with neurotransmitter receptors such as transient receptor potential channels (TRP), GABA, 5-HT, and DA receptors, producing anxiolytic or antidepressant effects.

Some research suggests that essential oils (EOs) may be absorbed through the respiratory system. When inhaled along with room air, EO molecules travel through the respiratory tract and reach the alveolar sacs. However, only soluble molecules can cross the air-blood barrier. EOs consist of various molecular compounds, with some being polar and others nonpolar. Most EO components belong to the lipid-soluble terpene family, making them lipophilic and hydrophobic. Nonetheless, certain EO components are water-soluble. The primary pathway for molecular delivery to the systemic circulation is through alveolar diffusion. Lipophilic EO molecules can traverse the blood-brain barrier (BBB) and reach the central nervous system (CNS). Previous studies have demonstrated that the systemic transport of volatile EO molecules can stimulate the CNS, leading to positive psychological and physiological effects.

Breathing is an involuntary function regulated by the autonomic nervous system. However, exposure to stress can alter respiration, activating the limbic system and triggering physiological responses that mirror emotional reactions. Consequently, there is a significant correlation between respiration and emotion. Furthermore, respiratory health is closely tied to brain function. Pulmonary diseases have been shown to impact brain cell growth through brain-lung communication. In addition, inflammation mediators induced by lung conditions can enter systemic circulation, prompting adaptive responses in the brain. Declining lung function can also reduce oxygen supply to the body, particularly the brain, resulting in brain injury and various neuropsychological and neurobehavioral disorders such as depression and anxiety. Conversely, the association between respiratory health and mental well-being is intricately interconnected.

2.3.3 TYPES OF AROMATHERAPY

Aesthetic Aromatherapy

This approach of Aromatherapy involves the use of specific essential oils in skincare, body care, facial, and hair care products. These products offer various benefits like cleansing, moisturizing, drying, and toning the skin. Essential oils incorporated into facial products helps to achieve healthy skin. On a personal level, indulging in cosmetic aromatherapy through full-body or foot baths offers a simple yet effective experience. Similarly, adding a few drops of suitable oil can provide a rejuvenating and revitalizing effect.

Therapeutic Massage Aromatherapy

Utilizing pure vegetable oils like grape seed, almond, or jojoba oil during massage sessions has demonstrated remarkable effects. This practice is often referred to as the healing touch of massage therapy.

Clinical Aromatherapy

Pioneered by modern aromatherapy founder René-Maurice Gattefossé, medical aromatherapy involves the application of essential oils to massage patients during surgery. This approach harnesses the therapeutic properties of essential oils to promote and treat clinically diagnosed medical conditions.

Olfactory Aromatherapy

Olfactory aromatherapy involves inhaling essential oils to enhance emotional well-being, induce calmness, relaxation, or rejuvenation. The inhalation of pleasant scents can help release stress and unlock olfactory memories. Essential oils complement medical treatment and should not be viewed as a substitute for it.

Psycho-Aromatherapy

Psycho-aromatherapy aims to evoke specific moods and emotions through the use of essential oils, providing sensations of relaxation, invigoration, or triggering pleasant memories. Inhalation is the primary method in this therapy, either directly or by infusing the patient's room with aromatic oils. Both psycho-aromatherapy and aromacology study the effects of aroma, whether natural or synthetic, but psycho-aromatherapy focuses solely on natural essential oils.

2.3.4 CLINICAL SIGNIFICANCES OF AROMATHERAPY

- ✓ Clinical study based evidence suggests that aromatherapy may be beneficial in managing several conditions, including stress, sleep disorders, menstrual cramps, and early labour.
- ✓ Some studies indicate that aromatherapy could potentially alleviate symptoms of dementia, such as behavioural, cognitive, and mood issues. However, conflicting findings exist, and a review published in 2020 concluded that there is insufficient evidence to support the effectiveness of aromatherapy in treating dementia.
- ✓ While aromatherapy is often touted as a remedy for various ailments, it is advisable to consult with a healthcare professional if you are considering it for a specific condition. Healthcare providers have access to up-to-date research and can help determine whether aromatherapy may offer potential benefits for your individual circumstances.
- ✓ Aromatherapy has shown promise in managing anxiety, particularly state anxiety, which arises from specific stressful situations such as medical procedures like MRI scans, surgery, or labour.
- ✓ Some studies suggest that aromatherapy may also be beneficial for trait anxiety, which is characterized by a more persistent feeling of anxiousness, such as that experienced by individuals with generalized anxiety disorder or those living with chronic illnesses.

2.3.5 AROMA THERAPY OILS

Aromatherapy oils, or essential oils, are highly concentrated plant's volatile oils. They are obtained from various parts of plants, including flowers, stems and leaves through distillation and cold press.

To explore the potential benefits of aromatherapy further, it is advisable to consult with healthcare provider and trained aromatherapist who can provide personalized guidance based on your specific needs and medical history.

2.3.6 SOME COMMONLY USED ESSENTIAL /VOLATILE OILS

Lavender oil

Lavender oil due to its gentleness and numerous benefits is preferred by aromatherapists. Lavender oil can be used in various ways, such as adding it to a bath or diffuser for aromatherapy, mixing it with water to create a room or body spray, or blending it with a base oil for a body oil.

Lavender oil is known to aid in stress relief, pain management, and improving sleep. However, it's important to note that studies have indicated a potential hormonal disruption in young boys from using lavender oil (as well as tea tree oil).

Tea tree oil

Mostly people use tea tree oil for its antiseptic, antimicrobial, or antifungal properties. It can be applied directly to acne without dilution, diluted with a carrier oil for conditions like athlete's foot or ringworm, or used cautiously due to its potential neurotoxicity around small children or pets.

Frankincense oil

Frankincense oil, often referred to as the "king of oils," is beneficial for inflammation, mood enhancement, and sleep improvement. Studies also suggest its potential in managing asthma and preventing gum disease. It has a distinct scent and is commonly used in aromatherapy and skincare products, but it should be diluted before skin application.

Peppermint oil

Peppermint oil is known for its anti-inflammatory, antifungal, and antimicrobial properties, along with its ability to alleviate headaches, fatigue, and digestive issues. It is recommended to dilute it when using topically and mentions its effectiveness in settling stomach discomfort, particularly for individuals with irritable bowel syndrome or gastric irritation.

Eucalyptus oil

Eucalyptus oil is beneficial during cold seasons as it helps clear nasal passages, provides pain relief, and fights against the herpes simplex virus. Caution is advised when using eucalyptus oil, including proper dilution for topical application and avoiding ingestion due to potential side effects, especially for children and pets.

Lemon oil

Lemon oil offers various benefits such as reducing anxiety, pain, and nausea, along with antibacterial properties. However, it can increase skin sensitivity to sunlight, so precautions should be taken to avoid sun exposure after use.

Lemongrass oil

Renowned for its strong citrus aroma, lemongrass oil is recognized for its ability to alleviate stress, anxiety, and depression. Its natural antibacterial properties make it an effective remedy for healing wounds and combating bacterial growth. Additionally, studies have indicated that lemongrass oil may help lower blood sugar levels in individuals with type 2 diabetes. It's important to dilute lemongrass oil with a carrier oil before applying it to the skin to avoid potential irritation.

Orange oil

Derived from citrus fruit rinds, orange oil can be diffused, applied topically with a carrier oil, or used as a natural household cleaner. It is known for its antibacterial properties and its ability to reduce anxiety and pain. However, caution should be taken as orange oil can increase skin sensitivity to sunlight.

Rosemary oil

Although commonly used in cooking for its flavor, rosemary oil offers additional benefits such as enhancing brain function, stimulating hair growth, reducing pain and stress, uplifting mood, and alleviating joint inflammation. It is safe for aromatherapy and topical use with a carrier oil, but individuals who are pregnant or have epilepsy or high blood pressure should avoid using rosemary oil.

Bergamot oil

Bergamot oil, known for its fruity and floral scent, is familiar to fans of Earl Grey tea. It can be diffused or applied topically with a carrier oil. Bergamot oil is recognized for reducing anxiety, boosting mood, and lowering blood pressure. However, it can also increase skin sensitivity to sunlight.

Cedarwood oil

With antioxidant and antibacterial properties, cedarwood oil is commonly found in insect repellents, shampoos, and deodorants due to its woodsy fragrance. It can also aid in promoting sleep and reducing anxiety. Cedarwood oil can be used in aromatherapy or topically with a carrier oil.

List of Aromatherapy oils in Common ailments

Volatile oil	Common Aromatherapy uses condition
✓ *Angelica archangelica rad. (angelica)* ✓ *Cistus ladaniferus (labdanum)* ✓ *Citrus aurantium var. amara fol.* ✓ *(petitgrain bigarade),* ✓ *Citrus aurantium var. amara per.* ✓ *(orange bigarade), Citrus bergamia* ✓ *(bergamot)* ✓ *Citrus sinensis (sweet orange)* ✓ *Cymbopogon martinii (palmarosa)* ✓ *Eucalyptus staigeriana (lemon-scented* ✓ *ironbark),* ✓ *Lavandula angustifolia (lavender)* ✓ *Litsea cubeba (may chang)* ✓ *Ocimum basilicum (basil)* ✓ *Origanum majorana (sweet marjoram)* ✓ *Pelargonium graveolens (geranium)* ✓ *Pogostemon patchouli (patchouli)* ✓ *Valeriana officinalis (valerian)* ✓ *Lavandula angustifolia (lavender)* ✓ *Santalum album (sandalwood)* ✓ *Boswellia carteri (frankincense)*	*Anxiety, agitation, stress, challenging behaviors*
✓ *Citrus paradisi (grapefruit)* ✓ *(exhaustion)* ✓ *Coriandrum sativum (coriander)* ✓ *(including mental)* ✓ *Cymbopogon nardus (citronella)* ✓ *Eucalyptus radiata (black peppermint)* ✓ *(chronic)* ✓ *Eucalyptus smithii (gully gum)* ✓ *Juniperus communis ram. (juniper twig)* ✓ *Mentha spicata (spearmint) (mental)* ✓ *Pelargonium graveolens (geranium)* ✓ *(nervous)* ✓ *Pinus sylvestris (Scots pine)* ✓ *Rosmarinus officinalis ct. cineole, ct.* ✓ *camphor, ct. verbenone (rosemary)* ✓ *Salvia sclarea (clary) (nervous)* ✓ *Zingiber officinale (ginger)* ✓ *Angelica archangelica rad. (angelica)* ✓ *Cistus ladaniferus (labdanum) (chronic)* ✓ *Citrus aurantium var. amara (neroli bigarade)*	*Fatigue*

Table *contd....*

Volatile oil	Common Aromatherapy uses condition
✓ *Angelica archangelica rad. (angelica)* ✓ *Cananga odorata (ylang ylang)* ✓ *Chamaemelum nobile (Roman* ✓ *chamomile)* ✓ *Citrus bergamia (bergamot)* ✓ *C. limon (lemon)* ✓ *Citrus reticulata (mandarin)* ✓ *Citrus sinensis (sweet orange)* ✓ *Citrus aurantium var. amara (neroli* ✓ *bigarade)* ✓ *Cistus ladaniferus (labdanum)* ✓ *Cuminum cyminum (cumin)* ✓ *Juniperus communis fruct. (juniper* ✓ *berry)* ✓ *Lavandula angustifolia (lavender)* ✓ *Litsea cubeba (may chang)* ✓ *Melissa officinalis (lemon balm)* ✓ *Myrtus communis (myrtle)* ✓ *Ocimum basilicum (basil) (nervous)* ✓ *Origanum majorana (sweet marjoram)* ✓ *Ravensara aromatica (ravensara)* ✓ *Thymus vulgaris ct. geraniol, ct.* ✓ *linalool (sweet thyme)* ✓ *Valeriana officinalis (valerian)*	*Insomnia*
✓ *Eucalyptus smithii (gully gum)* ✓ *Lavandula angustifolia (lavender)* ✓ *Matricaria recutita (German* ✓ *chamomile)* ✓ *Leptospermum scoparium (manuka)* ✓ *Origanum majorana (sweet marjoram)* ✓ *Pinus mugo var. pumilio (dwarf pine)* ✓ *Rosmarinus officinalis ct. camphor* ✓ *(rosemary)* ✓ *Zingiber officinale (ginger)*	*Pain management*

2.3.7 SAFETY CONCERN OF ESSENTIAL OILS USED IN AROMATHERAPY

Essential oils are generally considered safe with minimal adverse effects. Some of them have even been approved as food additives and are classified as generally recognized as safe by the U.S. Food and Drug Administration. However, there are some common adverse events associated with essential oils, such as eye, mucous membrane, and skin irritation, particularly with oils containing aldehydes and phenols. Essential oils that contain furocoumarins, like Citrus bergamia, may cause phototoxicity. Contact sensitization can occur due to the oxidation of monoterpenes, often because of improper storage conditions.

There's a possibility of cross-sensitization to other essential oils and foods. Allergic reactions from inhaling essential oils can happen, but there's limited data on exposure levels, with many reports focusing on perfumes rather than aromatherapy essential oils. An exceptional case of airborne contact dermatitis was reported in the context of aromatherapy without massage. Allergic reactions have also been reported in some instances, particularly with topical administration.

2.3.8 CARRIER OILS

Carrier oils, also considered as base oils or fixed oils, are substances made from plants which don't have a strong smell, and they don't evaporate like essential oils do.

Carrier oils act as a vehicle for safely getting essential oils into your body. It is essential to dilute essential oils in carrier oils. Because essential oils are so potent, usually use a much higher percentage of carrier oil compared to essential oil. Carrier oils also contain many ingredients like fat soluble vitamins, anti-oxidant unsaturated fatty acids that are good for skin. Examples of carrier oils:

Coconut oil.

Rosehip oil.

Grapeseed oil.

Sweet almond oil.

2.3.9 COMMON METHODS OF AROMATHERAPY INCLUDE

Inhalation: Essential oils can be inhaled through various methods. For instance, one can create a facial steam by adding essential oil to a bowl of hot water (up to six drops per ounce of water) and then leaning over the bowl with closing eyes to inhale the steam. Alternatively, a diffuser can be used to disperse the scent throughout your room or home. It's important to carefully follow the instructions provided with the specific diffuser you use.

Aromatherapy massage: A trained practitioner can perform a massage using lotion or oil infused with essential oils. However, it's essential to dilute the essential oil properly. For massage purposes, dilute the essential oil so that it is concentrated at approximately 1%.

Bath: Adding essential oils to bath water can be another method of aromatherapy. However, it's crucial to mix the essential oil with a carrier oil (such as jojoba oil) or dispersant (like solubol) beforehand. Using undiluted essential oil directly in the bath may not mix well with the water and could potentially irritate skin.

CHAPTER 3

Formulation Development of various Systems of Medicine

Traditional medicines play important role in global healthcare in disease management and treatment. According to WHO, "It is the sum total of the knowledge, skills and practices based on the theories, beliefs and experiences indigenous to different cultures, whether explicable or not, used in the maintenance of health, as well as in the prevention, diagnosis, improvement or treatment of physical and mental illnesses. The terms complementary/ alternative/non-conventional medicine are used interchangeably with traditional medicine in some countries. (WHO,2000)"

Today, traditional medicine has emerged as a worldwide trend, witnessing increasing demand as patients aim for greater control over their health and wellness journey. They seek compassionate and tailored healthcare experiences. For millions, particularly those in distant or rural regions, it remains the preferred option for healthcare, providing culturally appropriate, accessible, and cost-effective care.

Like modern allopathic medicine, various traditional medicines have different types of formulation to treat, prevent, cure and mitigate diseases. All Indian systems of medicine (except yoga) and Homoeopathy depend on different natural formulation for treating ailment along with other treatment strategies. Mostly these formulations are prepared with traditional knowhows, mentioned in indigenous texts. However, increasing demand of those formulations and global need of standardization requires more improvement and quality product development. In this chapter we will discuss Salient features of the techniques of preparation of some of the important class of Formulations as per different system's formulary, Pharmacopoeia and texts along with their standardization and stability studies. Most of the indigenous and traditional formulations are herbal/polyherbal/Herbo mineral/animal formulation.

3.1 AYURVEDIC FORMULATIONS

Several Ayurvedic formulations are mentioned in different Ayurvedic texts and Ayurvedic Formulary of India.

The first part of the Ayurvedic Formulary of India (AFI) was released in 1978 by the Government of India, under the Ministry of Health and Family Welfare, Department of Health, New Delhi, comprising 444 formulations. Its primary objective was to gather dispersed information on traditional Ayurvedic formulations and present it systematically, considering the needs of the pharmaceutical industry. The second part of the AFI outlines 191 classical formulations. The first edition of the third part of the AFI includes details on 350 classical formulations.

Ayurvedic formulations are broadly categorized in following classes:

(1) **Kasthausadhi** (predominantly plant drugs) e.g. Asava, aristha, churna, taila etc.

(2) **Rasausadhi** (predominantly metals and minerals) e.g. Bhasma, Pisti, Lauha, Kapibadkva, Rasayana etc.

Most ayurvedic formulations are polyherbal and Herbo mineral formulation and sometimes prepared with addition of animal products like Gomutra (cow urine), Ghrita (clarified butter), milk or honey.

There are approximately 21 types of compound formulations, incorporating various single drugs sourced from animal (52), mineral (55), and plant (351) origins. For detailed information on these single drugs and other relevant details, one can refer to the Ayurvedic Formulary of India, published by the Government of India, Ministry of Health and Family Welfare.

Ayurvedic medications are accessible in various forms such as powder, tablets, pills, liquid, and semi-solid, which are categorized into the following classifications:

- ✓ Arishta and Asavas
- ✓ Rasa Rasayana
- ✓ Lauha
- ✓ Bati
- ✓ Churna
- ✓ Avaleha
- ✓ Ghrita
- ✓ Parpati
- ✓ Taila
- ✓ Guggulu

ASAVA AND ARISHTA

Asava and Arishta are Ayurvedic fermented liquid formulation.

Asavas and Arishtas are prepared by soaking the crude drugs, either in powder form or in the form of Kasaya or decoction, in a solution of honey, sugar or jaggery, as the case may be, for a specified period of time, during which it undergoes a process of fermentation which is happened due to presence of adhered yeasts present on the surface of ***Woodfordia fruticosa*** (Dhataki Pushpa)and producing alcohol, thus facilitating the extraction of the active principles contained in the drugs. Generated alcohol is also serves as a preservative.

The difference between arishta and asava is in their raw materials form, arishta is made from the decoction of medicinal herbs while asava is prepared from fresh herbs powder. The following is the schematic representation of Arishta and Asava preparation:

ARISTA PREPARATION

Crude Drug/drugs mentioned in the formula

↓

Crude drug is coarsely powdered

|

Decoction(kasaya) is prepared and strained

↓

Transferred to Fermentation Vessel/pot/barrel

↓

Solution of Sugar, Jaggery or Honey is added (Heated to Dissolve)

↓

Any other additive/prakshepa dravya added along with Dhataki pushpa(*Woodfordia fruticosa*) added(if mentioned)

↓

Close the earthen lid sealed edges with clay smeared clothedges sealed with clay-smeared cloth wound in seven consecutive layers.

↓

Fermented at constant temp

↓

Set aside to settle down matter

↓

Fluid decanted & filtered

↓

Boil to avoid further fermentation

↓

Filled in bottle and sealed

ASAVA PREPARATION

Crude Drug mentioned in the formula

↓

Crude drug is coarsely powdered

↓

Transferred to Fermentation Vessel/pot/barrel

↓

Solution of Sugar, Jaggery or Honey is added (Heated to Dissolve)

↓

Any other additive/prakshepa dravya added along with Dhataki pushpa(*Woodfordia fruticosa*) added(if mentioned)

↓

Close the earthen lid sealed edges with clay smeared clothedges sealed with clay-smeared cloth wound in seven consecutive layers.

↓

Fermented at constant temp

↓

Set aside to settle down matter

↓

Fluid decanted & filtered

↓

Boil to avoid further fermentation

↓

Filled in bottle and sealed

Precaution

If fermentation is to occur in an earthen vessel, it is essential that the vessel is not new. Prior to use, water must be boiled in the vessel, and strict cleanliness is imperative throughout the process. Before pouring liquids into the vessel, the inner surface should be fumigated with Pippali churna (for sterilization purpose) and coated with ghee each time. In large-scale production, wooden vats, porcelain jars, or metal vessels are substituted for earthen vessels.

Properties:

Ashokarishta

- Asava or arishta should be clear
- Formulation should not generate any froth
- Should not become sour on keeping
- It has characteristic, aromatic & alcoholic odour
- During fermentation, Alcohol is generated which facilitates extraction of active constituents present in the drug
- Alcohol additionally functions as a preservative
- Earlier, the wooden pots are fumigated with pippali powder and smeared with ghee before pouring the liquid, drugs and fermenting agent.

Shelf Life

Asava and arishta can be kept indefinitely as it contains self-generated alcohol.

Storage Conditions

- Asava and Arishta should be stored in Narrow mouthed air tight container.
- Store in cool place.
- Keep away from sunlight.

Examples:

Asava: Kumariasva, Punarnavashava, Madhukasava

Aristha: Draksharishta, Ashokarishta

Standardization of Asavas and Arishta

Following parameters are to be considered for the standardization of the Arishta and Asava formulation:

✓ Physical appearance

✓ Alcohol content

✓ Water soluble extractive

✓ Alcohol soluble extractive

✓ pH

✓ Total solid

✓ Density

✓ Viscosity

✓ Surface tension

✓ TLC profile

Lehya or Avaleha

Lehya or Avaleha is defined as, "Avaleha or Lehya is a semi-solid preparation of drugs, prepared with addition of jaggery, sugar or sugar-candy and boiled with prescribed drug juice or decoction." They are also known as Modaka, Guda, Khanda, Rasayana, Leha etc.

Preparation comprises of:

✓ Decoction or other liquid of drugs mentioned in the formula

✓ Jaggery/ sugar/ honey

✓ Powder or Pulp of drug

✓ Ghee or Oil

- **Sugar/ Jaggery + Liquid+**strained to remove the foreign particles.

  ↓ Boiled & Dissolved (Ghee or Oil if any)
- When the Paka (Phanita) is thready (tantuvat)/when pressed between two fingers or when it sinks in water without getting easily dissolved, it should be removed from the fire.

  ↓
- Powdered drugs in small quantities

  ↓
- **Stirred continuously**

  ↓
- **Homogenous mass is formed**

Properties of Lehya

✓ The Lehya should possess a texture that is neither too hard nor overly thick.

✓ When the pulp of drugs is incorporated along with ghee or oil, it should be malleable enough to be rolled between the fingers.

✓ In cases where metals are mentioned, the bhasmas (ashes) of these metals are utilized.

✓ The color and fragrance of the Lehya are determined by the constituent drugs.

✓ Indicators of spoilage include the presence of fungus or signs of fermentation.

✓ It should be scoopable with a spoon.

✓ When pressed between fingers, it should exhibit threads during stretching.

✓ It should sink in water without rapidly dissolving.

✓ Lehya should retain impressions when touched by fingers.

✓ Its components are readily absorbed by the body, starting from the mouth.

Storage

✓ Lehya should be kept in Glass/ Porcelain Jar or suitable plastic or metal container which is inert.

✓ Lehya should be stored in wide mouthed air tight container

✓ Lehya should keep away from hot & humid conditions

Shelf Life

Used within a year.

Standardization Parameters:

- ✓ Description
- ✓ Colour
- ✓ Odour
- ✓ Taste
- ✓ Consistency
- ✓ Moisture content
- ✓ Total ash
- ✓ Acid- insoluble ash
- ✓ Alcohol- soluble extractive
- ✓ Water -soluble extractive
- ✓ pH (10% aqueous extract)
- ✓ Total acidity
- ✓ Specific gravity at 25°C
- ✓ Total solid content
- ✓ Fat content
- ✓ Reducing sugar/ Non-reducing sugar
- ✓ Total sugars
- ✓ Assay for major ingredients/Major constituents of main ingredients
- ✓ TLC/HPTLC/HPLC/LC-MS (any one or all)
- ✓ Test for heavy/toxic metals
- ✓ Lead, Cadmium, Mercury, Arsenic (Limits as per ASU Pharmacopoeia)
- ✓ Pesticide residue
- ✓ Organo chlorine pesticides, organophosphorus pesticides, pyrethroids
- ✓ (Limits as per ASU Pharmacopoeia)
- ✓ Microbial contamination
- ✓ Total viable aerobic count, Enterobacteriaceae, Total fungal count
- o Test for specific pathogen
- ✓ Escherichia coli, Salmonella spp., Staphyloccocus aureus, Pseudomonas aeruginosa (Limits as per ASU Pharmacopoeia)
- ✓ Aflatoxins (Limits as per ASU Pharmacopoeia (Bi, B2, Gi G2)

Churna

Churna is a fine powder of drug or drugs.

Properties

- Churna is fine of at least 80 mesh sieves.

- Churna Should not adhere together or become moist.
- The finer the Churna, the better is its therapeutic value.

Shelf Life

If churna stored properly, retains potency for one year.

General Method of preparation

Drugs mentioned in the formula are cleaned and dried properly

↓

powdered and sieved.

↓

weighed separately and mixed together uniformly

- ❖ drugs contain more fibrous matter than other, this method of powdering and weighing should be done separately and then mixing them together, is preferred.
- ❖ Salt, sugar, camphor etc., when mentioned are separately powdered and mixed with the rest at the end.
- ❖ Asafoetida (Hi´ngu) and salt may also be roasted, powdered and then added.
- ❖ Drugs like shatavari, Guduchi etc., which are to be taken fresh, is made into a paste, dried, and then added.

Storage Conditions

Churna should be preserved in air tight container and kept away from moisture. It should be **store in a cool & dry place**

Advantages:

Churna is easily administrable specially in the cases of children who cannot swallow pills, tablets or capsules.

Standardization Parameters

- ✓ Description
- ✓ Colour
- ✓ Odour
- ✓ Foreign matters
- ✓ Powder microscopy
- ✓ Particle size (80-100 mesh for Chuma)
- ✓ Moisture content
- ✓ Total ash value
- ✓ Acid - insoluble ash value

- ✓ pH (5% aqueous extract)
- ✓ Water- soluble extractive
- ✓ Alcohol- soluble extractive
- ✓ Bulk density and Tap density
- ✓ Assay for specific ingredients/chemical Constituents/group of compounds (if possible)
- ✓ TLC/HPTLC/HPLC with markers (any one or all)
- ✓ Test for heavy metals (Lead, Cadmium, Mercury, Arsenic (Limits as per Ayurvedic Pharmacopoeia)
- ✓ Pesticide residue (Organo chlorine pesticides, organophosphorus pesticides, pyrethroids
- ✓ Microbial contamination
- ✓ Total viable aerobic count
- ✓ Enterobacteriaceae
- ✓ Total fungal count (Limits as per ASU Pharmacopoeia)
- ✓ Aflatoxins (Limits as per ASU Pharmacopoeia)
- ✓ Test for specific pathogen Escherichia coli, Salmonella spp., Staphyloccocus aureus, *Pseudomonas aeruginosa* (Limits as per ASU Pharmacopoeia)
- ✓ Shelf life

Bhasma

Bhasma is Powder of a substance obtained by calcination. It is mainly applied to the metals and minerals and animal products which are, by special processes, calcined in closed cruibles in Puta (pits and with cow dung cakes).

Bhasma formulation is beneficial for reducing the toxicity of herbo-mineral formulation and animal products.

Stages of preparations

Generally, 2 stages are applicable for the Bhasma preparation which are as follows:

- ✓ Sodhana
- ✓ Marana

Sodhana

Bhasmas are prepared from purified minerals, metals and marine and animal products and the initial process of purification is known as **Sodhana.** Sodhana is beneficial to:

- Eliminate harmful matter from the drug;
- modify undesirable physical properties of the drug;
- helps in conversion of some of the characteristics of the drugs
- enhance the therapeutic action, thereby potentizing the drug.

Sodhan is performed in following ways:

(1) **Samanya sodhana:** This purification technique is applied to a large number of metals or minerals, as heating the thin sheets of the metals and immersing them in Taila, Takra, Gomutra etc.

(2) **Visesha sodhana:** Visesha sodhana is applied only to certain drugs and in certain preparations. consists of

- **Bhavana:** The substance is entirely immersed in the specified liquid and ground until it becomes dry.
- **Svedana:** metal or drug material is boiled in prescribed liquid using Dola Yantra method
- **Nirvapana:** Nirvapana involves the process of drying or evaporating moisture from medicinal substances.
- **Mardana:** Drug material is pulverized by continuous grinding with or without prescribed liquid.

Marana

Marana involves calcination of the drug and it can be done by the following processes:

Marana

- The purified drug is placed in a *khalva* (stone mortar and pestle) and ground with the juices of specified plants or the *kasayas* (decoctions) of the drugs recommended for a particular mineral or metal.
- This grinding continues for a specified duration. The resulting mixture is shaped into small cakes (*chakrikas*), with their size and thickness determined by the weight of the drug—heavier drugs result in thinner cakes.
- These cakes are thoroughly dried under sunlight, arranged in a single layer on a shallow earthen plate (*sarava*), and covered with another plate. The edges are sealed with cloth smeared with clay in seven consecutive layers and dried
- A pit is then dug in an open space, with its diameter and depth depending on the specific mineral or metal being calcined. Half of the pit is filled with cow dung cakes, the sealed earthen container is placed inside, and the remaining space is filledwith more cow dung cakes.
- Fire is ignited on all four sides and in the center of the pit. Once the burningprocess is complete, the setup is allowed to cool naturally. The earthen container is then removed, the seal is broken, and the contents are extracted. The resulting material is ground into a fine powder using the *khalva*
- This process — grinding with plant juice, forming *chakrikas*, and subjecting them to repeated heating cycles (*putas*)—is repeated as prescribed intraditional texts or until the desired fineness and quality are achieved.
- The *putas* are categorized by specific names, indicating the pit size, the number of cow dung cakes required, the intensity of heat, and the duration of burning. The commonly used *putas* in preparing *bhasmas*include:

1.Maha Puta
2.Gaja Puta
3.Varaha Puta
4.Kukkuta Puta
5.Kapota Puta
6.Bhanda Puta

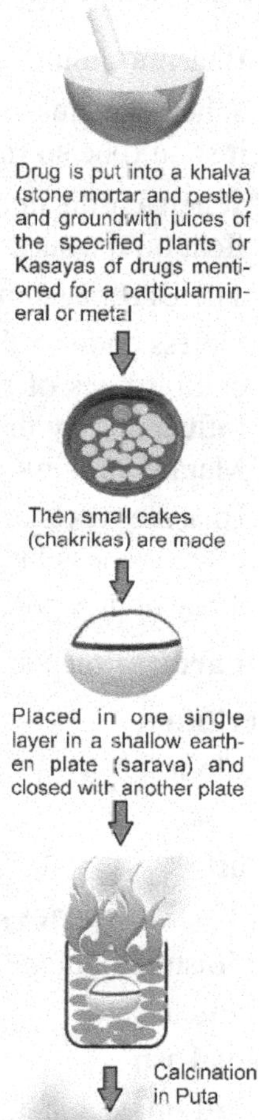

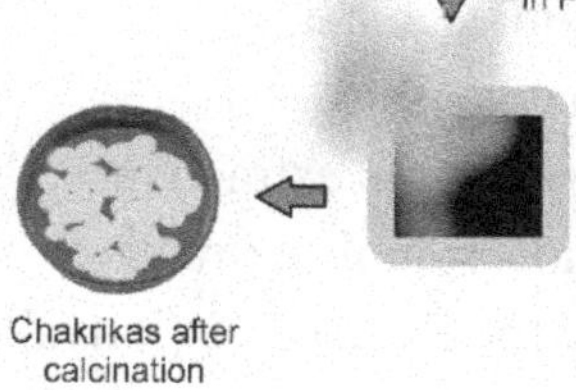

Characteristics and Preservation

(1) Bhasma should not show any Chandrika (metallic lustre) (Nischandrika)

(2) When Bhasma is placed between the index finger and thumb and spread, it should be so fine as to get easily into the finger lines (Rekha Purita)

(3) When a little amount of Bhasma is spread on cold and still water, it should float on the surface (Varitaram)

(4) The Bhasma should not revert to its original state (Apunarbhava).

(5) Unless indicated otherwise in specific formulations, Bhasmas typically exhibit hues of yellowish, black, pure white, grey, reddish black, or red, influenced by the primary drug and other components utilized during the Marana process.

(6) Bhasmas are stored in airtight glass or earthenware vessels and retain their effectiveness indefinitely.

(7) They do not possess any distinctive taste.

Standardization Parameters

Description

- Colour
- Odour
- Taste
- pH (1% aqueous extract)
- Moisture content
- Particle size
- Total ash
- Acid -insoluble ash
- Sulphated ash
- Water- soluble extractive
- Alcohol- soluble extractive
- Assay for element (s) (if available)
- IR/XRF/XPS/XRD/SEM/EDX/AFM (As per requirement)
- Nishchandrica (Lusterless)
- Rekha pumatva (Fine enough to enter within lines of finger)
- Varitara (Floats on water)
- Nirthoom (Smokeless)
- Niswadu (Tasteless)
- Apumar Bhav (Irreversible)
- Shelf life

Examples of Bhasma:

Bhasma	Main Ingredient
Louha bhasma	Iron oxide
Naga bhasma	Lead
Abhrak bhasma	Mica
Yasad Bhasma	Zinc Oxide
Swarn Bhasma	Gold

Gutika/vati

Medicines prepared in the form of tablet or pills are known as Vati and Gutika which are made of one or more drugs of plant, animal or mineral origin.

Preparation of Gutika/Vati

- The drugs of plant origin are dried and made into fine powders, separately.
- minerals are made into Bhasma or Sindura

↓

- put into a khalva and ground to a soft paste with the prescribed fluids.(if more than one liquid is mentioned for grinding, they are used in succession.)

↓

- When the mass is properly ground and is in a condition to be made into pills,

↓

- Sugandha Dravyas, Like Kasturi, Karpura, which are included in the formula, are added and ground again.

↓

- The criterion to determine the final stage of the formulation before making

↓

- pills is that it should not stick to the fingers when rolled. Pills may be dried in shade or insun as specified in the texts.

Characteristics and Preservation

- Plant-based pill formulations, when stored in airtight containers, remain suitable for use for a duration of two years.
- Pills containing minerals have an indefinite shelf life.
- Both pills and Vatikas should retain their original color, fragrance, taste, and shape.
- In formulations where sugar, salt, or Ksara is included, it is essential to keep the pills away from moisture.
- Similarly, when sugar or salt is present, moisture should be avoided.

Storage and Preservation

- Should be stored in an Air tight container
- Preparation containing vegetable drugs can be used for 2 years

- Preparations containing minerals or metals can be used for indefinite period
- Pills and vatis should not lose their original color, smell, taste and form.
- When sugar, salt is an ingredient, the pills should be kept away from moisture.

Standardization Parameters

- Description
- Colour
- Taste
- Odour
- Microscopic characters (if vegetable parts are used as ingredients)
- pH (5% aqueous extract)
- TLC/HPTLC/HPLC/LC-MS (any one of all)
- Moisture content
- Friability
- Hardness
- Uniformity of weight
- Disintegration time (not more than 35 minutes except guggulu)
- Total ash
- Acid- insoluble ash
- Alcohol- soluble extractive
- Water -soluble extractive
- Total sugar (if added)
- Reducing sugar/Non-reducing sugar (if added)
- Assay (active constituents of major ingredients) (if available)
- Test for heavy/toxic metals
- Lead, Cadmium, Mercury, Arsenic (Limits as per ASU Pharmacopoeia)
- Pesticide residue
- Organo chlorine pesticides, organophosphorus pesticides, pyrethroids (Limits as per ASU Pharmacopoeia)
- Microbial contamination

- Total viable aerobic count, Enterobacteriaceae,
- Total fungal count (Limits as per ASU Pharmacopoeia)
- Test for specific Pathogen
- Escherichia coli, Salmonella spp., Staphyloccocus aureus, Pseudomonas
- aeruginosa (Limits as per ASU Pharmacopoeia)
- Aflatoxins (Limits as per ASU Pharmacopoeia)
- (Bi, B2, Gi, G2)

Ghrita

Ghrita refers to preparations where ghee is boiled with specified decoctions (Kasayas) and paste of medicinal herbs according to the formulation outlined in the Ayurvedic formulary.

Parpati

Initially, Kajjali is created using refined Mercury and sulfur. Subsequently, additional herbs as per Ayurvedic formulations are incorporated and thoroughly mixed using a grinder. The resulting powder is heated in an iron vessel until it melts. This molten substance is purified following Ayurvedic protocols, cooled, and then the medicinal flakes are once again powdered.

Taila

Tailas are formulated by boiling prescribed decoctions (Kasayas) and paste of medicinal herbs in oils according to the Ayurvedic formulary guidelines.

Goggulu

Goggulu denotes Ayurvedic medicines derived from the resin of the Commiphora mukul plant. Although Ayurvedic texts list five variations of Goggulu, the commonly preferred ones are Mahishaksha and Kanaka for medicinal preparations.

The resin pieces are enclosed in a cloth and boiled in gomutra, milk, or Triphala decoction until the resin fully dissolves into the liquid through the cloth. After filtering, the liquid is boiled until it solidifies. Following drying, the solid mass is converted into a paste by adding ghee until it achieves a waxy consistency.

3.2 UNANI FORMULATIONS

Huboob And Aqras

Huboob (Pills) are round, small uniformly shaped Unani medicinal preparations. Aqras

(tablets) are circular and flat in shape oral solid preparation.

The size and weight of huboob and aqras range from 0.1 grams to 1 gram.

General methods of preparation

- ✓ Drug is powdered as per 'Daq-Wa-Sahaq' guidelines
- ✓ Lubdi (mass) is prepared by using a sufficient amount of water-dissolved adhesive like

Samagh-e-Arabi is used in case where the constituent drugs are not mucilaginous in nature.

- ✓ Sticking of the lubdi is avoided during the rolling between the fingers by using lubricants like Raughan-e-Zard or Raughan-e-Kunjad.
- ✓ The formulae wherein seemab (Mercury) and Kibreet (sulphur) are used together' the

  Kajli (See General Methods of Preparation) is made first and mixed with the powder of other drugs.
- ✓ Drugs like Darchikna, Raskapur, Halelajat, Aamla, Gul-e-Surkh, Post-e-Anar etc. should be pulverized in porcelain mortar; The use of iron spoon, knife etc. should be avoided.

Characteristics

The final products (pills, tablets, and banadiq) should have a moderate consistency, neither overly hard nor excessively soft.

Preservation:

Huboob and Aqras are stored in thoroughly dried, clean glass jars, stoppered bottles, phials, etc., and kept in a cool, dry environment to prevent contamination. Chalk or starch powder is applied inside the containers prior to use.

Example:

Habb-e-Aftimoon

Habb-e-Haiza

Qurs-e-Gul

Jauhar

The process of sublimation in Unani is called Tas-eed. According to The National formulary of Unani Medicine, Jauhar is defeined as follows:

"When the drugs like Kafoor, Sammul-Far, Gandhak and Raskapoor etc. are sublimated, therapeutically efficacious products for medicinal uses are produced. These products are called **"Jauhar"** and the process of **"Tas-eed"** in Urdu is called Jauhar-Ka-Urana. The drugs having this property are called Zawil Arwah."

Preparation Method

The medicinal herbs are finely ground into a powder using Sharab (Brandy). The powder is then placed between two earthen discs with smooth edges, which are tightly sealed using the process of sealing (Gil-e-Hikmat). This sealed apparatus is subjected to low heat, and periodically moistened with a water-soaked cloth to condense the material deposited inside the upper disc. As the lower disc's powdered drug is heated, it gradually transforms into vapors and accumulates in the upper disc. After approximately 4 hours of heating, the apparatus is removed from the fire and allowed to cool. Once cooled, the apparatus is opened, and the sublimate (Jauhar) adhering to the upper disc is scraped and collected.

General Precaution

Ensure that the earthen discs are tightly sealed, and the sublimation process occurs over low heat. Allow the apparatus to cool completely before opening.

Characteristics

The sublimate maintains the original color of the drug.

Preservation

The sublimate (Jauhar) can be preserved indefinitely. They are stored in glass phials, securely stoppered bottles, or glass jars in cool, dry, and clean environments.

Example

Jauhar-e-Kalan

Jauhar-e-Kafoor

Jauhar-e-Tila

Kohal

According to The National formulary of Unani Medicine, " **Kohal (Surma) is the finest powder form of the medicinal preparations used externally to strengthen the eye sight and to cure other eye ailments."**

Method of Preparation:

For the preparation of Surma Ingredients like lead, antimony, or other metallic compounds, along with medicinal herbs or substances like almond oil, rose water, or camphor, are chosen based on traditional formulations.

The selected ingredients are finely pulverized and mixed together thoroughly to form a homogeneous powder which is then heated and processed through specific techniques, like roasting, calcination using wick, or other traditional methods to enhance its medicinal properties and ensure purity.

The processed powder is carefully shaped into small sticks or cones, known as Surma sticks or Kohal sticks, using molds or by hand. These sticks are then cooled and solidify.

Packaging and Preservation

The finished Surma sticks or Kohl sticks are packaged in airtight containers prevent moisture and contamination. They are kept in a cool, dry place away from direct sunlight to maintain their efficacy and shelf life.

General Precautions

Kohal (Surma) should be pulverized to the finest degree of powder form.

Characteristics

When touched with fingers. Kohal (Surma) should not give the feel of grittiness.

Examples: Kohal-e-Asha, Kohal-e-Chashkham, Kohal-e-Tashmeezaj

Majoon

Majoon is a semi solid Unani formulation in which one or more single drugs of plant, animal or mineral origin are mixed in power or liquid forms in the base (Qiwam) made of purified honey, sugar. candy or jaggery. These include preparations like jawarish, Itrifal, Barshasha, Dawa-ul-misk. Mufarrehat, Luboob, Khamira and Laooq. etc.

Method of Preparation

- ✓ Ingredients like herbs, natural substances, and occasionally animal products are meticulously chosen based on traditional formula. These ingredients are specifically selected for their therapeutic attributes and compatibility with the intended purpose of the Majoon.
- ✓ The selected ingredients undergo a meticulous grinding process to form a fine powder, achieved through either traditional manual methods or modern mechanical equipment. The powdered herbs and substances are then thoroughly mixed together to ensure a consistent distribution of ingredients.

- ✓ To bind the powdered mixture and give the Majoon its semi-solid consistency, a binding agent like honey, ghee (clarified butter), or jaggery (unrefined sugar) is incorporated into the blend. This binding agent serves to hold the ingredients together effectively.
- ✓ The blended mixture undergoes heating and processing procedures aimed at enhancing its medicinal properties and ensuring optimal integration of ingredients. This heating method may involve gentle warming over a flame or in a controlled environment.
- ✓ When the blend achieves the desired consistency, it is meticulously shaped into small balls or tablets either by hand or utilizing molds. These individual Majoon doses are then allowed to cool and solidify, ready for consumption.

Packaging and Storage

The finalized Majoon balls or tablets are carefully packaged in airtight containers or securely wrapped in protective materials to safeguard against moisture and contamination. They are stored in a cool, dry environment away from direct sunlight to maintain their potency and extend their shelf life. Majoon containing Triphala as the primary ingredient should not be stored in metal containers.

General Precaution

- ✓ Utmost care should be taken to prevent moisture coming in contact with the Majoon.
- ✓ During the preparation of Majoon, the ingredient drugs should always be mixed one after the other with constant stirring to ensure uniform mixing.
- ✓ Majoon should maintain required consistency.

Characteristics

During preservation, if Majoon becomes dry, it can be brought to normal consistency with addition of purified honey or Qiwam made of sugar.

Examples: Majoon-e-Alkula, Majoon-e-Bhangra, Majoon-e-Gul

Jawarish

Jawarish is a Unani formulation where more than one single drugs of plant, animal of mineral origin are mixed in powder or liquid forms in the base (Qiwam) made of honey, sugar candy or jaggery.

Method of Preparation

For making Jawarish ingredients are finely powdered and mixed uniformly. Then the powder is mixed with base material made of honey, sugar candy or jaggery. The powder blend is slowly incorporated into the base substance and warmed-over low heat. Vigorous stirring is maintained throughout to evenly disperse the ingredients and avoid scorching. After getting desired consistency,

Jawarish is removed from the heat and allowed to cool slightly. semi-solid Jawarish is shaped into small balls, tablets, or lozenges by hand or using molds and packed in air tight container.

General Precautions

- ✓ Utmost care should be taken to prevent moisture coming in contact with the jawarish.
- ✓ During the preparation of Jawarish the ingredient drugs should always be mixed carefully one after the other and stirred constantly to achieve uniform mixing.
- ✓ Jawarish should be prepared according to the required consistency (Qiwam).

Characteristics

During preservation, if Jawarish becomes dry it can be brought to normal consistency on addition of purified honey or Qiwam made up of suger.

Preservation

- ✓ Jawarish can be preserved in dried, fungus free clean glass, china clay container.
- ✓ The Jawarish containing Triphala as ingredients, should not be preserved in metallic container.

Example:

Jawarish-e-Aamla Ambari, Jawarish-e-Kafoor, Jawarish-e-Safra Shikan

Itrifal

Itrifal is semi solid Unani medicinal preparation where more than one Single Drugs of Plant, animal or mineral origin are mixed in powder or liquid forms in the base (Qiwam) made of purified honey, sugar, candy or joggery.

Example

Itrifal-e-Atfimoon, Itrifal-e-Badiyan

Halwa

Halwa is semi solid Unani medicinal preparation where one or more single Drugs of Plant, animal or mineral origin are mixed in powder or liquid forms in the base.

Example

Halwa-e-Badam, Halwa-e-Bed Anjeer

Marham

According to National Formulary of Unani Medicine, Marham is defined as, "Marham (Ointment) is a semi-solid compound prepared in a base, like Mom (wax), Raughan (Oil) or other Shahmi (Fatty) ingredient. Preparations like Qairooti and Zimad are included in this category."

Method of Preparation

The prescribed oil is heated until wax of fat (shahm) is dissolved and thoroughly mixed in it.

Fine powder of drugs is added, continuously stirred well and allowed to cool till it forms a soft and semi solid mass.

General Precautions

- ✓ Ingredient drugs should be finely pulverized before mixing in the base. The powdering of drugs should strictly be done as per "Daq-wa-Sahaq" guidelines mentioned in National Formulary of Unani Medicine.
- ✓ Continuous stirring of the ingredient drugs is done after mixing in the base
- ✓ Excessive boiling should be avoided as it hardens the Marham.

Characteristics

- ✓ Marham and its related formulations typically exhibit shades of light brown, dark brown, or black.
- ✓ Marham should consistently maintain an opaque appearance.

Preservation

Marham and its related formulations must always be stored in airtight, clean, and dry glass or porcelain containers, kept in cool and dry environments.

Example

Marham-e-Misri, Marham-e-Sendu

3.3 SIDDHA FORMULATIONS

Like Ayurvedic formulations, siddha formulations are polyherbals, Herbo mineral and mineral preparation, Siddhar are pioneer of using mineral drugs and formulation. The ancient Siddha scripture Tirumantiram defines medicine as a remedy that not only heals physical and mental ailments but also serves as a preventive measure against diseases and promotes longevity. Siddha drugs are formulated using source materials derived from plants, minerals, and animal products. Essential Siddha texts such as 'Akattiyar Ku¸av¡ka¶am' and 'Pat¡rtta Ku¸acint¡ma¸i' provide valuable insights into the properties of raw medicinal ingredients utilized in both single and compound formulations.

Siddha Pharmacology or **Gunapadam** describes Pharmacology, Pharmacodynamics of Siddha medicine. Crude drugs are classified into three categories based on their origin: medicinal plants (Mooligai vakuppu), minerals (Thathu vakuppu), and animal products (Jeeva vakuppu). Siddha literature describes around 220 minerals, encompassing metals (ulokam – 11), salts (karasaram – 25), mercury and arsenic compounds (Paatanam - 64), and other minerals (uparasam – 120). Animal products such as coral, conch, deer horn, musk, and honey are also utilized.

Siddha medicines can be further classified based on their mode of application:

Internal Medicine (32 types)

Internal medicines are divided into 32 categories, each with its unique form and method of preparation, along with a specific shelf life. These categories range from medicines with short shelf lives to metallic preparations that can be used for extended periods, even up to hundreds of years.

External Medicine (32 types)

Among the thirty-two types of external applications and manipulations are ottradam (fomentation), vedhu (inhalation), pottanam (kizhi), nasiyam, kattu (bandaging), kombu kattal (splint application), and attai vidal (leech therapy), among others.

Siddha pharmacology revolves around the principles of the five basic elements, known as Pañcabhūtam, and the taste (Cuvai) of the drug. Siddha literature extensively mentions numerous varieties of medicinal plants, minerals, and animal products. This branch of Siddha medicine encompasses discussions on raw drugs (Mūlapporuḷkaṉ), the purification of raw drugs (Cūṭṭi), and methods for preparing medicines (Maruṇṭukaṉiṉ Ceymuḷai). Raw drugs are classified based on their origin into materials of medicinal plant (Mūlaikai Vakuppu), mineral (Tāṭu Vakuppu), and animal origin (Cīva Vakuppu).

Internal Medicine (32 types)

Internal medicines are classified according to dosage form and shelf life. The drugs which contain moisture like heat treated juice, decoction etc. have shorter shelf life than drugs which have no moisture like kattu, Kalanku, Urukku, Cattu etc., have longer shelf life.

Curacam (Heat treated juice)

Medicinal juice processed by placing a hot iron rod into it.

Juice (Caru)

Juice prepared by pressing / squeezing the fresh medicinal plants/raw materials.

Kuru Kulikai

Sublimated mercury is made into beads while in its amalgam state. Mercury stands as a cornerstone of Siddha therapeutics, and these mercury beads exhibit remarkable abilities to transform metals and revitalize the entire human body.

Kattu

Drugs like iron powder, magnetite, organic salts, poisonous drugs are pulverized well with egg white and placed in a crucible (Mucai) and blown; and the process is repeated 3 times. After that mercury, gold and sulphur are added to it and it is made into Centuram by burning process.

Kutinir (Decoction)

Kutinir is prepared by adding water to the crude drugs (dried or fresh ones) and boiling it till the water content is reduced to 1/16th 1/8th, $1/4^{th}$ of the initial or so as indicated in the process.

Herbal paste (Kurakam)

Paste is prepared by grinding wet drug or adding water or decoction to the dry powders of cruder rug.

Pudding (Utkali)

This formulation has the inner contents which are wet and paste-like while the external surface is dry. This is made by using raw or boiled rice, fried and pounded to a flour form or by grinding black gram and converted into paste or by powdering seeds and by adding enough water to make a paste and with this, sugar or jaggery is mixed and heated on a fire, placing the paste in a mud pot until it is cooked into a gruel form.

Pan cake (Atai)

Rice flour is mixed with a few leaves and ground thoroughly, possibly with a bit of water, and then baked in a hot oven after incorporating ghee.

Powder (Churnram)

The dried medicinal ingredients are individually purified, crushed separately, sifted, and blended according to the specified proportions, with the option of including jaggery or sugar.

Steamed medicinal powder (Pittu)

A Siddha formulation which is prepared by steaming moistened medicinal powder.

Lozenge / troche (Vatakam)

The natural ingredients are individually transformed into a fine powder, filtered through cloth, and combined thoroughly. Palm sugar or jaggery is subsequently introduced. An earthenware pot is filled with equal parts of cow's milk and water, covered with cloth at the mouth. The prepared mixture of ingredients is then placed on top, covered with a mud lid, and heated until the milk evaporates entirely. The resulting Pittu is then ground and shaped into small pills.

Medicated butter (Venney)

The powdered raw drugs are combined and blended with double their volume of butter in an iron spoon, then heated until the raw ingredients fully dissolve and blend with the butter. This mixture is then poured into an earthen pot filled with water and churned thoroughly to achieve a butter-like consistency.

Syrup (Manappaku)

Crude drugs are separately converted into decoction and boiled by adding sugar or jaggery till a sweet aromatic odour generates and then powdered raw materials are sprinkled over it.

Medicated ghee (Ney)

It is ghee-based preparation which is produced by boiling a mixture of ghee with specified medicinal pastes, juices, decoctions and milk, according to the composition formula.

Dry Confection (Iracayanam)

It is a semi-solid formulation which is prepared by adding sugar and ghee to a Churnam prepared from specified raw drugs.

Electuary (Ilakam/Lekiyam)

This formulation is prepared by heating certain decoctions, juices and milk with the addition of sugar till a viscous consistency is reached. At that stage, the specific drug powders are added and mixed to get homogenous mass after which ghee is mixed, and the mixture is cooled and then honey is added and preserved.

Medicated oil (Enney/Thailam)

Oily medications prepared by boiling decoctions, juices of herbs with milk and pastes of other raw materials in vegetable oil.

Pills/Tablet (Maththirai)

Crude drugs are triturated with the juices of herbs or decoction and rolled into different sizes of pills, dried and stored.

Sediments (Katuku)

Crude drugs are added to oil and boiled till granules or sediments form.

Processed medicines (Pakkuvam)

The medicinal substance to be prepared is first soaked in raw rice water or plain water. Afterward, it is soaked in either buttermilk, lime juice, ginger juice, or various leaf juices, and then preserved for medicinal purposes.

Honey infused drug (Thenural)

Ginger, Indian gooseberry, or gall nut are initially soaked in water and cut into small pieces. These pieces are then soaked in either honey or jaggery syrup.

Distilled extracts (Thinir)

This process involves boiling the medicinal substances with water in a unique distillation vessel. The steam from the medicated water is then cooled and gathered.

Medicinal wax (Meẕuku)

They come in two types: i) Araippu Meẕuku — Achieved by grinding specific mercurial compounds individually or with other medicinal ingredients, with the addition of juices or honey to form a semi-solid substance. ii) Curukku Meẕuku: Certain mercurial drugs or toxic substances are gently heated with the addition of oil substances or juices, forming a semi-solid substance that is finely ground.

Medicated semisolid mixture (Kuẕampu)

A combination of mixture of juices or a single juice is placed in a container, and then fine powder of medicinal ingredients is mixed in, heated, and consumed in liquid form. Additionally, certain substances are thoroughly ground with oily ingredients to form a semi-solid consistency.

Sublimates (Patankam)

Patankam is a sublimate prepared from inorganic substances through sublimation process by using a special sublimation apparatus (Patankak Karuvi).

Calcined red oxides / sulphides (Centuram)

Metallic substances or salts or toxic salts are converted red coloured powders, by the process of calcination or drying them or by exposing to the sunlight or keeping them in specific tubes with the addition of decoctions.

Calcined oxide/Calx (Parpam/Niru)

Calx (Parpam) is an atomized/nano sized mineral oxide preparation which facilitates high absorption.

Consolidation (Kattu) (Non-volatile form of volatile inorganic substances /materials)

In this formulation, where the volatile mercurial and the arsenic compounds, are converted into non-volatile form.

Solidification (Urukku)

Certain metals and some toxic minerals along with their incompatible materials are kept in crucibles and sealed properly and placed in intense heat using blowers utilising natural coal obtained from wood. The drugs in the crucible are melted by this process and cooled.

Amalgam (Kalanku)

These are the formulation containing metals and highly volatile substances like mercury, mercurial compounds, and arsenic compounds. Through this process, the metals become finely brittle. The metals and other components are finely melted together in a pan over moderate heat. The easily volatile substances are melted separately with extreme caution to prevent their evaporation. While they are still hot or in a molten state, specific plant juices or distillates mentioned in the formula are added gradually and in small quantities to ensure complete absorption.

Calcinated caustic compounds (Cunnam)

Cunnam is created by heating or calcining a metal, mineral, or animal product until it transforms into a calx following the steps outlined in the formula. These substances have alkaline characteristics akin to limestone. When combined with a small amount of turmeric powder, Cunnam changes to a red color.

Rejuvenating / Elixir drugs (Kaṟpam)

This process involves taking a specific dose of leaves, herbs, roots, salts, and minerals over a specified period, following the prescribed dietary guidelines. These substances can either be prepared daily or used as pre-prepared medicines.

Quintessence (Cattu)

Drugs like iron powder, magnetite, organic salts, poisonous drugs are pulverized well with egg white and placed in a crucible (Mucai) and blown; and the process is repeated three times. After that mercury, gold and sulphur are mixed with it and it is converted into Centuram by burning process.

Master pill (Kuru Kullikai)

The sublime mercury is converted into beads in its amalgam form. Mercury could be called as the sheet anchor of Siddha therapeutics. These mercurial pills possess marvellous properties of transmuting metals and rejuvenating the entire human system.

External formulations

Parru/Poultice

Parru/Poultice is a soft moist mass, usually made with herbs, and applied on areas affected by skin diseases like emollient, anti-microbial, anti-allergic, anti-inflammatory and analgesic.

Puccu (Topical application)

Puccu is atopical liquid formulation.

Mai (Collyrium /Medicated eye-liner)

Mai is an ophthalmic formulation which is applied in a paste format to inner eye margin of lower eyelid.

Piccu (Enema)

Piccu is a medicated oil/ water applied in enema form.

3.4 HOMOEOPATHIC MEDICINE

Homeopathic medicine and formulation are prepared from varieties of natural products and which includes:

Source	Example
Plant origin	*Aconitum napellus* *Strychnos nuxvomica* *Allium cepa*
Animal origin	*Blatta orientalis* *Tarentula hispanica* *Apis mellifica*
Mineraland chemical origin	Mag Phos Natrum Muriaticum
Sarcodes	Adrenalin (secretion of medulla of supra-renal gland) Pancreatinum (extract from pancreas of beef)
Nosodes	Influenzinum Anthracinum- lysate obtained without addition of antiseptic from the liver of rabbit suffering from Anthrax. Tuberculinum avis
Imponderabilia	Xray, Magnet, Moonlight

Sarcodes: Homeopathic medicines made from healthy animal tissues or secretions of animal tissue. In Greek, sarcode refers fleshly.

Nosodes: Homeopathic medicines prepared from disease products from humans or animals; from pathogenic organisms or their metabolic products; or from decomposition products of animal organs.

Imponderabilia: Homeopathic medicines made from energy, emanating from natural and physical reactions. It means "not weighable", i.e. which have no perceptible weights. Imponderabilia are energy forms such as sunlight (Sol), magnetic fields (Magnetis Polus Australis), radiation (X-ray).

Vehicle used for Homoeopathic medicine

Types	Examples
Solid	Lactose; pellet, globule, tabloids
Liquid	Alcohol, water, glycerin
Semisolid	Vaselin, lanolin, sparmaceti

Unlike other traditional/Complementary and alternative medicines, Homoeopathic medicines are single medicine formulation. Homoeopathic medicines mainly comprise of extract of plants and animal, crude minerals or their dilutions.

Mother tincture

Mother tinctures are the liquid preparations obtained from the extraction of suitable raw material (plant or animal crude drug) with alcohol/water mixtures which form the initial point for the production of most homeopathic medicines. Mother tincture is denoted as ɵ (Theta). Comminution or size reduction of crude drugs followed by standard percolation/ maceration extraction using alcohol and squeezing techniques are applied on fresh plant or crude drugs.

It is observed that the concentration of alcohol used in the extraction technique can affect the quality of the final mother tincture and that the ideal solvent is 70% w/v alcohol.

The resulting solutions are filtered and may contain one part drug to three parts mother tincture, although this strength can vary from 10 -50% based on the species and pharmacopoeial monograph being used. When the final tincture contains one-tenth of the concentration of original drug it is, in effect, a 1x dilution.

Method of Mother tincture preparation is variable and the process and time span of extraction differs between different Pharmacopoeias.

Insoluble drugs including minerals are triturated (grinding of powder in mortar and pestle) with lactose. The resulting triturate powder may be directly compressed into trituration tablets or administered as a powder if the remedy is required at potencies where it is still insoluble.

Mother tincture can be directly used for some remedies, for example Arnica or Calendula may be applied directly to the skin, or it can be used as diluted or gargle. However, mother tinctures are subjected to a specialized two stage process which involves dilution and sucussion. These 2 simultaneous steps increase the therapeutic strength of mother tincture, this process is known as

potentisation/dynamisation. There are several methods of potentisation, of which the Hahnemannian method, developed by the Founder after several series of experiments.

Dilutions

Dilutions are prepared to potentize the mother tincture to get better potent form of medicine and this is achieved by generally 2 scales referred in Hahnemannian method. These are Decimal and Centicimal scale. One drop of mother tincture is diluted with 9 or 99 drops of diluent in a new clean screw cap glass vial. In modern pharmaceutical practice, a triple-distilled alcohol and water system is commonly used, with strengths ranging from 20% to 60%, for preparing homeopathic dilutions.

Hahnemann introduced the **centesimal scale** during the early stages of homeopathy, featuring a dilution ratio of 1:100. This method entails diluting one part of the mother tincture in 99 parts of a water-alcohol solution, followed by succussion. This results in a 1C potency, where "C" denotes the 1:100 dilution ratio. Through serial dilution and succussion, higher potencies are achieved. Centesimal remedies are adaptable and effective for treating a wide range of acute and chronic illnesses in different presentations.

The **decimal scale**, which features a 1:10 dilution ratio, emerged as the second potency scale in the evolution of homeopathy. In this scale, one part of the mother tincture or potency is diluted in nine parts of a water-alcohol mixture (Represented with D or X), with ten succussions performed between each dilution step. Decimal potencies are user-friendly and can be administered in various forms, commonly employed for self-treatment of uncomplicated acute issues.

The Fifty Millesimal Scale, also referred to as the Quinquagintimillesimal Scale or simply LM or Q potencies, was introduced near the end of Hahnemann's life. Featuring an initial dilution ratio of 1:50,000 and a more intricate preparation method compared to the centesimal and decimal scales, these potencies are profound in their effects and adaptable. They are intended for liquid dispensation only and are usually recommended for professional use, as their proper prescription requires a deeper understanding of homeopathic principles.

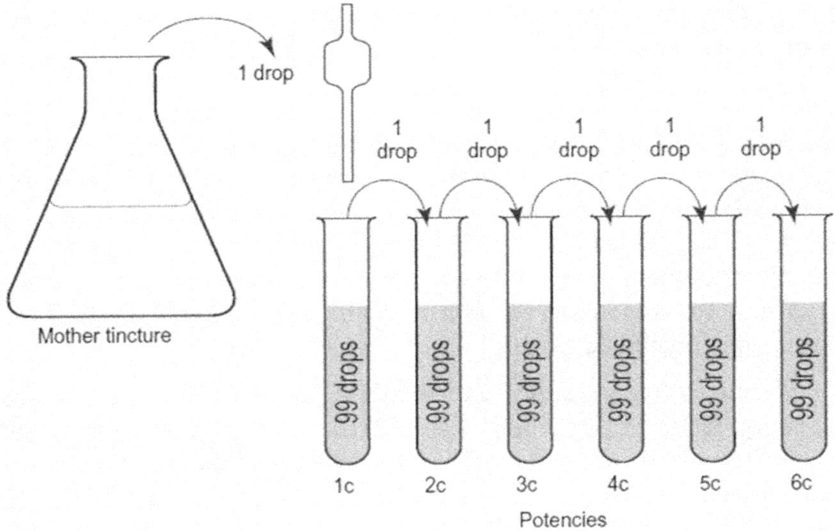

Succussion: The solution produced from admixture of the two liquids is subjected to the several shaking with impact known as succussion which is commercially done using mechanical shaker after each dilution is done.

Dilution	Concentration	Centesimal potency
1:100	10^{-2}	1c or 1cH
1:10 000	10^{-4}	2c or 2cH
1:1 000 000	10^{-6}	3c or 3cH
$1:10^{12}$	10^{-12}	6c or 6cH
$1:10^{30}$	10^{-30}	15c or 15cH
$1:10^{60}$	10^{-60}	30c or 30cH
$1:10^{400}$	10^{-400}	200c or 200cH
$1:10^{2000}$	10^{-2000}	1000c or M
$1:10^{20\,000}$	$10^{-20\,000}$	10 000c or 10M

List of centesimal potencies

Dilution	Concentration	Decimal potency
1:10	10^{-1}	1x or D1
1:100	10^{-2}	2x or D2
1:1000	10^{-3}	3x or D3
1:10000	10^{-4}	4x or D4
1:100000	10^{-5}	5x or D5
1:1000000	10^{-6}	6x or D6
$1:10^{30}$	10^{-30}	30x or D30

List of decimal potencies

Standardization of Homoeopathic Medicines

Plant crude drugs

Identification of source material	1. scientific name; 2. stage of growth; 3. part of plant used; 4. information about whether materials were cultivated or collected from the wild and the place of cultivation or collection from the wild; 5. comparison, by the manufacturer or by a recognized laboratory, with an illustrated description of an authentic specimen for macroscopic and microscopic characteristics as well as analytical determination of marker substances or standard substances (if applicable).
Limit tests:	1. Limit tests should be performed for: • pesticides (agricultural and veterinary chemicals), • heavy metals (if appropriate, for metals such as lead, mercury, arsenic and cadmium), • fungi, bacteria, mycotoxins (e.g. aflatoxins), and • any other relevant contamination (e.g. by-products of manufacture, radiolytic products derived from sterilization by ionizing radiation, or residues from other decontamination procedures). 2. Limit tests should be done on representative samples at an unprocessed or raw stage (if processed matter has to be used, a sample should be taken before any potentization is done). 3. Limit tests and ranges should comply with pharmacopoeial standards, as limits applicable to food may not be appropriate.

Tabled contd...

Complementary tests:	Where applicable, tests are performed for: 1. foreign matter; 2. total ash; 3. water content; 4. bitterness value; 5. loss on drying; 6. radioactive contamination.

Animal crude drugs

A clear description of the following characteristics should accompany every batch, or its absence needs to be justified:

- identification of the source of the animal material, including information on whether animals were bred or caught in the wild and the place of breeding or capture in the wild.;
- parts/material of animal used;
- anatomical description of the animal part;
- histological description of the animal part;
- identity tests;
- purity tests;
- moisture/water content;
- determination of content of toxic constituents (if applicable);
- method for preparation of the initial homeopathic preparation (reference to general procedure).

Human drugs

Clear documentation on the donor is a prerequisite for ensuring the safety of homeopathic medicines of human origin. A clear description (from tests and/or documentation of history of the material) of the following characteristics should accompany every batch, or its absence needs to be justified:

- identification of the source;
- material used;
- anatomical description;
- histological description;
- identity tests;
- purity tests;
- moisture/water content;
- method for preparing the initial homeopathic preparation (reference to general procedure).

Mineral drugs

For the first dilution/trituration, details of the following are required, or their absence needs to be justified:

- method of preparation;
- description and characteristics;
- identity tests;
- purity tests;
- determination of content;
- determination of toxic constituents.

Mother tincture

The following data should be presented, or their absence needs to be justified:

- method of preparation (reference to general procedure);
- appearance and description;
- identity tests;
- purity tests;
- procedure for stability tests;
- determination of content;
- determination of toxic constituents.

Additional test for Finished Product/mother tincture and potency upto 6x

- ✓ Alcohol content
- ✓ pH
- ✓ Wt/ml
- ✓ TDS
- ✓ Identification
- ✓ λmax
- ✓ TLC profile-Rf value

3.5 STANDARDIZATION, SHELF LIFE AND STABILITY STUDIES OF ISM FORMULATIONS

Standardization is a consensus-driven process grounded in scientific research and agreed upon by stakeholders most affected by it. It encompasses various aspects, including manufacturing processes, analytical tests, operational procedures, instrument calibration, and specific conditions necessary for a particular purpose. Its aim is to establish and implement rules in a systematic manner for the benefit of all involved parties. Key components of standardization include:

- **Authentication:** Ensuring the authenticity of raw materials used in the preparation of medicinal products based on botanical (pharmacognostic) characteristics.
- **Foreign Matter:** Ensuring that medicinal plants are free from visible contamination by insects, molds, and other contaminants. Foreign matter refers to any material other than the desired part of the drug and should be within prescribed limits set by pharmacopoeias.
- **Organoleptic Characteristics:** Assessing visual attributes such as size, color, texture, and fracture characteristics, as well as sensory attributes like odor and taste, to verify the authenticity of the material.
- **Macroscopic and Microscopic Characters:** Ensuring that the macroscopic and microscopic characteristics of the material align with pharmacopoeial standards.
- **Loss on Drying**
- **Total Ash**
- **Acid-insoluble Ash**
- **Extractable Value (Alcohol and Water)**
- **Heavy Metals (Lead, Cadmium, Mercury, Arsenic):** Observing prescribed limits for heavy metal content as specified in pharmacopoeias to ensure safety.
- **Microbial Load**: Monitoring microbial contamination levels to ensure safety standards are met, including absence of specific harmful bacteria and limits for total microbial plate count, yeast, and mold. Aflatoxins (Bi, B2, Gi, G2) - The limits as prescribed in ASU Pharmacopoeias i.e. B, - <2 ppb; B, +B2 +G, +G2 <5 ppb may be observed.
- **Chromatographic profiles (TLC, HPLC or GC)**
- **Assay of Marker Compounds**
- **Pesticide Residue (Organo Chlorine and Organo phosphorous)-**

By adhering to these standardization measures, the quality, safety, and efficacy of medicinal products can be assured, promoting public health and confidence in traditional medicine practices.

Standardization of Raw Drugs (with chemical profile)

↓

SOP of Extract (If used)

↓

Standardization of Extracts

↓

SOP of Formulation

↓

Standardization of Formulation/ Finished product and Shelf life studies

↓

Biological Screening

↓

Safety and Toxicity Studies

↓

Preservation, Packing and Storage

Steps involved in ISM formulation and quality control

3.6 SHELF LIFE AND STABILITY STUDIES OF ISM FORMULATIONS

Shelf life and stability studies of ISM formulations are highly essential due to following reason:

- Unlike the conventional medicine, ISM and traditional medicines are mostly susceptible to the microbial growth and decomposition.
- Prediction of the Stability of polyherbal/herbo-mineral/herbo- animal formulation used in ISM are difficult as physico-chemical stability may be altered during long time storage.
- Preparation of medicine in large scale using sophisticated machineries in compare to the ancient traditional method may alter the predicted stability of the formulation.

- Interaction with primary packaging material with ISM formulation are quite unpredictable.
- Global regulatory requirements are stringent and zone specific.

According to Gazette of India, G.S.R. 789(E), as per the 161-B of Drug and Cosmetics Rules 1945,

"1. The date of expiry of Ayurveda, Siddha and Unani medicines shall be conspicuously displayed on the label of container or package of an Ayurvedic, Siddhas and Unani medicines, and after the said date of expiry, these medicines shall not be in circulation.

2. The Shelf-life i.e. for Ayurveda, Siddha and Unani medicines shall be as follows:-

(i) Shelf life or date of expiry for Ayurvedic medicines.

Name of the Group of Ayurvedic Medicine	Shelf life and date of expiry with effect from the date of manufacture
Churna, Kwatha Churna	2 years
Gutika (Vati-Gutti, Pills, Tablets except Gutika with Rasa)	3 years
Gutika Tablet containing Kasth aushadhi	3 years
Gutika,Tablet containing Kasth aushadi and Rasa, Uprasa, Metallic Bhasmas, and Guggulu.	5 years
Rasaushadhies	No expiry date
Asava Arista	No expiry date
Avaleha	3 years
Guggulu	5 years
Mandura - Lauha	10 years
Ghrita	2 years
Taila	3 years
Arka	1 year
Dravaka, Lavana, Ksara	5 years
Lepa Churna	3 years
Dant Manjan Powder and paste	2years
Lepa Guti	3 years
Lepa Malahar (Ointment)/Liniment/Gels/ lotions /creams	3 years
Varti	2 years (one time use)
Ghana Vati	3 years
Kupipakva Rasayan	No expiry date
Parpati	No expiry date
Pisti and Bhasma	No expiry date
Capsules made of soft gelatin (depending upon the content material) for Kashtha aushadhi	3 years
Capsules of hard gelatin (depending upon the content material) -containing Kasth aushdhi with Rasa, Bhasma, Parad-Gandhak	5 years

Formulation like Asava, aristha, Kupipakva Rasayan, Pisti, Bhasma have long shelf life and it is mandatory to keep those items minimum 10 years for the record of stability studies.

Bhasmas, start solidifying after 5 years and they required one or two Puta'(calcination) again before using in the dosage form.

(ii) Shelf life or date of expiry for Siddha Medicines.

1. Karpam -No expiry date*
2. Cunnam - 5 years
3. Kalanku - No expiry date*
4. Kattu - No expiry date*
5. Parpam - No expiry date*
6. Centuram - No expiry date*
7. Karuppu - No expiry date*
8. Patankam- 5 years
9. Kulampu- 5 years
10. Meluku - 5 years
11. Tinir - 2 years
12. Tiravakam - 2 years
13. Mattirai - 3 years
14. Tailam 3- years
15. Ilakam- 3 years
16. Iracayanaam - 3 years
17. Ney -2 years
18. Manappaku- 3 years
19. Venney -3 years
20. Vatakam -3 years
21. Curanam- 2 years
22. Pura Maruntukal -5 years

(iii) Shelf life or date of expiry for Unani System of Medicines.

1. Habb (Pills)- 3 years
2. Qurs (Tablets) -3 years
3. Majoon/Dawa -3 years
4. Khamira -3 years
5. Itrifal -3 years
6. Tiryaq- 3 years

7. Laooq -2 years
8. Laboob -2 years
9. Halwa -2 years
10. Mufarreh/Yaqooti -2 years
11. Burood/Surma/Kohal- 3 years
12. Kushta -5 years
13. Raughaniyat -3 years
14. Marham/Zimad/Qairooti -3 years
15. Ayarij/Sufoof -2 years
16. Safoof (Namak wala/containing salt)- 1 year
17. Sharbat/Sikanjabeen -3 years
18. Jawarish- 3 years
19. Capsule -3 years
20. Arq -1 year
21. Qutoor -1 year
22. Nabeez- 5 years
23. Murabba- 1 year
24. Tila -2 years]....."

The expiry date of Ayurvedic, Siddha, or Unani medicines must be clearly shown on the label of the container or package. After this expiry date, the medicine cannot be sold, distributed, or used. However, this rule applies only to medicines seeking licensing or renewal after the notification date of these rules. Medicines manufactured and sold before this notification date are exempt from this rule.

Anyone applying for a license or license renewal to manufacture Ayurvedic, Siddha, or Unani medicines must provide scientific data on the shelf life or expiry date of the medicine based on real-time stability studies. These studies should follow the guidelines outlined in the Ayurvedic Pharmacopoeia of India. This sub-rule becomes applicable three years after the notification of the rules.

The stability study guidelines outlined in the Ayurvedic Pharmacopoeia of India, Part-I, Volume-VIII, apply to all Ayurvedic, Siddha, and Unani medicines.

Before granting or renewing a license for Ayurvedic, Siddha, or Unani medicine, the State Licensing Authority must verify the validity of the data provided by the manufacturer regarding the medicine's shelf life.

The State Licensing Authority has the power to request samples of the medicine and related information from the manufacturer at any time. This information may be shared with the Pharmacopoeial Laboratory for Indian Medicine, Ghaziabad, for analysis or independent validation. Failure to comply with such requests may result in the suspension of the manufacturing license after a fair hearing.

If a person is dissatisfied with an order issued by the State Licensing Authority, they can appeal to the Central Government within sixty days of the order. The Central Government will conduct a necessary inquiry and make a final decision, which will be binding.

Stability Studies of ISM formulation

The API guidelines for stability testing and determination of shelf life for both new and existing Ayurvedic drugs offer a framework for evaluating stability data and establishing shelf life. While the parent guideline provides a brief overview of stability data analysis, it lacks details, especially in scenarios involving multiple factors. This new guideline aims to address these limitations and provide a structured approach to determining shelf life through stability testing.

Scope and Objective

The primary objective of this guideline is to outline the methodology for determining shelf life through stability testing. The shelf life obtained through this process can be utilized to set an expiry date, particularly if manufacturers intend to extend shelf life beyond the specified duration mentioned in the GSR 764(E) notification dated October 15, 2009. This guideline applies to all patented and proprietary Ayurvedic medicines, regardless of whether they are new or existing products.

General Information on Stability

Shelf life information, also known as the expiry date, is a mandatory requirement for all licensed Ayurvedic medicines. Stability studies are crucial to demonstrate that the medicine maintains its suitability for consumption throughout its shelf life under specified storage conditions. If no specific storage condition is indicated on the product label, it is assumed that the product can be stored at room temperature (below 30° Celsius). For certain drug substances, a retest period may be more appropriate than an expiry date.

Purpose of Stability Testing

Stability testing aims to provide evidence on how the quality of a drug substance or product changes over time due to environmental factors like temperature, humidity, and light. This information helps establish a retest period for drug substances or a shelf life for drug products.

Approaches to Stability Monitoring

Stability monitoring can be conducted using two approaches: storing samples under standard and accelerated storage conditions and testing them periodically, or selecting samples from batches manufactured over the past five years and evaluating them simultaneously.

Selection of Batches

Formal stability studies should be conducted on at least three primary batches that represent the formulation proposed for marketing. For new products, these batches should be manufactured on a pilot scale using the same method and process planned for production batches.

Container and Closure System

Stability studies should use the same container and closure system intended for marketing, ensuring compatibility with storage and distribution conditions.

Specification

Stability studies should include testing for attributes susceptible to change during storage, covering physical, chemical, biological, and microbiological aspects. Specification limits should be derived from pharmacopoeias or release specifications, with justifiable differences between release and shelf-life acceptance criteria.

Testing Frequency

The frequency of testing should be sufficient to establish the stability profile, with more frequent testing during the initial stages and then annually thereafter. Reduced designs such as matrixing or bracketing can be applied if justified.

Storage Conditions

Recommended storage conditions include accelerated conditions at 40° Celsius ± 2° with 75% relative humidity for six months and long-term conditions at 30° Celsius ± 2° with 60% relative humidity for 12 months, specifically tailored for Zone IV climatic regions.

Evaluation

The goal of stability testing is to determine, through testing a minimum of three drug batches, a retest period for the drug substance or a shelf life with storage instructions for all future batches of the drug product manufactured and packaged under similar conditions. An Ayurvedic drug is considered stable if there is no significant change observed during testing under accelerated or real-time storage conditions.

A "significant change" in a drug is defined as:

- A deviation of ±20% from the initial assay value (for drugs analyzed based on their marker) or ±15% from the initial assay value (for drugs analyzed based on their active compound).
- Appearance of new spots or complete disappearance of existing spots in TLC identification (compared to samples stored at less than 10°C).
- Physico-chemical parameters (moisture, ash, particle size) should not vary more than 25% from the initial value.
- Failure to meet acceptance criteria outlined in individual monographs or specifications.
- Failure to meet acceptance criteria for appearance (physical attributes and functionality tests such as color, phase separation, caking, and hardness).

CHAPTER 4

Schedule T – Good Manufacturing Practice of Indian Systems of Medicine (ISM), Quality Assurance, Exports of ISM Medicine and Challenges in Monitoring the Safety of Herbal Medicines

4.1 SCHEDULE T – GOOD MANUFACTURING PRACTICE OF INDIAN SYSTEMS OF MEDICINE

Schedule T is the Good manufacturing practices (GMP) of Indian Systems of medicine including Ayurveda, Siddha and Unani (ASU). Schedule T is mentioned as Rule number 157 under Drug and Cosmetics Rules 1945.

Before understanding schedule T, it is essential to understand GMP and its basic objectives.

According to WHO, GMP can be defined as "GMP is the aspect of quality assurance that ensures that medicinal products are consistently produced and controlled to the quality standards appropriate to their intended use and as required by the product specification."

"*GMP defines quality measures for both production and quality control and defines general measures to ensure that processes necessary for production and testing are clearly defined, validated, reviewed, and documented, and that the personnel, premises and materials are suitable for the production of pharmaceuticals and biologicals including vaccines*"

GMP ensures consistent quality products and prevent mix up and cross contamination. GMP is the minimum set of practices that must be observed during manufacturing to ensure a quality product.

GMP guidelines do not provide specific directives for product manufacturing; rather, they outline general principles that must be adhered to throughout the manufacturing process. When establishing a quality program and manufacturing procedures, companies have various options for meeting GMP standards. It is the company's duty to identify the most suitable and efficient quality processes for compliance. Principles and guidelines of GMPs are variable and depends upon different global and regional regulatory authorities. However, all GMP guidelines fulfil the following objectives:

- Manufacturing procedures are meticulously outlined and supervised, with validation of all critical processes to ensure adherence to specifications and consistency.
- Any alterations to these processes undergo evaluation, with changes impacting drug quality subject to necessary validation.
- Instructions and protocols are drafted in clear, unambiguous language. Operators receive training to execute and document procedures effectively.
- Throughout manufacturing, records, whether manual or electronic, are maintained to verify adherence to defined procedures and instructions, as well as to confirm the expected quantity and quality of the drug.
- Any deviations are thoroughly investigated and documented.
- Additionally, comprehensive records of manufacturing (including distribution) are preserved in an understandable and easily accessible format, enabling complete batch tracing.

Why GMP of Herbal /Traditional medicine are challenging? /Need of special GMP for Herbal /Traditional medicine

- Herbal and traditional medicines are prepared mainly from Plant / animal sources which are highly dependent upon geo-climatic variation and unlike synthetic drugs they are not prepared from reproducible synthetic chemicals
- Mostly composed of polyherbal including several herbs, phytochemical and excipient
- More prone to microbial and pest attack
- Unobvious stability pattern
- Complex preparation techniques according to ancient text

Above reasons justify the specific special GMP guidelines for Traditional Indian Medicines /Ayurvedic, Siddha and Unani (ASU).

Schedule T [Rule number 157]/Good Manufacturing Practices for Ayurvedic, Siddha and Unani Medicines

In accordance with the Drugs and Cosmetics Act of 1940 and its accompanying Rules of 1945, the responsibility for enforcing legal provisions regarding Quality Control and the issuance of drug licenses for Ayurveda, Siddha, Unani, and Homoeopathic drugs lies with the State drug Controllers or State Licensing Authorities appointed by the respective State or Union Territory Governments. Rule 158-B in the Drugs and Cosmetics Rules, 1945 outlines the regulatory guidelines for granting licenses to manufacture Ayurvedic, Siddha, and Unani medicines, while Rule 85 (A to I) in the same Rules provides regulatory guidelines for issuing licenses to manufacture Homoeopathic medicines. Manufacturers are obligated to comply with specified requirements for licensing manufacturing units and medicines, including demonstrating safety and effectiveness, adhering to Good Manufacturing Practices (GMP) as outlined in Schedule T and Schedule M-I of the Drugs and Cosmetics Rules, 1945, and meeting the quality standards stipulated in the respective pharmacopoeias.

As per Rule 157 of Drugs and Cosmetics Rules, 1945 Schedule T is described under 2 parts (Part I and II) to ensure that:

"(i) Raw materials used in the manufacture of drugs are authentic, of prescribed

quality and are free from contamination.

(ii) The manufacturing process is as has been prescribed to maintain the standards.

(iii) Adequate quality control measures are adopted.

(iv) The manufactured drug which is released for sale is of acceptable quality.

(v) To achieve the objectives listed above, each licensee shall evolve methodology and procedures for following the prescribed process of manufacture of drugs which should be documented as a manual and kept for reference and inspection. However, under IMCC Act 1970 [THE INDIAN MEDICINE CENTRAL COUNCIL ACT, 1970] registered Vaidyas, Siddhas and Hakeems who prepare medicines on their own to dispense to their patients and not selling such drugs in the market are exempted from the purview of G.M.P."

Part I of Schedule T has following principles

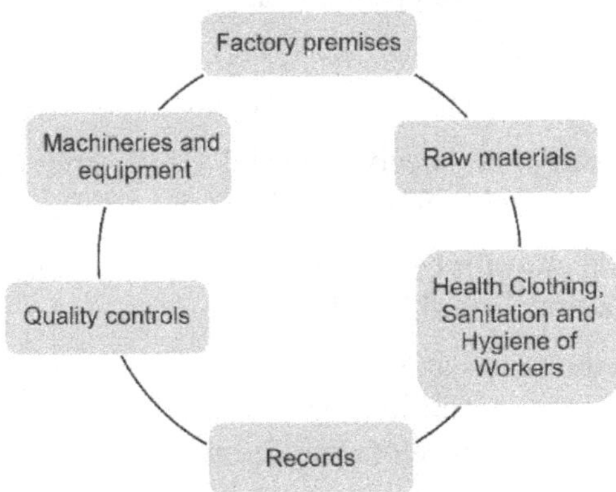

1.1 Factory Premises

The manufacturing plant should have adequate space for:

(i) Receiving and storing raw material section
(ii) Manufacturing process areas for the manufacturing of formulation
(iii) Quality control (QC) section
(iv) Finished goods store
(v) Office
(vi) Rejected drugs/ goods store.

1.1 General Requirements

1.1(A) Location and surroundings	"The factory building for manufacture of Ayurveda, Siddha and Unani medicines shall be so situated and shall have **such construction as to avoid contamination from open sewerage, drain, public lavatory for any factory** which produces **disagreeable or obnoxious odour or fumes or excessive soot, dust and smoke**." [Source: as per the 1.1(A) of Schedule T, Drug and Cosmetics Rule, 1945]
1.1(B) Buildings -	"The buildings used for factory shall be such as to permit production of drugs under hygienic conditions and should be free from cobwebs and insects/rodents. It should have adequate provision of light and ventilation. The floor and the walls should not be damp or moist. The premises used for manufacturing, processing, packaging and labelling will be in conformity with the provisions of the Factory Act. It shall be located so as to be: (I) Compatible with other manufacturing operations that may be carried out in the same or adjacent premises. (II) Adequately provided with working space to allow orderly and logical placement of equipment and materials to avoid the risk of mix-up between different drugs or components thereof and control the possibility of cross contamination by other drugs or substances and avoid the risk of omission of any manufacturing or control step. (III) **Designed, constructed and maintained to prevent entry of insects and rodents. Interior surface (walls, floors and ceilings)** shall be **smooth and free from cracks and permit easy cleaning and disinfection.** The walls of the room in which the manufacturing operations are carried out shall be impervious to and be capable of being kept clean. The flooring shall be smooth and even and shall be such as not to permit retention or accumulation of dust or waste products.

Table contd...

	(IV) Provided with **proper drainage system** in the processing area. The sanitary fittings and electrical fixtures in the manufacturing area shall be proper and safe. (V) **Furnace/Bhatti section could be covered with tin roof and proper ventilation**, but sufficient care should be taken to prevent flies and dust. (VI) There should be fire safety measures and proper exits should be there. (VII) Drying Space: -There **should be separate space for drying of raw material, in process medicine or medicines which require drying before packing**. This space will be protected from flies/ insects/dust etc., by proper flooring, wiremash window, glass panels or other material." [Source: as per the 1.1(B) of Schedule T, Drug and Cosmetics Rule, 1945]
1.1(C) Water Supply -	"The water used in manufacture shall be pure and of potable quality. Adequate provision of water for washing the premises shall be made." [Source: as per the 1.1(C) of Schedule T, Drug and Cosmetics Rule, 1945]
1.1(D) Disposable of Waste -	"From the manufacturing section and laboratories the waste water and the residues which might be prejudicial to the workers or public health shall be disposed off." [Source: as per the 1.1(D) of Schedule T, Drug and Cosmetics Rule, 1945]
1.1(E) Container's Cleaning -	"In factories where operations involving the use of containers such as glass bottles, vials and jars are conducted, **there shall be adequate arrangements separated from the manufacturing operations for washing, cleaning and drying of such containers**." [Source: as per the 1.1(E) of Schedule T, Drug and Cosmetics Rule, 1945]
1.1(F) Stores -	"Storage **should have proper ventilation** and shall be free from dampness. It should provide independent adequate space for storage of different types of material, such as raw material, packaging material and finished products." [Source: as per the 1.1(F) of Schedule T, Drug and Cosmetics Rule, 1945]

Specifications on different stores are as follows:

1.1. (F)(A) Raw Materials -	"All raw materials procured for manufacturing will be stored in the raw materials store. The manufacture based on the experience and the characteristics of the particular raw material used in Ayurveda, Siddha and Unani system shall decide the **use of appropriate containers which would protect the quality of raw**

Table contd...

	materials as well as **prevent it from damage due to dampness, microbiological contamination or rodent and insect infestation,** etc. If certain raw materials require such controlled environmental conditions, the raw materials stores may be sub-divided with proper enclosures to provide such conditions by suitable cabinization. While designing such containers, cupboard or areas in the raw materials store, care may be taken to handle the following different categories of raw materials:- 1. Raw material of metallic origin. 2. Raw material of mineral origin. 3. Raw material from animal source. 4. Fresh herbs. 5. Dry herbs or plant parts 6. Excipients etc. 7. Volatile oils/perfumes and flavours 8. Plant concentrates/ extracts and exudates/resins. Each container used for raw material storage shall be properly identified with the label which indicates name of the raw material, source of supply and will also clearly state the status of raw material such as **"UNDER TEST**' or **APPROVED** or **_REJECTED"**. The **labels shall further indicate the identity of the particular supply in the form of Batch No. or Lot No. and the date of receipt of the consignment.** All the raw materials shall be sampled and got tested either by the in-house Ayurvedic, Siddha and Unani experts (Quality control technical person) or by the laboratories approved by the Government and shall be used only on approval after verifying. The rejected raw material should be removed from other raw material store and should be kept in separate room. Procedure of **_First in first out**' should be adopted for raw materials wherever necessary. Records of the receipt, testing and approval or rejection and use of raw material shall be maintained." [Source: as per the 1.1(C) of Schedule T, Drug and Cosmetics Rule, 1945]
1.1. (F)(B) Packaging Materials. -	"All packaging materials such as bottles, jars, capsules etc. shall be stored properly. All containers and closure shall be adequately cleaned and dried before packing the products." [Source: as per the 1.1(F)(B) of Schedule T, Drug and Cosmetics Rule, 1945]
1.1. (F)(C) Finished Goods Stores. -	"The finished goods transferred from the production area after proper packaging shall be stored in the finished goods stores within an area marked —**Quarantine**. After the quality control laboratory and the experts have checked the correctness of finished

Table contd...

	goods with reference to its packing/labelling as well as the finished product quality as prescribed, then it will be moved to —**Approved Finished Goods Stock‖ area**. Only approved finished goods shall be dispatched as per marketing requirements. Distribution records shall be maintained as required." [Source: as per the 1.1(F)(C) of Schedule T, Drug and Cosmetics Rule, 1945] **If any Ayurvedic, Siddha and Unani drug needs special storage conditions, finished goods store shall provide necessary environmental requirements."** [Source: as per the 1.1(F)(C) of Schedule T, Drug and Cosmetics Rule , 1945]

1.1(G) Working space. -	"The manufacturing area shall provide adequate space (manufacture and quality control) for orderly placement of equipment and material used in any of the operations for which these employed so as to facilitate easy and safe working and to minimize or to eliminate any risk of mix-up between different drugs, raw materials and to prevent the possibility of cross contamination of one drug by another drug that is manufactured, stored or handled in the same premises." [Source: as per the 1.1(G) of Schedule T, Drug and Cosmetics Rule , 1945]
1.1(H) Health Clothing, Sanitation and Hygiene of Workers.-	"All workers employed in the Factory shall be free from contagious diseases. The clothing of the workers shall consist of proper uniform suitable to the nature of work and the climate and shall be clean. The uniform shall also include cloth or synthetic covering for hands, feet and head wherever required. Adequate facilities for personal cleanliness such as clean towels, soap and scrubbing brushes shall be provided. Separate provision shall be made for lavatories to be used by men and women, and such lavatories shall be located at places separated from the processing rooms. Workers will also be provided facilities for changing their clothes and to keep their personal belongings." [Source: as per the 1.1(H) of Schedule T, Drug and Cosmetics Rule, 1945]
1.1. (I) Medical Services:	"The manufacturer shall also provide: (a) adequate facilities for first aid; (b) medical examination of workers at the time of employment and periodical checkup thereafter by a physician once a year, with particular attention being devoted to freedom from infections. Records thereof shall be maintained." [Source: as per the 1.1(I) of Schedule T, Drug and Cosmetics Rule, 1945]
1.1(J) Machinery and Equipments -	"For carrying out manufacturing depending on the size of operation and the nature of product manufactured, suitable

Table contd...

	equipment either manually operated or operated semi-automatically (Electrical or steam based) or fully automatic machinery shall be made available. These may include machines for use in the process of manufacture such as crushing, grinding, powdering, boiling, mashing, burning, roasting, filtering, drying, filling, labelling and packing etc. to ensure ease in movement of workers and orderliness in operations a suitably adequate space will be ensured between two machines or rows of machines. These equipments have to be properly installed and maintained with proper cleaning. List of equipments and machinery recommended is indicated in Part II-A. Proper Standard Operational Procedures (SOPs) for cleaning, maintaining and performance of every machine should be laid down." [Source: as per the 1.1(J) of Schedule T, Drug and Cosmetics Rule, 1945]
1.1(K) Batch Manufacturing Records -	"The licensee shall maintain batch manufacturing record of each batch of Ayurvedic, Siddha and Unani drugs manufactured irrespective of the type of product manufactured (classical preparation or patent and proprietary medicines). Manufacturing records are required to provide an account of the list of raw materials and their quantities obtained from the store, tests conducted during the various stages of manufacture like taste, colour, physical characteristics and chemical tests as may be necessary or indicated in the approved books of Ayurveda, Siddha and Unani mentioned in the First Schedule of the Drugs and Cosmetics Act, 1940 (23 of 1940). These tests may include any in-house or pharmacopoeial test adopted by the manufacturer in the raw material or in the process material and in the finished product. These records shall be duly signed by Production and Quality Control Personnel respectively. Details of transfer of manufactured drug to the finished products store including dates and quantity of drugs transferred along with record of testing of the finished product, if any, and packaging, records shall be maintained. Only after the manufactured drugs have been verified and accepted quality shall be allowed to be cleared for sale. It should be essential to maintain the record of date, manpower, machine and equipments used and to keep in process record of various shodhana, bhavana, burning and fire and specific grindings in terms of internal use." [Source : as per the 1.1(K) of Schedule T, Drug and Cosmetics Rule, 1945]

Table contd...

1.1(L) Distribution Records -	"Records of sale and distribution of each batch of Ayurveda, Siddha and Unani Drugs shall be maintained in order to facilitate prompt and complete recall of the batch, if necessary. The duration of record keeping should be the date of expiry of the batch. Certain category of Ayurvedic, Siddha and Unani medicines like Bhasma, Rasa, Kupi-pakva, Parpati, Sindura, Karpu/Uppu/Puram, Kushta, Asavaarishta etc. do not have expiry date in contrast their efficacy increases with the passage of time. Hence, records need be maintained upto five years of the exhausting of stock." [Source: as per the 1.1(L) of Schedule T, Drug and Cosmetics Rule, 1945]
1.1(M) Record of Market Complaints -	"Manufacturers shall maintain a register to record all reports of market complaints received regarding the products sold in the market. The manufacturer shall enter all data received on such market complaints, investigations carried out by the manufacturers regarding the complaint as well as any corrective action initiated to prevent recurrence of such market complaints shall also be recorded. Once in a period of six months the manufacturer shall submit the record of such complaints to the licensing authority. The Register shall also be available for inspection during any inspection of the premises. Reports of any adverse reaction resulting from the use of Ayurvedic, Siddha and Unani drugs shall also be maintained in a separate register by each manufacturer. The manufacturer shall investigate any of the adverse reaction to find if the same is due to any defect in the product, and whether such reactions are already reported in the literature or it is a new observation." [Source: as per the 1.1(M) of Schedule T, Drug and Cosmetics Rule, 1945]
1.1(N) Quality Control. -	"Every licensee is required to provide facility for quality control section in his own premises or through Government approved testing laboratory. The test shall be as per the Auurveda, Siddha and Unani pharmacopoeial standard. Where the tests are not available, the test should be performed according to the manufacturers 'specification or other information available. The quality control section shall verify all the raw materials, monitor in-process quality checks and control the quality of finished product being released to finished goods store/warehouse. Preferably for such quality control there will be a separate expert. The quality control section shall have the following facilities:

Table contd...

	(1) There should be 150 sq. feet area for quality control section. (2) For identification of raw drugs, reference books and reference samples should be maintained. (3) Manufacturing record should be maintained for the various processes. (4) To verify the finished products, controlled samples of finished products of each batch will be kept till the expiry date of product for 3 years. (5) To supervise and monitor adequacy of conditions under which raw materials, semi- finished products and finished products are stored. (6) Keep record in establishing shelf life and storage requirements for the drugs. (7) Manufacturers who are manufacturing patent and proprietary Ayurveda, Siddha, and Unani medicines shall provide their own specification and control references in respect of such formulated drugs. (8) The record of specific method and procedure of preparation, that is, Bhavana, Mardana and Puta and the record of every process carried out by the manufacturer shall be maintained. (9) The standards for identity, purity and strength as given in respective pharmacopoeias of Ayurveda, Siddha and Unani systems of medicines published by Government of India shall be complied with. (10) All raw materials will be monitored for fungal, bacterial contamination with a view to minimize such contamination. (11) Quality control section will have a minimum of: – [(i) (a) Expert in Ayurveda or Sidha or Unani medicine who possesses a degree qualification recognized under Schedule II of Indian Medicine Central Council Act 1970; (b) Chemist, who shall possess at least Bachelor Degree in Science or Pharmacy or Pharmacy (Ayurveda), awarded by a recognized University; and (c) Botanist (Pharmacognosist), who shall possess at least Bachelor Degree in Science (Medical) or Pharmacy or Pharmacy (Ayurveda) awarded by a recognized University.] (ii) The manufacturing unit shall have a quality control section as explained under Section 35 (ii). Alternatively,

Table contd...

	these quality control provisions will be met by getting testing etc., from a recognised laboratory for Ayurveda, Siddha and Unani drugs; under Rule 160-A of the Drugs and Cosmetics Act. The manufacturing company will maintain all the record of various tests got done from outside recognised laboratory. (iii) List of equipments recommended is indicated in Part II C." [Source: as per the 1.1(N) of Schedule T, Drug and Cosmetics Rule, 1945]

1.2 Requirement for Sterile Product

(A) Manufacturing Areas: –	"For the manufacture of sterile Ayurvedic, Unani and Siddha drugs, separate enclosed areas specifically designed for the purpose shall be provided. These areas shall be provided with air locks for entry and shall be essentially dust free and ventilated with an air supply. For all areas where aseptic manufacture has to be carried out, air supply shall be filtered through bacteria retaining filters (HEPA Filters) and shall be at a pressure higher than in the adjacent areas. The filters shall be checked for performance on installation and periodically thereafter the record of checks shall be maintained. All the surfaces in sterile manufacturing areas shall be designed to facilitate cleaning and disinfection. For sterile manufacturing routine microbial counts of all Ayurvedic, Siddha and Unani drug manufacturing areas shall be carried out during operations. Results of such count shall be checked against established in-house standards and record maintained. Access to manufacturing areas shall be restricted to minimum number of authorized personnel. Special procedure to be followed for entering and leaving the manufacturing areas shall be written down and displayed. For the manufacturing of Ayurvedic, Siddha and Unani drug that can be sterilized in their final containers, the design of the areas shall preclude the possibility of the products intended for sterilization being mixed with or taken to be products already sterilized. In case of terminally sterilized products, the design of the areas shall preclude the possibility of mix-up between non-sterile products." [Source: as per the 1.2(A) of Schedule T, Drug and Cosmetics Rule, 1945]

Table contd...

(B) Precautions against contamination and mix:	"(a) Carrying out manufacturing operations in a separate block of adequately isolated building or operating in an isolated enclosure within the building, (b) Using appropriate pressure differential in the process area. (c) Providing a suitable exhaust system. (d) Designing laminar flow sterile air system for sterile products. (e) The germicidal efficiency of UV lamps shall be checked and recorded indicating the burning hours or checked using intensity. (f) Individual containers of liquids and ophthalmic solutions shall be examined against black-white background fitted with diffused light after filling to ensure freedom from contamination with foreign suspended matter. (g) Expert technical staff approved by the Licensing Authority shall check and compare actual yield against theoretical yield before final distribution of the batch. All process controls as required under master formula including room temperature, relative humidity, volume filled, leakage and clarity shall be checked and recorded." [Source: as per the 1.2 (B) of Schedule T, Drug and Cosmetics Rule , 1945]

Part II of Schedule T defines

A. List of Recommended Machinery, Equipment and Minimum Manufacturing Premises Required For The Manufacture Of Various Categories of Ayurvedic, Siddha System of Medicines.

Sl.No. (1)	Category of Medicine (2)	Minimum manufacturing space required (3)	Machinery/equipment recommended (4)
		1200 Square feet covered area with separate cabins or partitions for each activity. If Unani medicines are manufactured in same premises an additional area of 400 sq. feet will be required.	
1.	Anjana/Pisti	100 sq. feet.	Karel/mechanized/motorized, karel.End runner/Ball-Mill Sieves/Shifter.
2.	Churna / Nasya/ Manjan/Lepa/ Kwath Churn	200 sq feet	Grinder/disintegrator/Pulveriser/ Powder mixer/sieves/shifter.
3.	Pills/Vati /Gutika Matirai and tablets	100 sq. feet	Ball Mill, Mass mixer/powder mixer, Granulator, drier, tablet compressing machine, pill/vati cutting machine, stainless steel trays/container for storage and sugar coating, polishingpan in case of sugar-coated tablets,mechanised chattoo (for mixing guggulu) where required.

Table contd...

Sl.No. (1)	Category of Medicine (2)	Minimum manufacturing space required (3)	Machinery/equipment recommended (4)
4.	Sindura Karpu/ Uppu / Param /Kupi Parpati/ pakava/Ksara/ LavanaBhasmaSatva/	150 sq. feet	Multani Matti/Plaster of Paris, Copper Rod, Earthern container, Bhatti, Karahi, stainless steel Vessels/Patila Flask, Wooden/S.S.Spatula. Gaj Put, Bhatti, Muffle furnace End/EdgeRunner, Exhaust Fan,
5.	Kajal	100 sq. feet	S.S.Patila, Filling/ packing and manufacturing room with exhaust fan and ultraviolet lamps. earthen lamps for collection of Kajal, Triple Roller Mill, End Runner, Sieves
6.	Capsules	100 sq. feet	Capsule filling machine and chemical balance, Air Conditioner, De-humidifier, hygrometer, thermometer
7.	Marham Pasai, Ointment	100sq. feet	Tube filling machine, Crimping Machine/Ointment Mixer, End Runner/ Mill (Where required) S.S.Storage Container S.S.Patila.
8.	Khand/ Pak/Avaleh/Modak/La kayam	100 sq. feet	Bhatti section with exhaust fan and fly proof, Iron kadahi/S.S. Patila , S.S. Storage container.
9.	PravahiKwath Manapaku /Panak, Syrup	150 sq, feet	filter press / Gravity filter, liquid filling machine, tincture press, exhaust fan fitted andfly proof, Bhatti section, Bottle washing machine, P.P. Capping Machine.
10.	Asava/Arishta	200 sq. ft	Same as mentioned above. containers and distillation plant, Fermentation tanks, Filter Press.
11.	Sura	100 sq. ft	Same as mentioned above plus Transfer pump and Distillation plant

Table contd...

Sl.No. (1)	Category of Medicine (2)	Minimum manufacturing space required (3)	Machinery/equipment recommended (4)
12.	Ark Tinir	100 sq. ft	distillation plant,Liquid filling tank with tap/Gravity filter/Filter press, Maceration tank, Visual inspection box.
13.	Tail/Ghrit Ney	100 sq. ft	Kadahi/S.S. Patila S.S., Bhatti, Filtration equipment, filling tank with tap/Liquid filling machine, Storage Containers.
14.	Netra Malham Panir/Karn Bindu/Nasa- bindu Aschyotan /	100 sq. ft	collation mill,or ointment mill, tube filling equipment, hot air oven, kettle gas or electrically heated with suitable mixing arrangements, mixing and storage tanks made of stainless steel or of other suitable material sintered glass funnel, seitz filter /filter candle, liquid filling equipment, autoclave.
15.	Each manufacturing unit will have a distinct area for furnace boilers, Bhatti, puta, etc. This will have proper ventilation, removal of smoke, prevention of flies, insets, dust etc. The furnace area could havetin roof.	200 sq. ft	

B. "List of Machinery, Equipment and Minimum Manufacturing Premises Required For The Manufacture of Various Categories Of Unani System Of Medicines"

Sl.No. (1)	Category of Medicine (2)	Minimum space required for manufacturing (3)	Machinery/equipment recommended (4)
		"1200 square feet (sq.ft.) covered area with separate cabins, partitions for each activity. If Ayurveda / Siddha Medicines are also manufactured in same premises an additional area of 400 square feet will be required."	
1.	Jawarish Khamiras /Itrifal Tirya/majoon/ Laooq	100 sq. ft.	grinder/ Pulveriser, S.S. Patilas, Bhattiand other accessories, plant mixer for Khamiras. Sieves, powder mixer (if required),
2.	Arq.	100 sq. ft.	distillation plant (garembic) S.S. storage tank, boiling Vessel, bottle washing machine, Bottle drier, Gravityfilter, bottle filling machine,.
3.	Habb (Pills) and tablets.	100 sq. feet	Ball Mill, Mass Mixer/Powder mixer, polishing pan in case of sugar-coated tablets, Granulator drier, tablet compressing machine, pill/vati cutting machine, stainless steal trays/ container for storage and sugar coating, mechanized chattoo, (for mixingguggul) where required.
4.	Sufoof (Powder)	200 sq. feet	Grinder/pulveriser, Sieves, Trays, Scoops, Powder mixer (whererequired).
5.	Raughan (oils) (Crushing and boiling)	100 sq. ft.	S.S. Patilas, Oil filter bottle, Oil Expeller, Bottle drier, Bhatti, Filling machine
6.	Shiyaf, Surma, Kajal	100 sq. ft.	End runner, mixing S.S. Vessel.
7.	Zimad (Ointment), Marham,	100 sq. ft.	Kharal, Bhatti, Triple Roller Mill (if required), End runner, Grinder, Pulveriser,

Table contd...

8.	Qurs (Tab.)	100 sq. ft.	Grinder/Pulveriser, Granulator, Drier, Tablet Compressing Machine, Die punches Trays, O.T. Apparatus, Balance with weights, Sieves, Powder mixer (where needed), Scoops, Sugar Coating Pan, polishing pan, Heater.
9.	Kushta	100 sq. ft.	Bhatti, Sil Batta, Kharal, Earthen pots.
10.	Murabba	100 sq. ft.	Aluminium Vessels (50-100 kgs. Capacity), Bhatti, Gendna
11.	Capsule	100 sq. ft.	Pulveriser, humidifier, Balance with weights, storage containers, Powder mixer (where needed), capsule filling machine, Air conditioner
12.	Joshanda & Sharbat	100 sq. ft.	Tincture Press, exhaust fan fitted, Bhatti section, hot air oven, Bottle washing machine, Filter Press Gravity filter, Liquid filling tank with tap/liquid filling machine, electrically heated with thermostatic control, kettle.
13.	Qutoor-e- Chashm and Marham (Eye drops, eye ointment)	100 sq. ft.	Hot air oven, kettle.

(A)	Chemistry Section	(B)	Pharmacognosy Section
1.	Alcohol Determination Apparatus (completeset)	1.	Microscope Binoculor.
2.	Volatile Oil Determination Apparatus.	2.	Dissecting Microscope.
3.	Refractometer.	3.	Microtome.
4.	Polarimeter.	4.	Aluminium Slide Trays.
5.	Viscometer.	5.	Stage Micrometer.
6.	Boiling Point Determination Apparatus.	6.	Camera Lucida (Prism and MirrorType).
7.	Melting Point Determination Apparatus.	7.	Chemicals, Glassware etc.
8.	Tablet Disintegration Apparatus.	8.	Physical Balance.
9.	Moisture Meter.		

Table contd...

(A)	Chemistry Section	(B)	Pharmacognosy Section
10.	LPG Gas Cylinders with Burners.		
11.	Water Bath (Temperature controlled.)		
12.	Heating Mantles/ Hot Plates.		
13.	TLC Apparatus with all accessories (Manual)		
14.	Muffle Furnace.		
15.	Electronic Balance.		
16.	Hot Air Oven		•
17.	Magnetic Stirrer.		
18.	Refrigerator.		
19.	Glass/Steel Distillation Apparatus.		
20.	Paper Chromatography apparatus withaccessories.		
21.	Sieve size 10 to120 with Sieve shaker.		
22.	Centrifuge Machine.		
23.	Dehumidifier.		
24.	pH Meter.		
25.	Limit Test Apparatus.		

................."

4.2 QUALITY ASSURANCE IN ISM FORMULATION INDUSTRY

According to WHO (2004), Quality assurance ... "is a wide-ranging concept covering all matters that individually or collectively influence the quality of a product. It is the totality of the arrangements made with the object of ensuring that pharmaceutical products are of the quality required for their intended use. Quality assurance therefore incorporates GMP and other factors, including those outside the scope of this guide such as product design and development." Quality assurance in ISM formulation begins with standardization of the raw material. Most of the ISM formulations contains herbs and medicinal plants as raw materials. Quality parameters of herbs and medicinal plants were initiated during cultivation stages. To ensure the quality of medicinal plants and herbs, The National Medicinal Plants Board (NMPB), Department of AYUSH has prepared India centric Good Agriculture Practices (GAPs) (2009) on the pattern of Good Agriculture and Collection Practices (GACPs) developed by the World Health Organisation (WHO) for medicinal plants (2003).

WHO guidelines on good agricultural and collection practices (GACP) for medicinal plants can be defined as "Good Agricultural and Collection Practices for Medicinal Plants (or GACP for short) are a set of guidelines developed in 2003 by the World Health Organisation (WHO), aimed at improving the quality of medicinal plant material being used in herbal medicines in the market."

"The main objectives of these guidelines are to:

contribute to the quality assurance of medicinal plant materials used as the source for herbal medicines, which aims to improve the quality, safety and efficacy of finished herbal products;

guide the formulation of national and/or regional GACP guidelines and GACP monographs for medicinal plants and related standard operating procedures; and encourage and support the sustainable cultivation and collection of medicinal plants of good quality in ways that respect and support the conservation of medicinal plants and the environment in general."

4.3 GOOD AGRICULTURAL PRACTICES FOR MEDICINAL PLANTS DEVELOPED BY NATIONAL MEDICINAL PLANTS BOARD (NMPB), DEPARTMENT OF AYUSH

" 1. Background- Need for Good Agricultural Practices

1.1 India has a rich tradition of plant based health care systems contained in its classical texts like Charak Samhita (1) and Sushruta Samhita (2). In recognition of the diversity of health care practices, the Government of India have recognized Ayurveda, Yoga & Naturopathy, Siddha, Unani and Homoeopathy as the alternative systems of medicine under the National Health Policy.

1.2 Department of Ayurveda, Yoga and Naturopathy, Siddha, Unani and Homoeopathy (AYUSH) in the Ministry of Health and Family Welfare has the responsibility for quality assurance and standardization of the production processes of Ayurveda, Siddha and Unani (ASU) medicines and disseminate the guidelines for production of raw material used in ASU medicines.

1.3 To ensure and enhance the quality of ASU medicines, the Government of India have notified Good Manufacturing Practices under Schedule 'T' of the Drugs and Cosmetics Act 1940. These guidelines on Good Agricultural Practices (GAP) seek to lay down standards for production of raw material that goes in to the making of the ASU medicines and standardize the production processes from farm to factory.

1.4 The Good Agriculture Practices described in this document have been adapted from the WHO guideline on Good Agricultural & Collection Practices (GACP) to suit policy framework on environment and health in India(3).

2. Definition of Good Agricultural Practices; (4,5)

2.1 A good agricultural practice in the context of medicinal plants is a cultivation programme designed to ensure optimal yield in terms of both quality and quantity of any crop intended for health purposes.

3. Scope

3.1 This document is designed to play a facilitator role and shall be recommended to all stake holders.

3.2 In the current form, these GAPs are essentially meant for and applicable to commercial scale of farming.

4. Soil and Climatic Conditions

4.1 The grower should identify the best possible environment where the plant can express its full potential in terms of both quality and quantity during its entire growth period (germination, growth and maturity). Meteorological data collated for preceding three years should be taken into account while judging the suitability of the site.

4.2 The selected site should qualify in terms of overall soil health for the purpose of cultivation of medicinal plant species. The following should be avoided;

4.2.1 Sites designated with high-degree stress factors (salinity, acidity and toxicity), water logging conditions, industrial wastes and affluent.

4.2.2 Sites in proximity to grave yards, crematoria or having a traceable history of such usage.

4.3 A well drained fertile soil with optimum level of water holding capacity and productivity status should be used for medicinal plants cultivation.

4.4 In soils with low fertility levels use of soil amendments as per the specific site and requirement of species are to be followed. The latest soil test report on physico-chemical parameters and nutrient profile should be obtained to decide the nature and quantity of soil amendments required.

4.5 The site must be in proximity to a reliable source of irrigation water.

4.6 The quality of irrigation water should have been adequately understood and classified in the context of both soil type and the target crop in terms of total salt concentration, Sodium absorption ratio, Bicarbonate and Boron concentration etc.

4.7 When the end-product is required to conform to standards of residual contaminants, the irrigation water must be analyzed for heavy metals and residual pesticides also.

4.8 When shade-loving crop is planned for, availability of shade across the field should be ascertained. Provision for artificial shading should be examined in the light of crop economics.

5. Seeds and Propagation Material

5.1 The seed/planting material should be accompanied with the following information:

- Name as per pharmacopoeial nomenclature and trade name
- Botanical name
- Cultivar/ Selection / Phenotype/ Chemotype/ Genotype
- Projected quality of crop in terms of physico-chemical analysis/ marker based analysis – on the basis of earlier data/ reports

5.2 Marker based analytical projection for the end-product is mandatory requirement when the crop is meant for phyto-pharmaceutical industries.

5.3 When the planting material is obtained from wild resources as it happens during initial crop cycles, efforts should be made to establish its correct identity.

5.4 Precautions

5.4.1 Seed

- The seeds chosen for cultivation purposes must be physically free from pests, diseases, foreign and inert matter.
- The seed should be fresh and must have originated from recent harvests and in the accompanying document; the supplier should mention the date of harvest.
- The seed which is collected from wild sources must invariably be from recently collected lots and only mature seed should be collected.
- Prescribed seed treatment protocols if any, for the target species, must be completed well in advance so as to match the planting season.
- The process for seedling production under nursery conditions should be initiated as per the recommended agronomic practices for the target species and carried out reasonably well before the actual schedule of field transplantation. Only healthy seedlings should be transplanted.

5.4.2 Stem cutting

- When the grower takes the responsibility of root induction in stem cuttings under nursery conditions for eventual transplantation into the field, the source of cuttings should be well authenticated for both botanical identity and quality of vegetative propagules.
- The stem cuttings collected for root induction should be of uniform dimensions in terms of length and diameter and should be in tune with the requirements laid down for the target species. Only healthy stem cutting giving desired rooting should be used.

5.4.3 Root cutting

The propagation materials in form of 'ready-to-transplant saplings' or root cuttings should be of uniform size and maturity, both in terms of aerial and underground parts, and must be free from any disease and infection.

6. Crop Management for Cultivation

6.1 Field preparation

The soil should be brought to the desired tilth to facilitate favourable environment for growing seed and seedling. The field operation performed should provide better rhizospheric environment, soil porosity and texture, and keep it free from weeds for initial 20-30 days.

6.2 Sowing and transplanting

6.2.1 The recommended rate of seedlings per unit of land area should be adhered to. The placement of seeds should take place at the appropriate depth in the moist zone of the soil.

6.2.2 In cases where saplings are transplanted the spacing norms in terms of row- to-row and plant-to-plant distance should governed by the needs of target crop as envisaged in the agronomic protocol for target species.

6.2.3 The seedling at optimum stage of transplanting should be uprooted and transplanted immediately thereafter.

6.2.4 Replenishment of plant populations to compensate mortality losses should be carried out within a reasonable timeframe and in consideration of the gestation period of the target crop.

6.3 Manures and fertilizers

6.3.1 Use of organic manure is preferred for growing medicinal plants. However, mineral nutrition through inorganic source may be opted for in consideration of the nutritional needs of the target crop vis-à-vis the soil characteristics.

6.3.2 Use of compost, vermi-compost, poultry manure, green leafy manure is desirable. Similarly, use of microbial fertilizers for distinct purposes like, nitrogen fixing or for phosphate solubilizing is desirable.

6.3.3 The use of sludge, city waste, night soil and any other manure with known or assumed toxicities must be avoided.

6.3.4 Specialized nutritional care for distinct purposes such as root production or enhancement of leafy bio-mass etc should be opted for in the light of recommended agronomic practices for target species.

6.4 Irrigation

6.4.1 Total water requirement of the crop should be estimated in the light of available agronomic protocol. Accordingly, the irrigation cycles should be planned for and implemented to ensure optimal plant growth.

6.4.2 Water harvesting and water conservation methods should be followed wherever possible.

6.4.3 The quality of water should be considered in the light of prevailing soil conditions. A reasonably recent report of soil and water analysis should be taken into account for this purpose.

6.4.4 The soils having the problem of drainage should be dealt in specific manner so as to provide outlet for excess water, if any. The impounding of water through heavy rains should not be allowed.

6.5 Weeding and intercultural operations

6.5.1 Initial flush of weeds must be controlled effectively so as to ensure a weed free environment to young plants. The weeding and hoeing cycles should be so arranged as to keep the field free from weeds.

6.5.2 The prescribed schedule of all inter-cultural operations such as weeding, hoeing, topping, nipping of buds, pruning, shading and earthing up etc., must be adhered to in a manner to optimize the overall productivity.

6.5.3 Use of herbicides should be avoided as far as possible. In case of their inevitable usage, available evidence of safety to the target crop should be considered adequately.

6.6 Crop protection

6.6.1 Comprehensive preventive and control measures enumerated in the agronomic protocol should be used for disease, insect and pest management to minimize loss of the final crop and its quality.

6.6.2 In general crop protection plans should be limited to the use of bio-control agents and bio-pesticides. Under compulsive circumstances care should be taken to use smallest effective dosage of pesticides on the basis of crop protection protocols prescribed for the target species.

6.6.3 When chemical pesticides are used for crop protection, residue analysis should be carried out through appropriate testing agencies following standard procedures.

7. Harvest and Post Harvest Management

7.1. Harvesting

7.1.1 The principle of "maximizing sustainable production" as laid down for the subject crop should be adhered to.

7.1.2 The harvesting season should be determined and followed on the basis of qualitative parameters set for the end product of the constituents rather than the total vegetative yield.

7.1.3 Harvesting should be carried out only on favorable days avoiding the risks of dew, rain or exceptionally high humidity.

7.1.4 The containers used for harvested materials should be kept clean. Care should be taken to ensure freedom from the risks of cross contamination by other species, weeds and such other extraneous matter.

7.1.5 Cutting devices employed for harvesting should be selected so as to minimize the contamination by soil particles. While harvesting, care should be taken to avoid incidental and concurrent harvest of weeds.

7.2 Primary processing

7.2.1 Washing and cleaning methods for freshly harvested materials should be laid down in consideration of the target plant part. The procedure for this purpose should ensure removal of soil particles adhering to the materials.

7.2.2 Freshly harvested materials should not be stored as such and the drying process should be initiated in a continuum. Where necessary, the length of such storage should be minimized and handled in a manner to prevent degradation or rotting.

7.2.3 Processing yards or sites should be clean, well ventilated, and have the facilities for protection against sunlight, dust, rain, rodents, insects and livestock.

7.2.4 The drying procedure and the temperature employed for this purpose should be in conformity with the quality needs of the farm produce. In case the agronomic package prescribes specific procedures for this phase, compliance to the same should be ensured. In high humidity conditions, it may be necessary to dry the produce appropriately.

7.2.5 Sorting procedure, if any, should be ideally carried out after completion of drying phase and before the material is packed.

7.3 Packaging, storage and transportation

7.3.1 The selection of packaging material should be based on the quality requirements and possible length of storage before consumption. It should be clean, dry and undamaged.

7.3.2 Essential product description such as the product name, plant part, month and year of harvest and the name of farmer/farming agency must be legibly inscribed on every pack. If the material was tested before, an appropriate label may be used indicating quality approval.

7.3.3 While packaging, mechanical damages and undue compacting of the dried plant material that may result in undesirable quality changes should be avoided. Care should be taken to avoid overfilling of the containers.

7.3.4 The storage area should be a dry place protected from insects and rodents and such other factors that may be detrimental to the quality of the product.

7.3.5 Organic herbs must be stored separately from the non-organic products.

7.3.6 When multiple commodities are handled in the same storage area, care must be taken to prevent product mix up and cross contamination. Plant materials having strong aromatic compounds should be kept at a reasonably good distance from others.

8. Documentation

8.1 All the documents pertaining to entire cultivation process should be maintained in a manner that ensures easy accessibility and traceability for the concerned personnel. The content of documents should be simple and easily comprehensible for the key personnel engaged at the site.

8.2 Agronomic protocol for target crop involving all stages of cultivation including the component of pre-planning should be adopted.

Appropriate compliance reports should **be** generated for each stage and sub-stages of various operations and dates on which they were carried out. The records should include:

8.2.1 Meteorological data, reasonably recent reports of soil and water testing and any other grounds employed for site/ crop selection

8.2.2 The source, quantity and time of procurement/collection of seeds/ planting materials, relevant documents accompanying the supplies.

8.2.3 All procedures adopted for handling the planting materials and for procedures employed during the nursery phase.

8.2.4 Soil preparation and transplantation procedures

8.2.5 Crop management phase comprising irrigation cycles, the kind of manures and fertilizer used, and the time, amount and method of their use; the type of pesticides used- including insecticides, fungicides and herbicides – and the amount, time and method of their use, if any.

8.2.6 Compliance records to weeding cycles and inter-culture practices.

8.2.7 Procedural deviations that could affect the quality of crop

8.2.8 Extraordinary situations encountered (such as weather conditions or new types of diseases/ pest infestations etc.) during the crop cycle and spontaneous management practices that were adopted

8.2.9 Reports of any laboratory tests and/ or the observations by technical experts carried out on the standing crop or the materials used during cultivation, if any.

8.2.10 Adequate photographic records should support the documentation on a need and operational convenience basis.

8.2.11 The documents suggested above and any other documents having a relevance to the target crop must be maintained for a minimum period of 3 years for crops with gestation periods less than 1 year and for a minimum period of 5 years for those crops having a gestation periods exceeding one year.

9. Personnel and Equipment

9.1 Key resource persons engaged at the site (such as farm owner/ supervisor) must be conversant with all aspects related to the target crop such as, quality requirements of the end product, crop husbandry etc.

9.2 The personnel should have basic exposure to subject matters like safety and hygiene.

9.3 Appropriate measures/systems should be in place to ensure that personnel suffering from infectious diseases are not engaged at the site.

9.4 The machinery used in fertilizer and pesticide application must be calibrated at prescribed schedules and calibration certificates/records should be maintained.

9.5 Equipments must be clean and mounted where applicable, in an easily accessible manner. Scheduled servicing procedures must be adhered to keep them in working order.

9.6 Additional care should be taken for cleaning those machine parts that get into direct contact with the harvested medicinal plant.

9.7 The material used for the equipment, particularly that coming into direct contact, should be safe. Equipments, that pose a risk of hazardous metallic contamination of the harvested crop should be avoided."

4.3.1 ANNEXURE-I

A model structure for developing monographs on GAP for individual species of medicinal plants

1. Name of medicinal plant

I. Scientific name

II. Pharmacopoeial name of the medicinal plant

III. Local name (specify language)

2. Part to be employed as the medicinal plant material

(Description of the part of the plant used for medicinal purposes)

3. Characteristics of the medicinal plant

(Describe the agro-morphological and botanical characteristics of the medicinal plant concerned.)

4. Characteristics of medicinal plant material and major production areas

I. Characteristics of the medicinal plant material -------------------------------- ------------------

II. Major production areas of the medicinal plant material should be mentioned

5. Characteristics of strain(s) for cultivation

I. Taxonomical identity --

II. Ecological characteristics

III. Major chemical compound responsible for drug value along with chemical profile

IV. Preferred growing conditions

a) Climatic conditions

(Rain fall, Temperature and Daylight length)

b) Soil conditions

Soil type Soil condition (pH, water retention capacity; nutrient status as per soil test report etc.)

c) Shade requirements, if any.

6. Cultivation methods

I. Species and strains

II. Propagation methods III.Cultivation

a) Suitable cultivation conditions:

b) Propagation

c) Sowing

d) Planting/nursery

e) Manures & fertilizers including microbial fertilizers

f) Crop management

g) Diseases and pests management

h) Harvesting stage, time & procedures

i) Post harvest handling & processing

j) Expected yield with desired quality

7. Quality evaluation of the medicinal plant material

I. National quality standard of the medicinal plant material (Defined as the quality and quantity standard)

II. Name of major chemical/ chemicals constituents and its percentage

III. Chemical structure of selected major constituents

IV. Chemical profile, if known

8. Comparative summary table of the characteristics of different cultivated strains, if any

   Morphological characteristics of each strain chemotype, morphotype etc. being cultivated, including height, growth, morphology/shape of root, stem, leaf, flower, fruit and 'seed, resistance/tolerance to diseases/pests, and composition and quantitative indications of major chemical constituents of the medicinal plant.

9. Cultivation calendar

A tabulated schedule of cultivation practices whichever to be followed indicating the type of care and management work/ actions and their timing during the entire growing period.

10. Background data and other information

I. Source of seed, propagation material, etc ------------------------------------ -------------------

   To assess the appropriateness/suitability of cultivation and characteristics of seed/propagation material. Cultivation should be carried out according to the recommended cultivation practices.

II. Photographs (3-5)

   Plant and plant part material; also showing working methods/ equipment as appropriate

4.3.2 ANNEXURE-II

Sample record for cultivated medicinal plants

1. Identification of cultivated medicinal plant

   Scientific name
   Pharmacopoeial name
   Local name (language for)
   Plant part for medicinal use & harvested
   Identification of cultivation site   Field location
   State/District/Village

2. Identification of cultivator

   Name of cultivator
   Contact address
   Period of cultivation

3. Seeds and propagation materials

   Source of the planted material Physical description of the planted material
   Commercially available (circle): Yes/No

If yes, name of cultivar Name of supplier

4. Cultivation

4.1 Method of propagation materials establishment (circle): direct seed sowing/transplants

Date of sowing/transplantingPercentage emergence
Date of re-sowing/replantingPercentage stand establishment

4.2 Spacing

I. Row x Row (cm)

II. Plant x Plant (cm)

Covered area (m2)

Number of plants per unit area

Crop rotation

Soil and irrigation water analysis as per the standards methods:

4.3 Fertilizers and chemicals (if used)

Fertilizer applied before planting (circle): organic (composted animal manure)/chemical

Name Time/date (d/m/y)

Method

Rate

Fertilizer applied after planting (top dressing): organic (composted animal manure)/chemical

Name Time/date (d/m/y)

Method Rate

4.4 Herbicides applied before planting, if any

Name Time/date (d/m/y)

Method Rate

4.5 Herbicides applied after planting, if any

Name Time/date (d/m/y)

Method Rate

4.6 Special operations done, if any

Name

Time/date (d/m/y)

Method Rate

4.7 Plant protection chemicals applied, if any

Name Time/date (d/m/y)

Method Rate

5. Harvest/Collection

   Date of harvest   Conditions   Yield

   Time of day   Method

6. Drying practices

   Drying method

   (Sun drying/Shade/Mechanical)

   Duration of drying (days)
   Moisture content (after drying) (%)

7. Unusual circumstances that may influence quality

   (Extreme weather conditions, exposure to hazardous substances, pest outbreaks, etc):............

4.3.3 ANNEXURE III

Terminology

Chemotype: It is a chemically distinct entity in a plant or organism, with differences in the chemical constituents.

or

Phenotypically similar species i.e. indistinguishable morphological, when distinguished through chemical constituents are called chemotype

or

Plants of the same species that is chemically different but otherwise indistinguishable.

Genotype: The genetic constitution (the genome) of a cell, an individual or an organism. or

Phenotypically dissimilar species with minor mutation when identify through DNA profiling or genotypes

Irrigation: The application ofwater to soil to assist in the production of crops, especially during stress periods.

Irrigation water: Water which is artificially applied in the process of irrigation. It does not include precipitation

Inter crop: The crops raised in an orchard or other widely spaced crops for increasing the income from the same piece of land. e.g. short duration vegetables, pulses, oilseeds etc.

Inter cropping: Refers to growing of two or more generally dissimilar crops simultaneously on the same piece of land, base crop necessarily in distinct row arrangement. The recommended optimum plant population of the base crop is suitably combined with appropriate additional plant density of the associated crop, and there is crop intensification in both time and space dimensions.

Phenotype: The physical appearance of an organism as distinguished from its Genetic wake- up.

Ploughing: Operations carried out with the help of tractor drawn or bullock drawn implements known as plough, before the crops are sown.

Pollution: Contamination of natural environment by the addition to air or water of substances potentially toxic or otherwise harmful to man and animals for example, SO2, CO2, radio-active fall out insecticides etc.

Rouging: To remove weeds or off-type or diseased plants from a standing field crop.

Seedling: The juvenile stage of a plant grown from seed. U s u a l l y indicates plants which have up to and including about 4 true leaves.

Seed certification: A means to maintain and make available to the public, sources of high quality seeds and propagating materials of superior varieties so grown and distributed as to insure genetic identity. This is done by means of inspections of fields and seeds and by regulations for checking on the production, harvesting and cleaning of each lot of seed.

Tillage: The use of implements for mechanical manipulation to prepare seed beds conducive for field crop production……"

4.4 GLP IN ISM FORMULATION INDUSTRY

According to Organisation for Economic Co-operation and Development [OECD], Good Laboratory Practice or GLP is defined as, "***Good Laboratory Practice (GLP) is a quality system concerned with the organisational process and the conditions under which non-clinical health and environmental safety studies are planned, performed, monitored, recorded, archived and reported.***"

The OECD Principles of GLP apply to the non-clinical safety testing of test items contained in:

i) pharmaceutical products;
ii) pesticide products;
iii) cosmetic product;
iv) veterinary drugs;
v) food additives;
vi) feed additives; and
vii) industrial chemicals

Like other Pharmaceutical Products, ASU /ISM also required GLP to maintain the quality of laboratory standard for the testing of herbal/ASU drugs. GLP can be applied in ASU/ISM for the following:

- To prepare specifications and testing methods for raw materials and finished products.
- To sample, test, approve or reject RMs, PMs, semi-finished product and finished products.
- To supervise and monitor the adequacy of storage conditions.
- Maintenance of the records of each process where testing of finished product is not possible.

Along with the above parameters, GLP recordkeeping is essential:

- Batch Manufacturing Records (BMR)
- Distribution Records (to facilitate recall)
- Record of Market Complaints and Adverse Drug Reactions
- Shelf-life

According to the Statement Referred to In Reply to Lok Sabha Starred Question No. 256 * For 12th March, 2021,

(a) & (b) As per the provisions of Rule 157(1) of Drugs and Cosmetics Rules, 1945, the manufacture of Ayurvedic (Including Siddha) or Unani drugs are to be carried out in such premises and such hygienic conditions as are specified in Schedule-T (Good Manufacturing Practices). It is mandatory for the manufacturers to comply with GMP for obtaining license of Ayurveda, Siddha and Unani (ASU) drug manufacturing.

There are no separate guidelines of Good Laboratory Practice (GLP) for Ayurvedic Medicines. However, under Rule 160 A to J of Drug & Cosmetics Rules 1945, there are provisions for approval of laboratories for carrying out tests on Ayurvedic drugs and raw materials.

(c) As per Drugs & Cosmetics Act 1940 and Rules made thereunder, it is mandatory for all Ayurvedic medicines to comply with the standards prescribed under Ayurvedic Pharmacopeia of India (API), published by Ministry of AYUSH, Government of India from time to time, which includes pharmacopoeial standards for heavy metals content, microbiological limits, aflatoxins etc. and products are tested against the set standards. However, heavy metals are in built ingredients of certain ASU drugs and mentioned under Schedule E-1 of the Drugs & Cosmetics Rules, 1945. For such substances, 'Caution: to be taken under medical supervision' is to be conspicuously labelled on the container.

An advisory has been issued on 14th October, 2005 by this Ministry which prescribes limit and testing of heavy metals mandatory for export purposes in respect of every batch of purely herbal ASU drugs by every licensee.

(d) Ministry of AYUSH has a Central Sector Scheme of Pharmacovigilance of Ayurveda, Siddha Unani & Homeopathy Drugs already functional since June 2018 for inculcating the culture of Adverse Drug Events (ADE) reporting, documentation and analysis for further regulatory action. The Scheme has an established three tier network. All India Institute of Ayurveda (AIIA), New Delhi, has been designated as the National Pharmacovigilance Coordination Centre (NPvCC), 5 Intermediary Pharmacovigilance Centres (IPvC's) and 74

Peripheral Pharmacovigilance Centres (PPvC's).

Rule 158B in the Drugs & Cosmetics Act Rules, 1945, has mandatory provision relating to safety study and the experience or evidence of effectiveness for issuing license to ASU drugs.

The Government has established Pharmacopoeia Commission for Indian Medicine and Homoeopathy under the Ministry of AYUSH. The prime mandate of the Commission is to publish and revise Ayurvedic Pharmacopoeia of India (API), Siddha Pharmacopoeia of India (SPI), Unani Pharmacopoeia of India (UPI) and Homoeopathic Pharmacopoeia of India (HPI). The Pharmacopoeial standards are basic need to ensure quality, safety and efficacy of Ayurvedic, Siddha, Unani and Homoeopathic medicines.

Approval of Institutions for Carrying Out Tests on Ayurvedic, Siddha and Unani Drugs and Raw Materials Used In Their Manufacture On Behalf of Licensees For Manufacture For Sale of Ayurvedic, Siddha and Unani Drugs [Rule 160 A-J]

"**160-A.** Application for grant of approval for testing Ayurvedic, Siddha and Unani drugs. - Application for grant or renewal of approval for carrying out tests for identity, purity, quality and strength of Ayurvedic, Siddha and Unani drugs or the raw materials used in the manufacture thereof on behalf of licensees for manufacture for sale of the said Ayurvedic, Siddha and Unani drugs, shall be made in Form 47 to the Licensing Authority appointed by the State Government for the purposes of Part XVI, XVII or XVIII of these rules, as the case may be, and referred to as the approving authority' under this Part and shall be accompanied by an inspection fee of six thousand rupees in respect of the drugs specified in the books prescribed in First Schedule to the Act.

Provided that the applicant shall furnish to the approving authority such additional information as may be required by it in connection with the application in Form 47:

Provided further that if the applicant applies for renewal of approval after its expiry but within six months of such expiry, the inspection fee payable shall be six thousand rupees plus an additional inspection fee at the rate of one thousand rupees per month in the case of testing of Ayurvedic, Siddha and Unani drugs specified in First Schedule to the Act.

Explanation: For the purpose of this Part, the words Ayurvedic, Siddha and Unani

Drugs shall also mean and include the raw materials used in the manufacture of Ayurvedic, Siddha and Unani drugs, as the case may be.

160B. Form in which approval to be granted for carrying out tests on Ayurvedic, Siddha and Unani drugs on behalf of licensees for manufacture of Ayurvedic, Siddha and Unani drugs and conditions for grant or renewal of such approval.-- (1) Approval for carrying out such tests of identity, purity, quality and strength of Ayurvedic, Siddha and Unani drugs as may be required under the provisions of these rules, on behalf of licensee for manufacture of Ayurvedic, Siddha and Unani drugs shall be granted in Form 48.

(2) Before approval in Form 48 is granted or renewed, the following conditions shall be

complied with by the applicants, namely: -

(i) The premises where the tests are carried out shall be well lighted and properly ventilated except where the nature of tests of any Ayurvedic, Siddha and Unani drug warrants otherwise. Wherever necessary, the premises shall be air-conditioned so as to maintain the accuracy and functioning of laboratory instruments or to enable the performance of special tests such as sterility tests and microbiological tests.

(ii) (a) The applicant shall provide adequate space having regard to the nature and number of samples of drugs proposed to be tested:

Provided that the approving authority shall determine from time to time whether the space provided continues to be adequate:

Provided further that separate section shall be provided for (i) Chemistry, (ii) Pharmacognosy,

(iii) Ayurveda, Siddha and Unani,

(iv) Microbiology, (v) Sample Room, (vi) Office-cum-Record Room, with proper partitions and minimum required area is 800 sq. ft.

1 [(b) The applicant shall provide a list of persons who may be employed with him as experts, such as Chemist, Botanist and expert in Ayurveda/Siddha/Unani or Pharmacist who shall possess a degree in Chemistry, Botany, Ayurveda/Siddha/Unani/Bachelor in Pharmacy from a recognized University or equivalent, with experience for 2 years for carrying out tests or analysis as per the Ayurvedic, Siddha and Unani Pharmacopoeias].

The applicant shall provide adequate equipment essential for carrying out tests for identity, purity, quality and strength of Ayurvedic, Siddha and Unani drugs as per Pharmacopoeial standards or other available standards.

List of equipment recommended is given below:

Chemistry Section

1. Alcohol determination apparatus complete set.
2. volatile oil determination apparatus.
3. Boiling point determination apparatus.
4. Melting point determination apparatus.
5. Refractometer.
6. Polarimeter.
7. Viscometer (Ostwalds, Redwood Viscometer).
8. Tablet disintegration apparatus.
9. Moisture determination apparatus (IC filtrator).
10. U.V. Spectro-photometer.
11. Muffle furnace.
12. Electronic Balance.
13. Hot air oven(s) different range of temperature/vacuum oven.
14. Refrigerator.
15. Glass distillation apparatus/plant.
16. Water supply demineralised exchange equipment/distillation equipment.
17. Air conditioner.
18. LPG Gas cylinder with burners.
19. Water bath (temperature controlled).
20. Heating mantle (4) or as required.
21. TLC apparatus with all accessories.
22. Sieves 10 to 120 with sieve shaker.
23. Centrifuge machine.
24. Dehumidifier.
25. pH meter.
26. G.L.C. with F.I. detector.
27. Silica crucible.

28. Tablet friability tester.
29. Tablet dissolution tester.
30. Other related equipment, reagents, glasswares etc.

Pharmacognosy Section

1. Microscope binocular.
2. Dissecting Microscope.
3. Microtome.
4. Chemical balance.
5. Microslide cabinet.
6. Aluminium slide trays.
7. Hot air oven.
8. Occular Micrometer.
9. Stage Micrometer.
10. Camera Lucida Prism type and mirror type.
11. Hot plates.
12. Refrigerator.
13. LPG Cylinder with burners.
14. Other related equipments, reagents, glasswares etc.

Note: Instruments like HPLC, HPTLC, Atomic Absorption spectrophotometer could be arranged by tie up with other laboratories.

Microbiology section

1. Laminar air flow bench (L.A.F.)
2. B.O.D. Incubator.
3. Plain Incubator.
4. Serological water bath.
5. Oven.
6. Autoclave/sterilizer.
7. Microscope (high power).
8. Colony counter.
9. Other related equipment and reagents.

(1) The applicant shall provide and maintain suitable equipment having regard to the nature and number of samples of Ayurvedic, Siddha and Unani drugs

intended to be tested which shall be adequate in the opinion of the approving authority.

(2) The testing of Ayurvedic, Siddha and Unani drugs, as the case may be, for identity, purity, quality and strength shall be carried out under the active direction of one of the experts stated in clause (b) of sub-rule (2) who shall be the person-in-charge of testing and shall be held responsible for the reports of test issued by the applicant.

(3) The testing of Ayurvedic, Siddha and Unani drugs, as the case may be, for identity, purity, quality and strength shall be carried out by persons whose qualifications and experience of testing are adequate as stated in clause (b) of sub-rule (2).

(4) The applicant shall provide books of standards recognized under the provisions of the Act and the rules made thereunder and such books of reference as may be required in connection with the testing or analysis of the products for the testing of which approval is applied for.

(5) The applicant shall provide list of standard Ayurvedic, Siddha and Unani drugs (Reference samples) recognized under the provisions of the Act and rules made thereunder and such reference samples kept in the laboratory may be required in connection with the testing or analysis of the products of which approval is applied for.

160C. Duration of approval. - An approval granted in Form 48 or renewed in Form 49 unless sooner suspended or withdrawn, shall be valid for a period of three years from the date on which it is granted or renewed:

Provided that if an application for the renewal of an approval in Form 40 is made before its expiry or if the application is made within six months of its expiry after the payment of the additional inspection fee, the approval shall continue to be in force until orders to the contrary are passed on the application and approval shall be deemed to have expired if the application for renewal is not made within six months of expiry.

160D. Conditions of approval. An approval in Form 48 shall be subject to the following conditions, namely: -

I. The Institution granted approval under this Part (hereinafter referred to as the approved laboratory) shall provide and maintain adequate staff and adequate premises and equipment as specified in rule 160-B.

II. The approved laboratory shall provide proper facilities for storage so as to preserve the properties of the samples to be tested by it.

III. The approved laboratory shall maintain records of tests for identity, purity, quality and strength carried out on all samples of Ayurvedic, Siddha and Unani drugs and the results thereof together with the protocols of tests showing the readings and calculation in such form as to be available for inspection and such records shall be retained in the case of substances for which date of expiry is assigned; for a period of two years from such date of expiry and in the case of other substances, for a period of three years.

IV. The approved laboratory shall allow the Inspector appointed under this Act to enter with or without prior notice the premises where testing is carried out and to inspect the premises and the equipment used for test and the testing procedures employed. The laboratory shall allow the Inspectors to inspect the registers and records maintained under these rules and shall supply to such Inspectors such information as they may require for the purpose of ascertaining whether the provisions of the Act and rules made thereunder have been observed.

V. The approved laboratory shall from time to time report to the approving authority any changes in the person-in-charge of testing of Ayurvedic, Siddha and Unani drugs or the expert staff responsible for testing, as the case may be, and any material alterations in the premises or changes in the equipment used for the purposes of testing which have been made since the date of last inspection made on behalf of the approving authority before the grant or renewal of approval.

VI. The approved laboratory shall furnish reports of the results of tests or analysis in Form 50.

VII. In case any sample of Ayurvedic, Siddha and Unani drug is found on test to be not of standard quality, the approved laboratory shall furnish to the approving authority and the licensing authority of the State where the manufacturer and/or sender of the Ayurvedic, Siddha and Unani drugs is located, a copy of the test report of the sample with the protocols of tests applied.

VIII. The approved laboratory shall comply with the provisions of the Act and rules made thereunder and with such further requirements, if any, as may be specified in the rules made from time to time under Chapter IV-A of the Act of which the approving authority has given the approved laboratory not less than four months ‘notice.

IX. The approved laboratory shall maintain an inspection book to enable the Inspector to record his impression or defects noticed.

160 E. Inspection before grant of approval.— Before an approval in Form 48 is granted, the approving authority shall cause the laboratory at which the testing of Ayurvedic, Siddha and Unani drugs, as the case may be, is proposed to be carried out to be inspected jointly by the Inspectors appointed or designated by the Central Government and State Government for this purpose, who shall examine the premises and the equipment intended to be used for testing of drugs and verify into the professional qualifications of the expert staff who are or may be employed by the laboratory.

160F. Report of inspection.— The Inspectors appointed by the Central Government as stated in Rule 160-E shall forward to the approving authority a detailed report of the results of the inspection.

160G. Procedure of approving authority. - (1) If the approving authority after such further enquiry, if any, as it may consider necessary, is satisfied that the requirements of the rules made under the Act have been complied with and that the conditions of the approval and the rules made under the Act have been observed, it shall grant approval in Form 48.

(2) If the approving authority is not satisfied, it shall reject the application and shall inform the applicant of the reasons for such rejection and of the conditions which shall be satisfied before approval could be granted.

160 H. Application after rejection. - If within a period of six months from the rejection of an application for approval, the applicant informs the approving authority that the conditions laid down have been satisfied and deposits inspection fee of two thousand rupees, the approving authority may, if, after causing a further inspection to be made and after being satisfied that the conditions for grant of approval have been complied with, grant the approval in Form 48.

160 I. Renewal. - On an application being made for renewal, the approving authority shall, after causing an inspection to be made and if satisfied that the conditions of the approval and the rules made under the Act have been complied with, shall issue a certificate of renewal in Form 49.

160 J. Withdrawal and suspension of approvals. - (1) The approving authority may, after giving the approved laboratory an opportunity to show cause why such an order should not be passed, by an order in writing stating the reasons therefor, withdraw an approval granted under this Part or suspend it for such period as it thinks fit either wholly or in respect of testing of some of the categories of Ayurvedic, Siddha and Unani drugs to which it relates, if in his opinion the approved laboratory had failed to comply with any of the conditions of the approval or with any provision of the Act or the rules made there under.

(2) Any approved laboratory, whose approval has been suspended or withdrawn, may, within three months of the date of the order of suspension or withdrawal, appeal to the State Government which shall dispose of the appeal in consultation with a panel of competent persons appointed by the Department of Indian Systems of Medicine & Homoeopathy, Government of India in this behalf and notified in the Official Gazette.]"

4.5 PREPARATION OF DOCUMENTS FOR NEW DRUG APPLICATION AND EXPORT REGISTRATION FOR ISM OR AYUSH DRUGS

Traditional medicine is gaining increasing acceptance worldwide, and most countries have now established regulations for these products. Ayush products, in particular, have been experiencing a consistent growth in exports and are tapping into new markets. However, despite India's export growth, the regulatory environment varies across different international markets. Unlike the modern pharmaceutical industry, navigating regulatory requirements for Ayush products in these global markets is not consistently straightforward, and registering Ayush pharmaceuticals remains a significant challenge.

Nevertheless, Indian exporters have shown resilience and have developed export strategies within the existing legal frameworks. Understanding the regulatory landscape of export destinations, along with the associated challenges and opportunities, is crucial for all stakeholders, including the Ministry of Ayush. This understanding opens up possibilities for expanding exports by identifying regulatory pathways for these products, while also highlighting the obstacles that need to be addressed for market entry or expansion.

The major exports of Ayush products include medicinal plants/herbs, extracts, pharmaceuticals, and health/dietary supplements. The primary export destinations for Ayush products are the USA, EU, and UAE. The study provides an overview of the regulatory environment concerning these commodities and outlines the strategies adopted by exporters to access markets and distribution channels more easily. It also examines both tariff and non-tariff barriers to exports. Additionally, services and service providers in the traditional medicine sector play a crucial role in drug distribution.

According to Research Information System in Developing countries, RIS (2021), the global herbal sector was valued at USD 657.5 billion in 2020 and is expected to reach USD 746.9 billion by 2022. This sector encompasses medicinal and aromatic plants (MAPs), herbal medicines, herbal extracts, plant derivatives, and supplements. While the overall sector grew at a rate of 7.4 percent annually from 2014 to 2020, the growth performances of its sub-sectors varied significantly. Particularly, the herbal pharmaceutical sector expanded at an impressive rate of 18.5 percent during the same period, capturing a market share of 14.1 percent in 2020 (RIS, 2021). This growth pattern indicates that higher value-added sub-sectors are growing faster than primary sectors, and the industry is expected to witness an expansion of the value chain based on trade among economies.

The COVID-19 pandemic has further fueled a surge in global demand for biodiversity-based goods and services, including phytopharmaceuticals (UNCTAD, 2022). Herbal medicines have experienced a higher-than-expected demand across all regions compared to pre-pandemic levels. Several reports have revised their estimates for the size of the herbal medicine market, albeit using different methodologies. Fortune Business Insights (2022) projects the global herbal medicine market to grow from USD 165.66 billion in 2022 to USD 347.50 billion by 2029, at a compound annual growth rate (CAGR) of 11.16 percent. Meanwhile, a Zion Market Research study (2022) estimated the global herbal medicine market size at around USD 166 billion in 2021, with a CAGR of approximately 11.2 percent expected between 2022 and 2028.

However, export of AYUSH /ISM medicine has to face several challenges to export in other countries and which includes:

- Traffic rate or custom duties of developing countries are higher in compare to the developed countries.
- Sanitary and Phytosanitary (SPS) measures SPS measures for AYUSH medicines are challenging as those drugs are prone to microbial and pest attack.
- Technical barrier to trade includes production equipment and specific processes, labelling and packaging, product performance and quality control, environmental impacts, traceability and product identity, testing and certification are challenging and diverse for the AYUSH products.

USA

The United States is the primary destination for India's Ayush exports, holding the largest share. As of 2022, the herbal medicines market in the USA is valued at USD 24.5 billion, representing an 18.4 percent share in the global market (Fortune Business Insights, 2022). The high per capita spending in the USA allows for access to high-value products. Additionally, limited pricing restrictions and direct-to-consumer advertising create an advantageous environment for exporters, enabling them to set higher prices. However, challenges such as high operating costs and limited public health financing can restrict the potential for exports.

Apart from the market size, India's Ayush industry is interested in the favorable epidemiological trends in the USA. The country has a developed-country epidemiological profile with a high prevalence of non-communicable diseases (NCDs). The leading causes of NCD deaths include cardiovascular diseases (38 percent), cancer (25 percent), respiratory diseases (9 percent), and diabetes (6 percent), accounting for nearly four out of every five deaths (79 percent). This trend is expected to worsen due to factors like population growth, aging, urbanization, and increased exposure to risk factors. The Ayush industry's strength in addressing NCDs provides a promising consumer base interested in alternative healthcare solutions.

Furthermore, the wellness trend is gaining traction, potentially driving further demand for Ayush products and services. The practice of complementary and alternative medicine (CAM) is permitted in eleven states in the US, which could boost Ayush drug sales in the market. Currently, most Ayush goods, including medicinal and aromatic plants (MAPs) and pharmaceuticals, are marketed as dietary or food supplements.

In terms of export trends to the USA, Ayush product exports from India have grown at a rate of 8.02 percent during 2017-2021. Extracts accounted for the largest proportion of India's export basket in 2021 (57.3 percent), while Ayurvedic drugs contributed significantly to Ayush pharmaceuticals exports (96.4 percent).

4.6 REGISTRATION REQUIREMENT OF AYUSH DRUG EXPORT

AYUSH drugs in USA mostly treated as Botanical drugs. All formulations and drugs, including traditional medicines, must undergo a series of tests and clinical studies to demonstrate their effectiveness, safety, quality, and dosage standards before being approved for market release. There are three types of new drug registration applications allowed:

Investigational New Drugs (INDs)

New Drug Applications (NDAs)

Abbreviated New Drug Applications for Generic Drug products (ANDAs)

The fundamental food and drug law in the United States is the Federal Food, Drug, and Cosmetics Act of 1938 (FD&C Act), which is governed by the Code of Federal Regulations (CFR). The Food and Drug Administration (FDA) is responsible for enforcing this law.

For AYUSH pharmaceuticals, the most suitable regulatory pathway would likely involve registration as 'botanical drugs.' The term 'botanicals' is defined by the FDA as products that include plant materials, algae, macroscopic fungi, and combinations thereof, excluding animal products or minerals except when they are a minor component in a traditional botanical preparation, such as traditional Chinese medicine or Ayurvedic medicine.

A botanical product can be classified as a food (including dietary supplements), drug (including biological drugs), medical device, or cosmetic under the FD&C Act, depending on its intended use. Intended use is determined by factors like the product's labeling, advertising, and how it is distributed. A botanical product intended for diagnosing, curing, mitigating, or treating disease would be considered a drug under the FD&C Act. Similarly, a product intended to prevent disease would generally also be classified as a drug.

However, certain circumstances may subject an article that meets the drug definition to a different regulatory scheme. For instance, if a conventional food or dietary supplement makes a health claim about reducing disease risk in accordance with authorized regulations, it would not be regulated as a drug solely because of that claim.

It's important to note that manufacturers of dietary supplements making nutritional deficiency, structure/function, or general well-being claims must substantiate that these claims are truthful and not misleading, as required by Section 403(r)(6) of the FD&C Act. Therefore, a botanical product can be categorized as either a drug or a food supplement based on its labeling claims and related regulatory adherence.

AYUSH drugs as Dietary Supplements

AYUSH exports to the US, which include herbs, extracts, and pharmaceuticals, are primarily marketed and distributed as dietary supplements. This approach is adopted due to the significant regulatory hurdles faced by herbal medicinal products in obtaining registration as drugs, making the sale of such products as food supplements the most legal and feasible marketing option. In the US, the sale of food supplements is governed by the Dietary Supplement Health and Education Act (DSHEA) of 1994, while labeling requirements are regulated by the Nutrition Labeling and Education Act of 1990.

Under Section 3 of DSHEA, supplements are broadly defined as anything that supplements the diet, encompassing vitamins, minerals, herbs, amino acids, enzymes, organ tissues, metabolites, extracts, or concentrates. Unlike drugs, manufacturers of dietary supplements, including herbs, are not mandated to obtain premarket approval from the FDA before making their products available to consumers. Instead, the FDA must demonstrate that a supplement is unsafe before taking regulatory action.

DSHEA permits manufacturers to make certain health-related statements about their supplements, provided they have substantiated evidence for these claims. However, such statements do not require FDA evaluation before marketing use. Nonetheless, manufacturers are still subject to DSHEA provisions concerning supplement safety and marketing.

Dietary supplements may face legal consequences under DSHEA if deemed adulterated. Reasons for adulteration include posing a significant risk of illness or injury as per label directions, containing insufficiently researched new ingredients, posing an imminent public health hazard, or containing poisonous or unsanitary components. The FDA has the authority to require recalls or halt the sale of supplements if they pose hazards under normal use conditions. However, unless a herbal product is proven to be adulterated based on these criteria, it can remain on the market.

Key Barriers to Marketing Ayush Products in the US:

- ***Premarket Safety Notification for New Dietary Ingredients:***

  Under section 413(a)(2) of the FD&C Act, manufacturers or distributors introducing a New Dietary Ingredient (NDI) into interstate commerce must submit a premarket safety notification to the FDA at least 75 days prior to the product's introduction. Failure to do so results in the dietary supplement containing the NDI being deemed adulterated.

- ***Quality Standards for Herbal Ingredients According to USP-NF:***

  The quality standards applied to natural ingredients and finished products in the US vary depending on the product's regulatory classification as a botanical drug, herbal dietary supplement, or natural food product. Official monographs in the USP-NF designate FDA-approved or USP-accepted uses for these articles, with botanical monographs being FDA-enforceable and containing detailed descriptions, requirements, tests, analytical procedures, and acceptance criteria.

- ***Restrictions on Health Claims for Dietary Supplement Labeling:***

  Since Ayush drugs are marketed as supplements, limitations on health claims pose challenges to their sales potential. Section 6 of the DSHEA specifies acceptable claims for supplement labels or promotional materials, including those related to nutrient deficiency diseases, nutrient roles in human structure or function, documented mechanisms of nutrient actions, and general well-being from nutrient consumption. However, manufacturers must include a disclaimer stating that the FDA has not evaluated the claim. Additionally, supplement manufacturers cannot make disease-related claims, which are reserved for drugs rather than dietary supplements.

European Union

Under the EU Directive 2001/83/EC, which was amended in 2004 by Directive 2004/24/EC (the Herbal Directive), traditional medicines such as Ayush products can be registered through three regulatory pathways: Traditional use registration, Well-established use registration, and Stand-alone or mixed application. Each of these pathways presents its own distinct challenges.

Traditional use registration, also known as the simplified registration procedure, was established by Directive 2004/24/EC. This type of registration is intended for herbal medicinal products with a long history of traditional medicinal use (at least 30 years, including 15 years within the EU). These products can be used without medical supervision and are administered orally or topically. However, obtaining evidence of traditional use within the EU is a significant challenge for registering Ayush herbal medicinal products through this procedure, requiring bibliographic or expert evidence.

For traditional use registration, the product:

- Does not require clinical safety and efficacy trials.
- Requires submission of bibliographic safety and efficacy data.
- Must have a history of at least 30 years of traditional use, including 15 years within the EU.
- Is intended for use without medical supervision and is not administered via injection.

Well-established use marketing authorization (MA) applies to medicinal products with published scientific literature or studied data demonstrating acceptable efficacy and safety, along with at least 10 years of use within the EU. This category may not be suitable for most Ayush pharmaceuticals.

The stand-alone or mixed application for MA is only applicable to novel herbal medicinal products developed through research and development. This application requires a comprehensive dossier of clinical data, similar to the process for Western medicine MA applications. There is also an option to combine this with bibliographic data.

Traditional use registration can be pursued through national competent authorities for national, mutual recognition, or decentralized procedures. Well-established use MA and stand-alone or mixed application for MA can also be sought through these procedures, including the centralized procedure at the European Medicines Agency (EMA). Traditional use registration is relatively simpler compared to the other pathways for registering Ayush herbal medicinal products in the EU market.

United Arab Emirates (UAE)

Simplified Regulatory Systems for Ayush Registration as Drugs in UAE:

The UAE has embraced traditional medicine as a vital aspect of disease management and has established a regulatory framework for the registration and importation of these medicines as drugs. This regulatory setup has been a key factor contributing to the high export volume of Ayush products, despite the UAE's smaller geographic size and population compared to the US and EU. Traditional, complementary, and alternative medicine (TCAM) is overseen jointly by two departments within the Ministry of Health. The Drug Department manages the registration of herbal, homeopathic, Ayurvedic, and Chinese medicines, as well as natural products in drugstores and pharmacies. On the other hand, the Complementary and Alternative Medicine Unit coordinates the licensing and regulation of TCAM practitioners.

According to Article 1 of UAE Federal Law No. 4 of 1983, medicines are defined as any substance containing elements for treating or protecting humans and animals. This definition encompasses traditional, herbal, complementary, and alternative medicines. Market authorization for herbal medicines like Ayurveda is obtained through the registration of 'Pharmaceutical Products Derived from Natural Sources.' As per Article 65 of Federal Law No. 4 of 1983, all pharmaceutical products imported into the UAE must be registered with the Ministry of Health. Registration requirements include evidence of quality, safety, and efficacy, such as the Certificate of Pharmaceutical Product (CoPP) or a certificate of free sale from the country of origin.

Due to Islamic regulations, restrictions are imposed on products containing pork materials, and alcohol must be declared with reasons specified. Labeling regulations require all labels and stickers to be approved by UAE authorities before use. Importers must provide copies of the product's label, packaging, and official certificates for assessment and approval. A committee at the Ministry of Health reviews the pharmaceutical product and determines the CIF (cost, insurance, and freight) price during registration.

Regulation of Traditional Medicine Health Professional License:

The UAE also simplifies the regulation of traditional medicine services, making it an attractive destination for service exports. Professional licenses are issued for TCAM fields **such as** Ayurveda, Chiropractic Medicine, Homeopathy, Naturopathic Medicine, Osteopathic Medicine, Therapeutic Massage, Traditional Chinese Medicine, and Unani Medicine. License requirements vary by emirate, but generally, an Ayurveda practice license requires a degree from an accredited university, five years of clinical experience, English proficiency, and other criteria.

Key Barriers:

Import requirements mandate 51% UAE ownership, making it challenging to sell products without a local agent. Thorough due diligence on commercial agents and compliance with the Commercial Agency Law are crucial. Import licenses are typically granted only to UAE-registered companies with at least 51% UAE ownership, though this requirement doesn't apply to goods imported into free zones like the Dubai Healthcare City.

High SPS (Sanitary and Phytosanitary) and TBT (Technical Barriers to Trade) measures are imposed on imports of Medicinal and Aromatic Plants (MAPs) and Extracts, adding complexity to trade compared to the US and EU. Additionally, UAE imposes relatively higher tariffs on Ayush commodities compared to these regions.

4.7 CHALLENGES IN MONITORING THE SAFETY OF HERBAL MEDICINES: REGULATION, QUALITY ASSURANCE AND CONTROL, NATIONAL/REGIONAL PHARMACOPOEIAS

Consumers often mistakenly believe that natural products are always safe and free from risks, but this is not always the case, as some medicinal plants can be inherently toxic. Herbal medicines, like all medicines, can have adverse side effects, often linked to quality issues. Problems such as adulteration with undisclosed substances like corticosteroids and non-steroidal anti-inflammatory drugs, using the wrong plant species, incorrect dosages, errors in usage by both consumers and healthcare providers, interactions with other medications, and contamination with harmful substances like toxic metals and pathogens can lead to adverse events.

***Examples illustrate these challenges*:**

- Some herbal products contained betamethasone, causing corticosteroid-like effects.
- Misidentification led to aristolochic acid-containing products, causing severe kidney failure.
- Ginkgo biloba use was linked to bleeding disorders and haemorrhages.
- Traditional herbal medicine caused interstitial pneumonia when used with interferon, leading to severe cases, sometimes fatal.
- Use of Traditional/CAM medicine along with allopathic medicine, nutraceuticals, specific food may cause herb-drug, food -drug, herb-herb interaction which may be fatal.
- Taking of herbal medicine of indigenous system of medicine with practitioner's prescription and supervision may developed undesired adverse effect.
- Complexity of polyherbal medicine may create unpredictable adverse reaction in individual

Adverse events related to herbal products are often due to quality issues or improper use, making it challenging to distinguish genuine adverse reactions until the cause is determined.

National regulations for herbal medicines vary globally, categorizing them as prescription or non-prescription medicines or other products. The regulatory status impacts access and distribution routes. International trade may lead to reclassification based on importing country regulations, not the product's medical value. Quality assurance, including good manufacturing practices and labeling, is crucial for safety and efficacy. Weak regulation can lead to adverse reactions due to poor quality, including adulteration and contamination. Quality control for herbal products is complex, influenced by raw materials and agricultural practices. National pharmacopoeias define standards, but differences exist between regions. Health professionals need better education on herbal medicines to ensure safe use and monitoring. Patients should disclose herbal medicine use to all healthcare providers for comprehensive care and risk prevention.

To address this issue following steps have been taken by WHO Pharmacovigilance program (Pharmacovigilance is the science and activities relating to the detection, assessment, understanding and prevention of adverse effects or any other possible drug-related problems.).

Regulation

Regulation and registration of herbal medicines vary globally, with different countries categorizing them as prescription or non-prescription drugs. Additionally, herbal products may be classified differently, not always as medicines. The regulatory status can differ between countries and determines the access and distribution of these products, involving qualified providers and distributors.

When trading herbal products between countries with different regulatory statuses, the reclassification in the importing country depends on its own regulatory framework, not the product's inherent characteristics. The popularity of herbal products categorized outside of medicine and food is rising, posing risks due to insufficient regulation, weaker quality control, and lax distribution channels like online sales.

National regulatory information on herbal medicines is often not fully shared among authorities or with safety monitoring centers. While new medicines typically start as prescription drugs, some transition to non-prescription status over time, becoming major sources of self-medication. However, in many countries, herbal products often enter the non-prescription category directly rather than transitioning from prescription status.

Quality assurance and control

Quality assurance and control measures for herbal medicines, including national quality standards, good manufacturing practices (GMP), labeling, and licensing schemes, must be implemented in countries where these medicines are regulated. These measures are crucial for ensuring the safety and effectiveness of herbal medicines. Inadequate regulation and quality control can lead to a higher incidence of adverse reactions due to poor-quality herbal products, such as adulteration with undisclosed substances or contamination with harmful residues.

The requirements and methods for quality control of finished herbal products, especially mixtures, are more complex compared to other pharmaceuticals because the quality depends on the raw materials used. Good agricultural and collection practices (GACP) for medicinal plants, including proper plant selection and cultivation, are essential.

National and regional pharmacopoeias

National and regional pharmacopoeias establish quality specifications and standards for herbal materials and preparations like essential oils and powdered herbal materials. The inclusion of herbal materials in these pharmacopoeias depends on their local availability, which is linked to specific ecological habitats of medicinal plants. However, discrepancies may arise among pharmacopoeias regarding the same herbal material due to differences in original plant species and processing methods.

It is essential to have a drug regulatory framework for herbal medicines similar to other human medicines to ensure they meet safety, quality, and efficacy standards.

Appropriate use

Healthcare providers who offer herbal medicines vary depending on each country's healthcare system. In countries where herbal medicines are prescription drugs, certain providers may not be included in current reporting systems. Nurses, alongside other healthcare professionals, are increasingly involved in monitoring the safety of non-prescription herbal medicines, highlighting the need for trust and knowledge-sharing among providers.

Healthcare professionals often lack sufficient knowledge about herbal medicines, their effects on patients, and potential interactions with other medicines. Patients' attitudes towards herbal medicines, believing them to be inherently safe due to their natural origin, can lead to underreporting of their use to healthcare providers.

Therefore, education for healthcare professionals, herbal medicine providers, and patients is crucial to prevent potential risks associated with the misuse of herbal medicines.

CHAPTER 5

TKDL, Geographical Indication Bill, Government Bills in AYUSH, ISM, CCRAS, CCRS, CCRH, CCRU

5.1 TKDL

Full form of TKDL is Traditional Knowledge Digital Library [available at https://www.tkdl.res.in/]. It is an online repository to preserve the available traditional knowledge of India. It is the joint initiative of Council of Scientific and Industrial Research (CSIR) and the Ministry of AYUSH and established in 2001. The major objective of setting up TKDL repository to prevent the misinterpretation of Indian Traditional Knowledge (TK) at international Patent office and to protect Indian TK.

5.1.1 OBJECTIVES OF TKDL

- to protect Indian traditional medicinal knowledge and prevent its misappropriation at International Patent Offices.
- To overcome the language barrier associated with ancient text associated with Indian systems of Medicine and represent ancient Medical text with modern interpretation.
- Proper digital preservation of Indian systems of Medicine knowledge and TK
- Development of innovative classification system - Traditional Knowledge Resource Classification (TKRC) to classify Indian Traditional Medicine System into several thousand subgroups which are effective in International Patent classification system.
- Beneficial to set a benchmark in TK protection around the world and to prevent exploitation of TK globally.
- Act as a bridge between these books (prior art) and International patent examiners.

5.1.2 KEY FEATURES OF TKDL

Background of TKDL Creation

TKDL was set up in 2001 to prevent exploitation and to protect Indian traditional knowledge at different Patent Offices worldwide.

The TKDL is a digital repository of India's traditional on systems of medicine from classical/ traditional books pertains to Ayurveda, Unani, Siddha and Sowa Rigpa as well as practices of Yoga.

- TKDL has scientifically converted and structured the available ancient texts on Indian Systems of Medicines i.e. Ayurveda, Unani , Siddha and Sowa Rigpa and Yoga, into 5 international languages i.e. English, French, Japanese, German and Spanish, with the help of information technology and also created innovative classification system dedicatedly for Traditional Knowledge - Traditional Knowledge Resource Classification (TKRC).

TKDL incorporated about 200 sub-groups under A61K 36/00 in International Patent Classification system instead of few sub-groups which were previously available on medicinal plants under A61K 35/00, thus enhancing the quality of search and investigation of prior art with respect to the application of patent in traditional knowledge (TK).

- TKDL has established standard and specification for the creation of International databases on TK and those specification was adopted in 2003 by the Committee in fifth session of the Intergovernmental Committee (IGC) of World Intelectual Property Organiztion on Intellectual Property and Genetic Resources, Traditional Knowledge and Expression of folklore.

TKDL was initiated on 2001, however 2 cases of exploiting traditional knowledge may results the formation of this organized digital database. As traditional medicines and Indian systems of medicine are the potential source of treating various diseases and development of new drugs for modern medicine. So, TK on Indian knowledge on medicines are highly susceptible to misappropriation as there was language barrier to interpret the information (all are mentioned in regional languages). It was difficult for the most of the patent offices to search this information as prior art, before granting patents. It was easy for individual and organization to utilize this time-tested formulation for misappropriation and bio-piracy.

Two infamous cases of bio-piracy have highlighted the situation prominently.

Turmeric Patent: In 1995, 2 expatriate Indians at the University of Mississippi Medical Centre (Suman K. Das and Hari Har P. Cohly) were granted a US patent (no.5, 401,504) on use of turmeric (*Curcuma longa*) , an age old Indian herb rhizome of *Curcuma longa* in wound healing. Turmeric is a common spice was used in Indian cuisine and also essential medicine in Indian systems of medicine for wound healing, skin diseases and other ailments.

On objection of The Council of Scientific & Industrial Research (CSIR), India, who has filed a re-examination case with the US PTO challenging the patent on the grounds of existing of prior art, The US Patent Office revoked this patent after 2 years in 1997, after confirming that there was no novelty; the findings by innovators having been known in India for centuries. CSIR's claim was justified by documentary evidence of traditional knowledge, including ancient Sanskrit text and a paper published in 1953 in the Journal of the Indian Medical Association.

Neem Patent: In 1994, American chemical company W.R. Grace had, along with a number of other international corporations, been granted patents on various uses of the substance Azadirachtin, compound present in Neem, *Azadirachta indica. The patent was granted by* European Patent Office (EPO) patent (EPO patent No.436257) for a method for controlling fungi on plants by the aid of hydrophobic extracted Neem oil. Neem oil was used for centuries in Indian agriculture to protect crops, and therefore it cannot be considered for granting a patent. a group of international NGOs and representatives of Indian farmers filed legal opposition and on this basis EPO revoked this patent on 2000.

In international patent offices, while examining the patentability of any claimed subject matter, Patent officers use available resources for searching the appropriate non-patent literature sources. Availability of distinctive databases and patent literature can be beneficial for search and retrieved whereas non-patent literature prior art is often buried somewhere in the many and diverse sources. Therefore, a need was felt to create more easily accessible language- barrier free non-patent literature databases on traditional knowledge of Indi

5.1.3 PRESENT STATUS OF TKDL

TKDL database repository amalgamates diverse disciplines and languages such as ISM (Ayurveda, Siddha, Yoga Unani, Homeopathy), Arabic, Urdu, Persian, Sanskrit, Tamil, English, Japanese, Spanish, French, German, modern science & modern medicine. TKDL is based on ancient texts of Indian Systems of Medicine (ISM), which are accessible in public domain and can be obtained by any individual or organization at both national and international level. This database acts as a bridge between these books (prior art) and international patent examiners.

Presently TKDL is available and accepted to 16 patent offices on the basis of approval Cabinet Committee on Economic including

1. European Patent Office,
2. United State Patent & Trademark Office,

3. Japan Patent Office,
4. United Kingdom Patent Office,
5. Canadian Intellectual Property Office,
6. German Patent Office,
7. Indian Patent Office,
8. Intellectual Property Australia,
9. Intellectual Property Corporation of Malaysia,
10. Chile Patent Office,
11. Rospatent- Intellectual Property Office of Russia,
12. Peru Patent Office,
13. Spanish Patent and Trademark Office,
14. Danish Patent and Trademark office,
15. National Industrial Property Institute, France
16. Eurasian Patent Office),

under TKDL Access (Non-disclosure) Agreement. On the basis of prior terms and conditions of the Access agreement of TKDL database, patent examiners of different patent offices can utilize TKDL for search and examination purposes only and cannot reveal the contents to any third party unless it is required for the citation purpose.

On the basis of prior art evidences from TKDL, according to TKDL website more than 324 patent applications have either been withdrawn/ set aside/ amended, based on the prior art proofs available in the TKDL database without any financial cost and in few weeks/months of time.

TKDL is presently hosting an information of more than 4.24 lakh formulations from the texts of traditional medicine systems of India including Ayurveda, Unani and Siddha. TKDL is hosting 119 Ayurveda, 55 Unani, 91 Siddha, 1 Sowa- rigpa, 15 yoga.

5.2 TKRC

Traditional Knowledge Resource Classification is one of the structured classification system on Traditional Knowledge on Indian Systems of Medicine developed by TKDL to facilitate International Patent offices to prevent the grant of wrong patents for non-original discoveries relating to traditional knowledge systems.

TKRC system structure:

"TKRC has major 4 sections including:

A = Ayurveda

B = Unani

C = Siddha

Y = Yoga

Section A is further divided into the following classes:

01 – Pharmaceutical preparations (Kalpana)

02 – Personal Hygiene Preparations

03 – Dietary (Food / Food stuff or Beverages)

04 – Biocides, Fumigatives (Dhupana, Krimighna)

Class 1 under Section A is further categorized under following sub classes

01A – Based on Plants (Audbhida)

01B – Based on Animals (Jangama)

01C – Based on Minerals (Parthiva)

01D – Characterised by Diseases (Roga)

01E – Characterised by Actions (Karma)

01F – Mode of Administration

01G – Miscellaneous .."

Group A01A-1/00 is for Whole Medicinal Plants (Audbhida). The TKRC code for the plant Nigella sativa is A01A-1/1326. This plant belongs to the Ranunculaceae family and falls under the sub-group A61K 36/71 in the IPC classification. Consequently, the TKRC code A01A-1/326 is associated with A61K 36/71, allowing for the search of Nigella sativa using either of these codes interchangeably.

Presently 80 formulation codes which completely describe a particular method of formulation.

Chronological development of TKDL

Pre- Development	
Year	**Milestone**
1999 **October, December**	Approach paper on establishment of TKDL; presenting approach paper to Standing Committee on Information Technology (SCIT), World Intellectual Property Organisation (WIPO).
2000	Setting up of the interdisciplinary (inter-ministerial Task Force on

Table *contd...*

January	TKDL.
2000 **May**	Submission of TKDL Task Force Report to Department of Indian System of Medicine and Homeopathy; and presenting TKDL Concept & Vision at International forum.
2001 January	Cabinet Committee of Economic Affairs (CCEA's) approval for the establishment of TKDL Project.
2001 June	Memorandum of Understanding (MoU) between Department of ISM&H now AYUSH) and National Institute of Science Communication (now CSIR-National Institute of Science Communication and Information Resources).
Development	
2001 **July**	Development of TKDL software, specifications and design.
October,2001 to March, 2002	Establishing TKDL team of Project Assistants (IT), Ayurveda, Patent Examiners, etc.
February, 2001	Presentation on Traditional Knowledge Resource Classification (TKRC) at International Patent Classification (IPC) Union for getting established WIPO-TK Task Force consisting of USPTO, EPO, JPO, China and India.
Year	**Milestone**
Post Development	
February, 2002	WIPO-TK Task Force recommended addition of a new subclass under A 61; Committee of Experts recommended: (i) inclusion of approx. 200 subgroups on TK against earlier few sub-groups on medicinal plants, (ii) linking of TKRC to IPC and (iii) continuation of work on biodiversity, TK and TCE.
November December, 2002; July, 2003	Internationally recognized specifications and standards for setting up of TK databases and registries based on TKDL specifications, their drafting presentation and adoption of recommendations at the 5th Session of IGC.
August, 2002	Constitution of Access Policy Issue Committee (APIC).
March, 2003	First batch of data abstraction work on 36,000 Ayurveda formulations for creating TKDL in five languages, i.e. English, German, Spanish, French and Japanese.
October, 2003	Release of demo TKDL CD containing a sample of 500 formulations.
June ,2004	Initiation of the TKDL Unani project.
August, 2004	Initiation of TKDL Ayurveda Phase II.
October, 2004	Concordance between IPC and TKRC and approval on linking of TKRC with IPC.
August, 2005	Initiation of project on TKDL Siddha. Creating of TKRC containing approx. 25,000 subgroups.
June 2006	Approval on Access to TKDL database to international patent offices by Cabinet Committee on Economic Affairs.

Table *contd...*

January 2008	Initiation of activities on creation of TKDL Yoga.
February 2009	TKDL Access Agreement with European Patent Office (EPO).
July 2009	TKDL Access Agreement with USPTO.
July 2009	The first prior art evidence based on TKDL citations under Third Party observations against 35 patent applications submitted to EPO leading to development of a formalised structure for filing Third Party Objections (TPOs)/oppositions at various international patent offices.
October, 2009	TKDL Access Agreement with German Patent and Trademark Office (DPMA).
February, 2010	TKDL Access Agreement with United Kingdom Intellectual Property Office. TKDL Access Agreement with Canadian Intellectual Property Office (CIPO).
January, 2011	TKDL Access Agreement with Intellectual Property Australia (IP Australia).
March 22-24, 2011	International Conference on 'Utilization of the Traditional Knowledge Digital Library (TKDL) as a Model for the Protection of Traditional Knowledge.
April, 2011	TKDL Access Agreement with Japan Patent Office (JPO).
July, 2012	First Amending Agreement to TKDL Access Agreement with European Patent Office (EPO).
Year	**Milestone**
August, 2012	First Amending Agreement to TKDL Access Agreement with Canadian Intellectual Property Office (CIPO).
January, 2014	First Amending Agreement to TKDL Access Agreement with United Kingdom Intellectual Property Office (IPO).
May, 2014	TKDL Access Agreement with Chile Patent Office (INAPI).
June, 2014	First Amending Agreement to TKDL Access Agreement with Japan Patent Office (JPO).
October 2015	TKDL Access Agreement with Intellectual Property Corporation of Malaysia (MyIPO)
June, 2017	TKDL Access Agreement with Rospatent (Russia).
June, 2017	TKDL Access Agreement with INDECOPI (Peru).
October, 2017	First Amending Agreement to TKDL Access Agreement with Chile Patent Office (INAPI).
September, 2018	Initiation of Project on Ayurveda from Kerala manuscripts.
October 2018	Initiation of Project on Sowa Rigpa.
April, 2019	TKDL Access Agreement with Spanish Patent and Trademark Office.
October, 2019	Second Amending Agreement to TKDL Access Agreement with IP Australia.
October, 2021	TKDL Access Agreement with Danish Patent and Trademark Office.
August 2022	Cabinet approves **widening access of the Traditional Knowledge digital library database to users, besides patent offices.**
September 2022	TKDL Access Agreement with National Industrial Property Institute, France.
February, 2023	TKDL Access Agreement with Eurasian Patent Office.

Home page of TKDL website

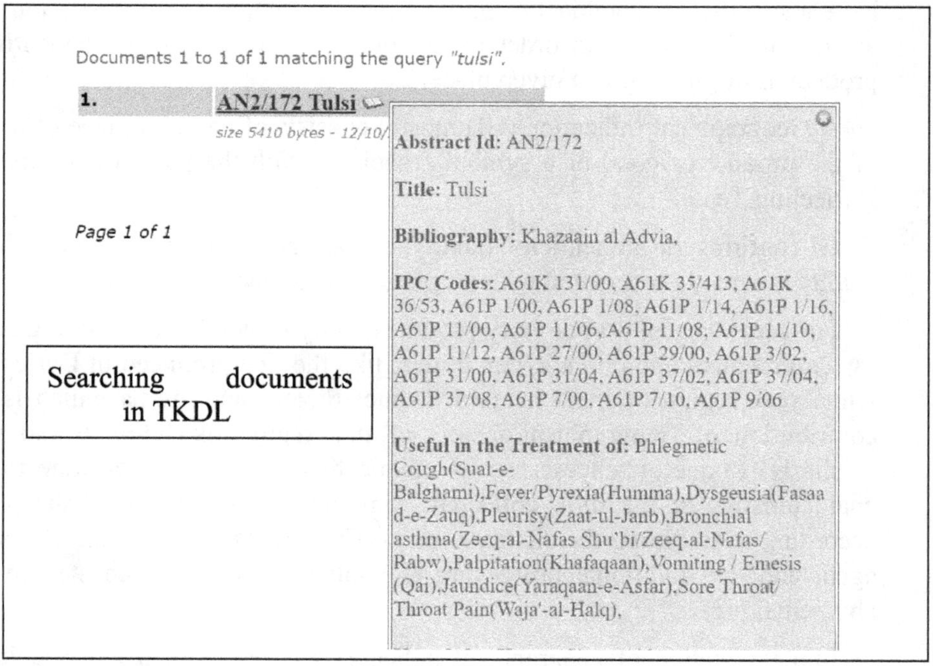

Searching documents in TKDL

5.3 GEOGRAPHICAL INDICATIONS (GI)

Geographical Indications of Goods is considered as an Intellectual Property Rights. It was originated to ascertain the assurance of quality and distinctness of a good or product along with its geographical origin. It was conceptualized in Article 1(2) of the Paris Convention for the Protection of Industrial Property of 1883 (Paris Convention) which refers to "indications of source" and "appellations of origin" as objects of industrial property. Paragraph (3) of the same article indicates that the term "industrial property" is not limited to "industry and commerce" proper, but applies also to agricultural and extractive industries and to all manufactured or natural products, like "wines, grain, tobacco leaf, fruit, cattle, minerals, mineral waters, beer, flowers and flour.

According to TRIPS Agreement Article 22.1 GI is defined as "*...indications which identify a good as originating in the territory of a Member [of the World Trade Organization], or a region or locality in that territory, where a given quality, reputation or other characteristic of the good is essentially attributable to its geographical origin.*"

According to World Intellectual Property Organization (WIPO), GI is defined as "A geographical indication (GI) is a sign used on products that have a specific geographical origin and possess qualities or a reputation that are due to that origin. In order to function as a GI, a sign must identify a product as originating in a given place."

A Geographical Indication (GI) mostly consists of name of place of origin of the product or good or a symbol associated with the place of origin. Eg. Darjeeling Tea.

GI confirms the authenticity, quality, characteristic of a good for which the quality is directly associated with its geographical place of production.

For some agricultural or dairy product quality of good is directly regulated by geographical and climatic conditions; like the Tea produced in Darjeeling Himalayan region of India bears a distinct flavour and aroma which is the contribution of Geographical factors of that region like climate and soil. Similarly, Roquefort cheese has its unique features and softness due to the characteristics of the milk collected from indigenous breeds of sheep fed according to tradition, the characteristics of the caves in which the cheese is aged, and the traditional processing technologies used in each step of the cheesemaking.

Implementation of geographical indications is not limited to agricultural products. A GI may also highlight specific qualities of a product that are produced due to human factors found in the product's place of origin, like specific manufacturing knowhows and traditions. It may include handicrafts, which are usually handmade using local natural resources, skills and usually embedded in the traditions of local communities.

5.3.1 PURPOSE OF GI

- GI is considered as one of the important IPR, Under Articles 1 (2) and 10 of the Paris Convention for the Protection of Industrial Property. GI is also covered under Articles 22 to 24 of the Trade Related Aspects of Intellectual Property Rights (TRIPS) Agreement, which was part of the Agreements concluding the Uruguay Round of GATT negotiations.
- GI helps in assuring the quality, authenticity and characteristic of good or produce which are directly governed by Geographical and climatic condition of place of origin.
- It helps to protect traditional method of production of good and preserve the cultural heritage associated with the production of those product.
- Implementation of GI protects traditional agricultural practices, handicraft knowhows and other Traditional knowledges.
- It gives stakeholders confidence about the authenticity of the genericity of the product associated with its place of origin.
- A geographical indication right enables people who have the right to use the indication to prevent its use by a third party whose product does not conform to the applicable standards.
- It promotes rural development by enhancing marketability of product by increasing demand of the GI good and ultimately enhance the economic development of the entire region of the place of origin.
- GI indirectly promotes environmental sustainability, agricultural diversity, cultural and social identity of place of origin.
- GI prevents unauthorized utilization of a registered geographical indication by third parties.
- It provides legal protection and promotes the export of local goods.

5.3.2 GI AND INDIA

As a participant in the World Trade Organization (WTO), India implemented the Geographical Indications of Goods (Registration & Protection) Act in 1999, which became effective on September 15, 2003.

According to Section 2 (1) (e) of THE GEOGRAPHICAL INDICATIONS OF GOODS (REGISTRATION AND PROTECTION) ACT, 1999,

GI is defined as...... *"geographical indication", in relation to goods, means an indication which identifies such goods as agricultural goods, natural goods or manufactured goods as originating, or manufactured in the territory of a country, or a region or locality in that territory, where a given quality, reputation or other characteristic of such goods is essentially attributable to its geographical origin and in case where such goods are manufactured goods one of the activities of either the production or of processing or preparation of the goods concerned takes place in such territory, region or locality, as the case may be.*

In December 1999, the Parliament of India had passed the Geographical Indications of Goods (Registration and Protection) Act,1999. It seeks to provide for the registration and better protection of GI relating to goods in India. The Act would be administered by the Controller General of Patents, Designs and Trade Marks- who is the Registrar of Geographical Indications. The Geographical Indications Registry is situated at Chennai.

Geographical Indications of Goods (Registration and Protection) Act, 1999 extends to the whole of India contains the following chapters which contains several sections (87 sections):

Chapter I: Preliminary

Chapter II: The Register and Conditions for Registration

Chapter III: Procedure for and Duration of Registration

Chapter IV: Effect of Registration

Chapter V: Special Provisions Relating to Trade Marks and Prior Users

Chapter VI: Rectification and Correction of the Register

Chapter VII: Appeals to the Appellate Board

Chapter VIII: Offences, Penalties and Procedure

Chapter IX: Miscellaneous

In the exercise of the powers conferred by sub-section 87 of Geographical Indications of Goods (Registration & Protection) Act,1999 (48 of 1999), the Central Government makes the **Geographical Indications Of Goods (Registration and Protection) Rules, 2002** which was further amended in **2020.**

5.3.3 APPLICANT FOR THE REGISTRATION OF GI

According to chapter III, section 11 of this Act, Any association of persons, producers, organisation or authority established by or under the law can apply:

- The applicant must represent the interest of the producers The application should be in writing in the prescribed form
- The application should be addressed to the Registrar of Geographical Indications along with prescribed fee.

5.3.4 KEY FACTS OF GI ACT

Registered proprietor of GI

Registered proprietor of GI is

Any association of persons, producers, organisation or authority established by or under the law can be a registered proprietor whose name should be entered in the Register of Geographical Indication as registered proprietor for the Geographical Indication applied for.

Authorised user of GI

A producer of goods can apply for registration as an authorised user. One should apply in writing in the prescribed form along with prescribed fee.

Producer in Relation to GI

The persons dealing with three categories of goods are covered under the term Producer:

i. Agricultural Goods includes the production, processing, trading or dealing
ii. Natural Goods includes exploiting, trading or dealing
iii. Handicrafts or Industrial goods includes making, manufacturing, trading or dealing.

Validity of GI Registration

GI registration in India is valid for the period of 10 years. However, it can be renewed time to time for further period of 10 years each.

Steps for GI Registration Application

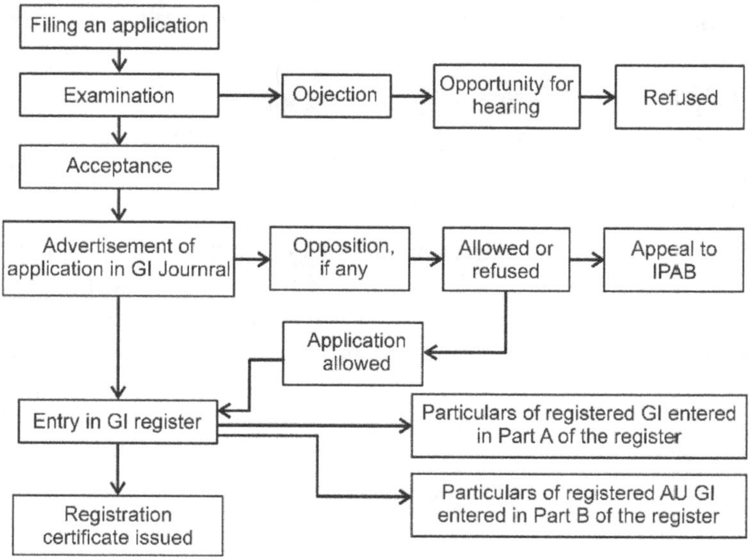

GI and Trademark

A trade mark is a sign which is applied in the course of trade and it differentiates goods or services of one enterprise from those of other enterprises. Whereas a GI is an indication used to identify goods having special characteristics originating from a definite geographical territory.

Trademarks assist consumers in connecting a product or service with a particular standard or standing, relying on details about the company responsible for manufacturing or providing it.

GI assure customers about identity of good as originating from a *particular place*; based on its place of origin, consumers may related a good with a particular quality, characteristic or reputation.

A trademark typically comprises a unique or arbitrary symbol that can be utilized by its owner or an authorized individual. It has the flexibility to be assigned or licensed globally as it is tied to a specific company rather than a particular location. In contrast, the symbol representing a geographical indication usually mirrors the name of the place where the product originates or the name it is known by in that region. All individuals in the area of origin who adhere to specified standards for producing the product may use a geographical indication. However, due to its association with the place of origin, a geographical indication cannot be transferred or licensed to someone external to that region or not affiliated with the authorized producers.

Appellations of Origin

Appellations of origin are a special kind of geographical indication which is used in the Paris Convention and defined in the Lisbon Agreement.

According to, Article 2 of the Lisbon Agreement appellations of origin can be defined as

"(1)… the geographical denomination of a country, region, or locality, which serves to designate a product originating therein, the quality or characteristics of which are due exclusively or essentially to the geographical environment, including natural and human factors."

This definition suggests that appellations of origin consist of the name of the product's place of origin. However, it is interesting to note that a number of traditional indications that are not place names, but refer to a product in connection with a place. E.g. Reblochon (cheese) and Vinho Verde (green wine))

REGISTRATION DETAILS OF GEOGRAPHICAL INDICATIONS OF DIFFERENT AGRICUTURAL AND NATURAL PRODUCTS

S. No As per registe r of GI	Application No.	Geographical Indications	Goods (As per Sec 2 (f) of GI Act 1999)	State
		FROM APRIL 2004 – MARCH 2005		
1	1 & 2	Darjeeling Tea (word & logo)	Agricultural	West Bengal
		FROM APRIL 2005 – MARCH 2006		
20	25	Kangra Tea	Agricultural	Himachal Pradesh
27	33	Coorg Orange	Agricultural	Karnataka
		FROM APRIL 2006 – MARCH 2007		
28	34	Mysore Betel leaf	Agricultural	Karnataka
29	35	Nanjanagud Banana	Agricultural	Karnataka
		FROM APRIL 2007 – MARCH 2008		
37	69	Mysore Malligae	Agricultural	Karnataka
38	70	Udupi Malligae	Agricultural	Karnataka
39	71	Hadagali Malligae	Agricultural	Karnataka
40	17	Navara Rice	Agricultural	Kerala
41	36	Palakkadan Matta Rice	Agricultural	Kerala
47	49 & 56	Malabar Pepper	Agricultural	India (Kerala, Karnataka & Tamilnadu)
48	50	Allahabad Surkha Guava	Agricultural	Uttar Pradesh
54	85	Monsooned Malabar Arabica Coffee	Agricultural	India (Karnataka & Kerala)
55	114	Monsooned Malabar Robusta Coffee	Agricultural	India (Karnataka & Kerala)
56	72	Alleppey Green Cardamom	Agricultural	India (Kerala & Tamil nadu)
57	78	Coorg Green Cardamom	Agricultural	Karnataka
		FROM APRIL 2008 – MARCH 2009		
72	110	Eathomozhy Tall Coconut	Agricultural	Tamil Nadu
86	81	Pokkali Rice	Agricultural	Kerala
94	111	Malda Laxman Bhog Mango	Agricultural	West Bengal
95	112	Malda Khirsapati (Himsagar) Mango	Agricultural	West Bengal
96	113	Malda Fazli Mango	Agricultural	West Bengal
99	109	Naga Mircha	Agricultural	Nagaland

Table *contd...*

100	116&117	Nilgiri (Orthodox)	Agricultural	Tamil Nadu
101	115 &118	Assam (Orthodox)	Agricultural	Assam
103	124	Virupakshi Hill Banana	Agricultural	Tamil Nadu
104	126	Sirumalai Hill Banana	Agricultural	Tamil Nadu
FROM APRIL 2009 – MARCH 2010				
108	125	Mango Malihabadi Dusseheri	Agricultural	Uttar Pradesh
112	130 & 141	Vazhakulam Pineapple	Agricultural	Kerala
113	131	Devanahalli Pomello	Agricultural	Karnataka
114	132	Appemidi Mango	Agricultural	Karnataka
115	133	Kamalapur Red Banana	Agricultural	Karnataka
122	143	Guntur Sannam Chilli	Agricultural	Andhra Pradesh
131	154	Mahabaleshwar Strawberry	Agricultural	Maharashtra
135	163	Central Travancore Jaggery	Agricultural	Kerala
137	186	Wayanad Jeerakasala Rice	Agricultural	Kerala
138	187	Wayanad Gandhakasala Rice	Agricultural	Kerala
140	165	Nashik Grapes	Agricultural	Maharashtra
147	129	Byadagi Chilli	Agricultural	Karnataka
FROM APRIL 2011 – MARCH 2012				
152	185	Gir Kesar Mango	Agricultural	Gujarat
153	192	Bhalia Wheat	Agricultural	Gujarat
158	199	Udupi Mattu Gulla Brinjal	Agricultural	Karnataka
172	229	Ganjam Kewda Flower	Agricultural	Odisha
FROM APRIL 2012 – MARCH 2013				
181	238	Madurai Malli	Agricultural	Tamil Nadu
189	211	Bangalore Blue Grapes	Agricultural	Karnataka
FROM APRIL 2013 – MARCH 2014				
194	205	Kalanamak Rice	Agricultural	Uttar Pradesh
199	242	Kaipad Rice	Agricultural	Kerala
209	240	Kolhapur Jaggery	Agricultural	Maharashtra
215	385	Nagpur Orange	Agricultural	India (Maharashtra & Madhya Pradesh)
FROM APRIL 2014 – MARCH 2015				
217	212	Bangalore Rose Onion	Agricultural	Karnataka
220	374	Naga Tree Tomato	Agricultural	Nagaland
221	375	Arunachal Orange	Agricultural	Arunachal Pradesh
222	376	Sikkim Large Cardamom	Agricultural	Sikkim
223	377	Mizo Chilli	Agricultural	Mizoram

Table *contd...*

226	435	Assam Karbi Anglong Ginger	Agricultural	Assam
227	436	Tripura Queen Pineapple	Agricultural	Tripura
228	479	Chengalikodan Nendran Banana	Agricultural	Kerala
230	438	Tezpur Litchi	Agricultural	Assam
231	465	Khasi Mandarin	Agricultural	Meghalaya
232	466	Kachai Lemon	Agricultural	Manipur
FROM APRIL 2015 – MARCH 2016				
236	437	Memong Narang	Agricultural	Meghalaya
238	145	Basmati	Agricultural	India (Punjab / Haryana / Himachal Pradesh / Delhi / Uttarkhand / Uttar Pradesh / Jammu & Kashmir)
248	470	Ajara Ghansal Rice	Agricultural	Maharashtra
249	472	Mangalwedha Jowar	Agricultural	Maharashtra
250	474	Sindhudurg & Ratnagiri Kokum	Agricultural	Maharashtra
255	476	Waghya Ghevada	Agricultural	Maharashtra
256	477	Navapur Tur Dal	Agricultural	Maharashtra
257	489	Vengurla Cashew	Agricultural	Maharashtra
258	491	Lasalgaon Onion	Agricultural	Maharashtra
FROM APRIL 2016 – MARCH 2017				
262	490	Sangli Raisins	Agricultural	Maharashtra
265	494	Beed Custard Apple	Agricultural	Maharashtra
266	495	Jalna Sweet Orange	Agricultural	Maharashtra
267	520	Uttarakhand Tejpat	Agricultural	Uttarakhand
268	471	Waigaon Turmeric	Agricultural	Maharashtra
269	500	Purandar Fig	Agricultural	Maharashtra
270	501	Jalgaon Bharit Brinjal	Agricultural	Maharashtra
271	502	Solapur Pomegranate	Agricultural	Maharashtra
278	473	Bhiwapur Chilli	Agricultural	Maharashtra
279	478	Ambemohar Rice	Agricultural	Maharashtra
280	493	Dahanu Gholvad Chikoo	Agricultural	Maharashtra
281	498	Jalgaon Banana	Agricultural	Maharashtra
282	499	Marathwada Kesar Mango	Agricultural	Maharashtra
287	439	Joha Rice of Assam	Agricultural	Assam
FROM APRIL 2017 – MARCH 2018				
295	241	Banaganapalle Mangoes	Agricultural	India (Telangana & Andhra Pradesh

Table *contd...*

297	531	Gobindobhog Rice	Agricultural	West Bengal
300	530	Tulapanji Rice	Agricultural	West Bengal
305	543	Nilambur Teak	Agricultural	Kerala
311	551	Bhagalpuri Zardalu	Agricultural	Bihar
312	553	Katarni Rice	Agricultural	Bihar
313	554	Magahi Paan	Agricultural	Bihar
FROM APRIL 2018 – MARCH 2019				
322	558	Boka Chaul	Agricultural	Assam
324	139	Alphonso	Agricultural	Maharashtra
326	552	Shahi Litchi of Bihar	Agricultural	Bihar
327	496	Sangli Turmeric	Agricultural	Maharashtra
331	604	Coorg Arabica Coffee	Agricultural	Karnataka
332	605	Wayanaad Robusta Coffee	Agricultural	Kerala
333	606	Chikmagalur Arabica Coffee	Agricultural	Karnataka
334	607	Araku Valley Arabica Coffee	Agricultural	India (Andhra Pradesh & Odisha)
335	608	Bababudangiris Arabica Coffee	Agricultural	Karnataka
336	432	Himachali Kala Zeera	Agricultural	Himachal Pradesh
337	464	Sirsi Supari	Agricultural	Karnataka
340	231	Erode Manjal (Erode Turmeric)	Agricultural	Tamil Nadu
341	613	Marayoor Jaggery (Marayoor Sharkara)	Agricultural	Kerala
343	611	Jeeraphool	Agricultural	Chhattisgarh
FROM APRIL 2019 – MARCH 2020				
344	610	Kandhamal Haladi	Agricultural	Odisha
346	616	Kodaikanal Malai Poondu	Agricultural	Tamil Nadu
353	593	Gulbarga Tur Dal	Agricultural	Karnataka
354	641	Tirur Betel Leaf (Tirur Vettila)	Agricultural	Kerala
356	618	Khola Chilli	Agricultural	Goa
361	609	Kaji Nemu	Agricultural	Assam
362	572	Chokuwa Rice of Assam	Agricultural	Assam
364	602	Chak - Hao	Agricultural	India (Manipur & Nagaland)
FROM APRIL 2020 – MARCH 2021				
366	635	Kashmir Saffron	Agricultural	Jammu & Kashmir
FROM APRIL 2021 – MARCH 2022				
372	628	Sojat Mehndi	Agricultural	Rajasthan
382	663	Balaghat Chinnor	Agricultural	Madhya Pradesh

Table *contd...*

383	660	Kuttiattoor Mango (Kuttiattoor Manga)	Agricultural	Kerala
387	642	Harmal Chilli	Agricultural	Goa
388	662	Edayur Chilli	Agricultural	Kerala
390	651	Munsyari Razma	Agricultural	Uttarakhand
394	680	Myndoli Banana	Agricultural	Goa
399	650	Kumaon Chyura Oil	Agricultural	Uttarakhand
401	206	Rataul Mango	Agricultural	Uttar Pradesh
402	590	Tamenglong Orange	Agricultural	Manipur
406	675	Kanniyakumari Clove	Agricultural	Tamil Nadu
407	592	Hathei Chilli	Agricultural	Manipur
408	640	Naga Cucumber	Agricultural	Nagaland
411	401	Mahoba Desawari Pan	Agricultural	India (Uttar Pradesh and Madhya Pradesh)
413	629 & 630	Mizo Ginger	Agricultural	Mizoram
414	636	Dalle Khursani	Agricultural	India (Sikkim and West Bengal)
FROM APRIL 2022 – MARCH 2023				
421	696	Mithila Makhana	Agricultural	Bihar
424	685	Alibag White Onion	Agricultural	Maharashtra
425	686	Attappady Aattukombu Avara	Agricultural	Kerala
426	687	Attappady Thuvara	Agricultural	Kerala
427	736	Onattukara Ellu	Agricultural	Kerala
428	749	Kanthalloor Vattavada Veluthulli	Agricultural	Kerala
429	752	Kodungallur Pottuvellari	Agricultural	Kerala
430	706	Tandur Redgram	Agricultural	Telangana
431	729	Ladakh Raktsey Karpo Apricot	Agricultural	Ladakh (UT)
435	669	Nagri Dubraj	Agricultural	Chhattisgarh
437	707	Rewa Sunderja Mango	Agricultural	Madhya Pradesh
438	699	Sharbati Gehu	Agricultural	Madhya Pradesh
440	715	Adamchini Chawal	Agricultural	Uttar Pradesh
441	720	Ramnathapuram Mundu Chilli	Agricultural	Tamil Nadu
442	788	Vellore Spiny Brinjal	Agricultural	Tamil Nadu
452	668	Pratapgarh Aonla	Agricultural	Uttar Pradesh
462	716	Banaras Langda Aam (Mango)	Agricultural	Uttar Pradesh
463	717	Ramnagar Bhanta (Brinjal)	Agricultural	Uttar Pradesh
464	719	Authoor Vetrilai	Agricultural	Tamil Nadu

Table *contd...*

467	730	Banaras Pan (Betel Leaf)	Agricultural	Uttar Pradesh
468	734	Cumbum Panneer Thratchai	Agricultural	Tamil Nadu
469	745	Indi Limbe	Agricultural	Karnataka
473	789	Sholavandan Vetrilai	Agricultural	Tamil Nadu
474	800	Marthandam Honey	Natural	Tamil Nadu
475	843	Kari Ishad Mango	Agricultural	Karnataka
FROM APRIL 2023 – MARCH 2024				
484	727	Ladakh Seabuckthorn	Agricultural	Ladakh (UT)
485	688	Bhandara Chinoor Rice	Agricultural	Maharashtra
489	757	Kanyakumari Matti Banana	Agricultural	Tamil Nadu
490	758	Mushqbudji Rice	Agricultural	Jammu & Kashmir
492	763	Agsechi Vayingim (Agassaim Brinjal)	Agricultural	Goa
494	790	Sat Shiro Bheno (Sat Shirancho Bhendo)	Agricultural	Goa
495	801	Marcha Rice	Agricultural	Bihar
497	728	Goa Mankurad Mango	Agricultural	Goa
503	768	Bhaderwah Rajmash	Agricultural	Jammu & Kashmir
504	772	Ramban Sulai Honey	Natural	Jammu & Kashmir

5.4 AYUSH

AYUSH is the acronym of Ayurveda, Yoga, Unani, Siddha and Homoeopathy. AYUSH is considered as Indian Systems of Medicine and Homoeopathy. AYUSH is now considered as a Ministry of Government of India to promote and regulate Indian Systems of Medicine and Homoeopathy. The Ministry of AYUSH was established on 9th November 2014 to promote the optimal development and dissemination of AYUSH systems of health care. Previously it was established as the Department of Indian System of Medicine and Homeopathy (ISM&H) in March 1995 and renamed as Department of Ayurveda, Yoga and Naturopathy, Unani, Siddha and Homoeopathy (AYUSH) in November 2003.

Presently AYUSH acronym stands for Ayurveda, Yoga and Naturopathy, Unani, Siddha, Sowa Rigpa and Homoeopathy.

Ministry of AYUSH was established as a ministry to promote and strengthen AYUSH system of medicine in India and other countries. Along this AYUSH ministry is responsible for research, education and promoting health care under AYUSH.

To ensure transparency and enhance the quality and functioning of institutes offering Ayurveda, Siddha, Unani, Sowa-Rigpa, and Homoeopathy (ASUSR&H) systems of medicine nationwide, the **National Commission for Indian System of Medicine Act, 2020, and the National Commission for Homoeopathy Act, 2020** were officially announced and published in the Official Gazette of India on September 21, 2020. These Acts were implemented with the goal of establishing a medical education system that facilitates improved access to high-quality and affordable medical education.

The objective is to ensure the availability of sufficient and well-trained medical professionals in Indian Systems of Medicine and Homoeopathy across the country. The Acts aim to promote equitable and universal healthcare, fostering a community health perspective and making the services of these medical professionals accessible and affordable for all citizens. Additionally, they seek to align with national health goals, encourage professionals to integrate the latest medical research into their practice, and contribute to ongoing research efforts. The Acts also include provisions for periodic and transparent assessments of medical institutions, the maintenance of a medical register for Indian Systems of Medicine in India, and the enforcement of high ethical standards in all aspects of medical services.

The legislative framework is designed to be adaptable to evolving needs, incorporating an effective grievance redressal mechanism. The Acts further stipulate the dissolution of the Indian Medicine Central Council Act, 1970, and the Homoeopathy Central Council Act, 1973, on June 11, 2021, and July 5, 2021, respectively, with the establishment of the National Commission for Indian System of Medicine (NCISM), the National Commission for Homoeopathy (NCH), and their respective Autonomous Boards on the same days. These Commissions operate as statutory bodies in accordance with the NCISM & NCH Act, 2020, contributing to the establishment of a robust and responsive medical education and healthcare system.

To foster evidence based Research and Development in the field of every discipline of AYUSH system of medicine Ministry of AYUSH has established 5 research councils which are as follows:

1. Central Council for Research in Ayurvedic Sciences (CCRAS)
2. Central Council for Research in Yoga and Naturopathy (CCRYN)
3. Central Council for Research in Unani Medicine (CCRUM)
4. Central Council for Research in Siddha (CCRS)
5. Central Council for Research in Homoeopathy (CCRH)

To promote research and innovation in the field of AYUSH system, Ministry of AYUSH has also created Ayurgyan Scheme (Central Sector Schemes). Major objectives of this scheme are:

- Capacity building and continuing medical education in AYUSH system of medicine.
- Promote Research and innovation in AYUSH to harness the capabilities of medical, scientific, and research and development institutions, universities, and organizations.

The Ministry of Ayush has devised the **National Ayush Research Consortium**, collaborating with the Ministry of AYUSH, DSIR, DBT, and DST, in consultation with NITI Aayog. This initiative aims to establish a systematic and high-quality research framework for Ayush systems, meeting global standards. The consortium adopts a multidisciplinary approach, bringing together scientists from both basic science and Ayush domains to collectively engage in Ayush research. This collaborative effort involves addressing healthcare challenges, planning, and implementing research and development initiatives to achieve the overarching objective of ensuring health for all.

To foster the medicinal plants sector, the Indian government established the National Medicinal Plants Board (NMPB) on November 24, 2000. Currently situated within the Ministry of AYUSH (Ayurveda, Yoga & Naturopathy, Unani, Siddha & Homoeopathy), Government of India, the NMPB is tasked with creating a suitable mechanism for coordinating efforts among different ministries, departments, and organizations in India. Its primary objective is to implement supportive policies and programs to facilitate the comprehensive development (including conservation, cultivation, trade, and export) of the medicinal plants sector at both the Central/State and international levels.

Ministry of AYUSH and different research in under its domain are involved in the following research:

- Medico-Ethno Botanical Survey
- Collection of medicinal plants
- Documentation & Digitization of Herbarium specimens
- Revision of Pharmacopoeia
- Cultivation of medicinal plant
- Standardization of ASU and Homoeopathic drugs and medicines
- Pre-clinical and clinical studies in AYUSH system
- Validation studies on safety and efficacy of ASU and H formulations
- Translation and digitalization of Ancient texts on AYUSH
- Publication of AYUSH literature and popularization of AYUSH in India and abroad
- Pharmacovigilance studies on AYUSH

The Ministry of Ayush operates a Drug Policy Section (DPS) responsible for overseeing regulatory and quality control functions related to Ayurveda, Siddha, Unani, and Homoeopathy (ASU&H) drugs, as well as implementing initiatives related to drugs. The DPS manages the provisions outlined in the Drugs and Cosmetics Act, 1940, and its associated rules, along with the Drugs and Magic Remedies (Objectionable Advertisements) Act, 1954, specifically concerning ASU&H drugs and related matters.

Serving as a central framework for drug control in the ASU&H domain, this section collaborates with State Licensing Authorities, Drug Controllers, and drug manufacturers associations to ensure consistent administration of legal provisions. Additionally, it provides regulatory guidance, clarification, and direction in this context.

5.5 CENTRAL COUNCIL FOR RESEARCH IN AYURVEDIC SCIENCES (CCRAS)

The Central Council for Research in Ayurvedic Sciences (CCRAS) is an independent entity under the Ministry of AYUSH (Ayurveda, Yoga & Naturopathy, Unani, Siddha, and Homeopathy), Government of India. It serves as the foremost organization in the country dedicated to formulating, coordinating, developing, and promoting research in Ayurveda and the Sowa-Rigpa system of medicine based on scientific principles.

Historical development of CCRAS

- The Central Council for Ayurvedic Research was established as an advisory body in 1962.
- Subsequently, the Central Council for Research in Indian medicine & Homoeopathy (CCRIM&H) was formed in 1969, initiating research programs across India and coordinating nationally for the first time.
- Later, the Central Council for Research in Ayurveda & Siddha (CCRAS) was established in 1978, following the reorganization of CCRIM&H. This council was registered under the Societies Registration Act XXI of 1860 on July 29, 2011, and was reconstituted with its present name on April 11, 2011, becoming an autonomous body under the Ministry of AYUSH, Government of India.
- It serves as the apex organization for formulating, coordinating, developing, and promoting research in Ayurveda and Sowa-Rigpa systems of medicine.
- CCRAS conducts research programs through a network of 30 peripheral Institutes/Centres/Units, with its headquarters overseeing control, monitoring, and supervision. Additionally, it recently established a

Collaborative Research Centre for Veterinary Ayurveda at Guru Angad Dev Veterinary and Animal Sciences University (GADVASU) in Ludhiana.

Objective of CCRAS

According to the Memorandum by laws, following are the objectives of CCRAS formation:

1) To formulate aims and patterns of research on scientific lines in Ayurvedic Sciences.
2) To undertake any research or other related programmes in Ayurvedic Sciences including undergraduate, post-graduate and post-doctoral educational programmes in Ayurvedic Sciences.
3) To prosecute and assist in research, the propagation of knowledge and experimental measures generally in connection with the causation, mode of spread and prevention of diseases.
4) To initiate, aid, develop and coordinate scientific research in different aspects, fundamental and applied aspects of Ayurvedic Sciences and to promote and assist institutions of research for the study of diseases, their prevention, causation, treatment and remedy
5) To provide technical and financial support for research for the furtherance of objectives of the Central Council.
6) To exchange information with other institutions, associations and societies interested in the objects similar to those of the Central Council and especially in observation and study of diseases in East Asia and in India, in particular.
7) To establish, equip and maintain laboratories, libraries, Institutions and other facilities necessary to fulfil the Objectives of the Central Council.
8) To prepare, print, publish and exhibit any papers, posters, pamphlets, periodicals, standard treatment protocols and books for furtherance of the objectives of the Central Council and to contribute to development of such literature.
9) To issue appeals and make applications for money and funds in furtherance of the objectives of the Central Council and to accept for the aforesaid purpose gifts, donations and subscriptions of cash and securities and of any property whether movable or immovable.
10) To borrow or raise monies with or without security or on security mortgage charge, hypothecation or pledge of all or any of the immovable or movable properties belonging to the Central Council or in any other manner whatsoever.
11) To invest and deal with the funds and monies of the Central Council or entrusted to the Central Council not immediately required in such manner

as may from time to time be determined by the Governing Body of the Central Council.

12) To permit the funds of the Central Council to be held by the Government of India.
13) To acquire and hold, whether temporarily or permanently any movable or immovable property necessary or convenient for the furtherance of the objectives of the Central Council.
14) To sell, lease, mortgage and exchange, and otherwise transfer any of the properties movable or immovable of the Central Council provided prior approval of the Central Government is obtained for the transfer of immovable property.
15) To purchase, construct, maintain and alter any buildings, including for establishment of research laboratories, libraries or works necessary or convenient for the purpose of the Central Council.
16) To undertake and accept the management of any endowment or trust fund for donation, the undertaking or acceptance whereof may seem desirable.
17) To offer prizes and grant fellowship, scholarships, or financial assistance including travelling assistance in furtherance of the objectives of the Central Council.
18) To create administrative, scientific, technical and ministerial and other posts under the Society and to make appointments thereto in accordance with the rules and regulations of the Society.
19) To engage administrative, technical, ministerial and other staff under the project on contract basis in accordance with the procedure laid down by the Executive Committee.
20) To establish a provident fund and/or pension fund for the benefit of the Central Council's employees and/or their family members.
21) To organize and participate in national and international programmes in Ayurvedic Sciences.
22) To undertake R&D Consultancy projects and transfer of patents on drugs and process to industry.
23) To undertake R&D projects sponsored by industries in Public/Private Sector.
24) To undertake International and inter-agency collaboration.
25) Utilization of results of research conducted and payment of share of royalties/ consultancy fees to those who has contributed towards pursuit of such research.
26) To enter into arrangements with scientific agencies of other countries for exchange of scientists, study tours, training in specialized areas, conducting joint projects etc.

27) To provide technical assistance to Govt./Private agencies in matters consistent with the activities of the Council.
28) To collaborate with, Government of India in Research and Scientific Institutions, Academics in achieving its objectives.
29) To constitute Management Committees consisting of eminent Scientists/Physicians to monitor the R&D activities and suggest remedial measures for the improvement of activities of the Central Council as well as all Research Institutes of the Council.
30) To do all such other lawful things either alone or in conjunction with others, as the Central Council, may consider necessary or as being incidental or conducive to the attainment of the above objectives.
31) The property of the Central Council shall be vested in the Governing Body and in any proceedings; civil or criminal may be described as the property of the Governing Body.
32) In any proceedings, the Central Council may sue or be sued in the name of the Director General or such other member as shall in reference to the matter concerned be appointed by the Governing Body. "

Research Institutes under CCRAS network:

Following are the different research institutes under CCRAS network:

1. Central Ayurveda Research Institute for Cardiovascular Diseases, New Delhi
2. National Ayurveda Research Institute for Panchakarma, Cheruthuruthy
3. Central Ayurveda Research Institute for Hepatobiliary Disorders, Bhubaneswar
4. Central Ayurveda Research Institute for Drug Development, Kolkata
5. Central Ayurveda Research Institute for Respiratory Disorders, Patiala
6. Raja Ramdeo Anandilal Podar Central Ayurveda Research Institute for Cancer, Mumbai
7. National Institute of Indian Medical Heritage, Hyderabad
8. Regional Ayurveda Research Institute for Eye Diseases, Lucknow
9. M.S. Regional Ayurveda Research Institute for Endocrine Disorders, Jaipur
10. Regional Ayurveda Research Institute for Drug Development, Gwalior
11. Regional Ayurveda Research Institute for Skin disorders, Vijayawada
12. Regional Ayurveda Research Institute for Mother and Child Health, Nagpur
13. Regional Ayurveda Research Institute for Metabolic Disorders, Bangalore

14. Regional Ayurveda Research Institute for Life style related Disorders, Thiruvananthapuram
15. Regional Ayurveda Research Institute for Infectious Diseases, Patna
16. Regional Ayurveda Research Institute for Gastro- Intestinal Disorders, Guwahati
17. Regional Ayurveda Research Institute, Gangtok
18. Regional Ayurveda Research Institute, Itanagar
19. Regional Ayurveda Research Institute for Urinary Disorders, Jammu
20. Regional Ayurveda Research Institute for Nutritional Disorders, Mandi
21. Regional Ayurveda Research Institute for Skin Disorders, Ahmedabad
22. Regional Ayurveda Research Institute, Ranikhet
23. Regional Ayurveda Research Institute, Jhansi
24. Regional Ayurveda Institute for Fundamental Research, Pune
25. Captain Srinivasa Murthy Regional Ayurveda Drug Development Institute, Chennai
26. Advanced Center for Ayurveda in Mental Health & Neurosciences, Bangalore
27. Dr. Achanta Lakshmipati Research Centre for Ayurveda, Chennai
28. Regional Research Center of Ayurveda, Port Blair
29. National Research Institute for Sowa-Rigpa, Leh
30. Herbal Ayurveda Research Centre (HARC), Nagaland University, Lumami, Nagaland

Main research areas under CCRAS:

- Medicinal plant research
- Clinical research on Ayurveda therapy
- Pharmacological Research
- Standardization of Ayurvedic medicine and quality control
- Revival, Retrieval &Documentation ofAyurveda and Indian Medical Heritage texts
- OPD & IPDs
- Research Oriented Public Health Care Activities
- AYUSH Wellness clinics

Organogram of CCRAS

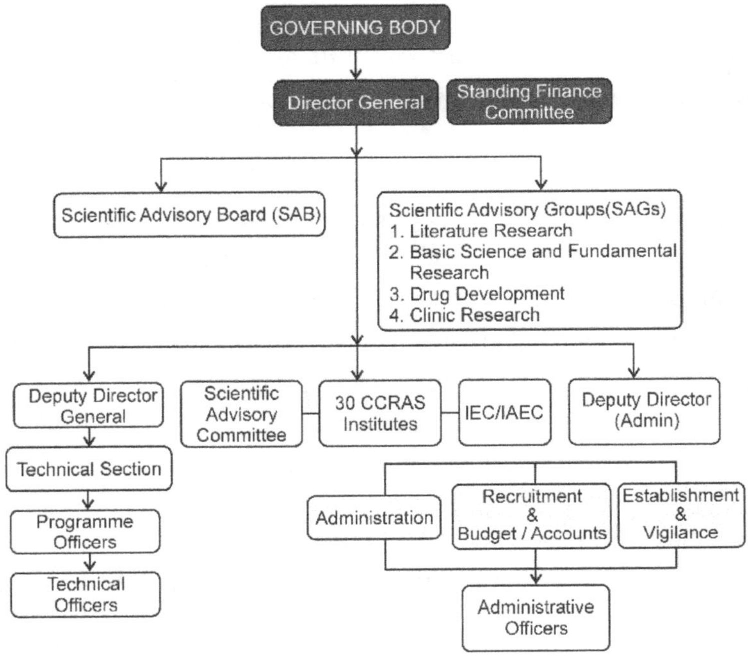

5.6 CENTRAL COUNCIL FOR RESEARCH IN SIDDHA (CCRS)

Central Council for Research in Siddha (CCRS) under Ministry of AYUSH is an apex research organization is responsible for conducting the research in Siddha system of medicine. It has 8 peripheral units/ institutes and 5 co-located units. CCRS is involved in:

- Clinical and preclinical trials on Siddha Medicine
- Standardization and quality control of Siddha Medicine
- Restoration of Siddha medicine ancient text
- Toxicological studies
- Public health care
- Medicinal plant research

Development of CCRS

The Central Council for Research in Siddha (CCRS) was established as an independent entity on July 27, 2010. Its formation followed the division of the former Central Council for Research in Ayurveda and Siddha (CCRAS) into two separate bodies, with the creation of the Central Council for Research in Siddha (CCRS). The Registered Office of the Society is situated in the State of Tamil Nadu and presently at Central Research Institute (Siddha), Arumbakkam, Chennai 600106, Tamil Nadu.

Objectives of CCRS: According to Memorandum bylaws of CCRS, following objectives are mentioned as object of CCRS:

(i) The formulation of aims and patterns of research on scientific lines in Siddha.

(ii) To undertake any research or other related programmes in Siddha.

(iii) The prosecution of and assistance in research, the propagation of knowledge and experimental measures generally in connection with the causation, mode of spread and prevention of diseases.

(iv) To initiate, aid, develop and coordinate scientific research in different aspects, fundamental and applied aspects of Siddha and to promote and assist institutions of research for the study of diseases, their prevention, causation and remedy.

(v) To finance enquiries and researches for the furtherance of objects of the Central Council.

(vi) To exchange information with other institutions, associations and societies interested in the objects similar to those of the Central Council and specially in observation and study of diseases in India in particular.

(vii) To prepare, print, publish and exhibit any papers, posters, pamphlets, periodicals and books for furtherance of the objects of the Central Council and contribute to such literature.

(viii) To issue appeals and make applications for money and funds in furtherance of the objects of the Central Council and to accept for the aforesaid purpose gifts, donations and subscriptions of cash and securities and of any property whether movable or immovable.

(ix) To borrow or raise funds with or without security or on security mortgage charge, hypothecation or pledge of all or any of the immovable or movable properties belonging to the Central Council or in any other manner whatsoever.

(x) To invest and deal with the funds and monies of the Central Council or entrusted to the Central Council not immediately required in such manner as may from time to time be determined by the General Body of the Central Council.

(xi) To permit the funds of the Central Council to be held by the Government of India.

(xii) To acquire and hold, whether temporarily or permanently any movable or immovable property necessary or convenient for the furtherance of the objects of the Central Council.

(xiii) To sell, lease, mortgage and exchange, and otherwise transfer any of the properties movable or immovable of the Central Council provided prior approval of the Central Government is obtained for the transfer of immovable property.

(xiv) To purchase, construct, maintain and alter any buildings or works necessary or convenient for the purpose of the Central Council.

(xv) To undertake and accept the management of any endowment or trust fund for donation, the undertaking or acceptance whereof may seem desirable.

(xvi) To offer prizes and grant of scholarships, including travelling scholarships in furtherance of the objects of the Central Council.

(xvii) To create administrative, technical and ministerial and other posts under the Society and to make appointments thereto in accordance with the rules and regulations of the Society.

(xviii) To establish a provident fund and/or pension fund for the benefit of the Central Council's employees and/or their family members.

(xix) To do all such other lawful things either alone or in conjunction with other; as the Central Council may consider necessary or as being incidental or conducive to the attainment of the above objects.

(xx) To undertake R & D Consultancy projects and transfer of patents on drugs and process to industry.

(xxi) To undertake R & D projects sponsored by industries in Public/private sector

(xxii) To undertake international and inter-agency collaboration.

(xxiii) Utilization of results of research conducted and payment of share of royalties/consultancy fees to those who has contributed towards pursuit of such research.

(xxiv) To enter into arrangements with scientific agencies of other countries for exchange of scientists, study tours, training in specialized areas, conducting joint projects etc.

(xxv) To provide technical assistance to Govt./Private agencies in matters consistent with the activities of the Council.

(xxvi) To assist Medicinal Plants Board, Government of India in achieving its objectives.

(xxvii) To constitute Management Committees consisting of eminent Scientists/Physicians to monitor the R & D activities and suggest remedial measures for the improvement of activities of ail Central as well as Research institutes of the Council."

List of CCRS Institutes

1. Siddha Central Research Institute (SCRI), Govt. Anna Hospital Campus Arumbakkam, Chennai – 600106.
2. Siddha Regional Research Institute (SRRI), Chellaperumal Street, Kuyavarpalayam Puducherry – 605013.
3. Siddha Regional Research Institute (SRRI), Poojappura, Thiruvananthapuram – 695 012
4. Siddha Medicinal Plants Garden 17, SDO Quarters, Opp. Ulavar Sandhai Cauvery Nagar,, Mettur Dam – 636 401
5. Siddha Clinical Research Unit, Govt. Siddha Medical College Campus, Palayamkottai, Tirunelveli – 627 002
6. Siddha Clinical Research Unit, New Delhi Room No.108, first Fl.M.S.Office Building, Safdarjung Hospital. New Delhi-110029.
7. Siddha Clinical Research Unit, Sri Jayachamarejendra Govt. Ayurvedic Hospital Campus Dhanvantri Road, Bengaluru – 560009
8. Siddha Clinical Research Unit Sri Venkateswara Institute of Medical Sciences (SVIMS) Campus Alipiri Road, Tirupati – 517507

5.7 CENTRAL COUNCIL FOR RESEARCH IN HOMOEOPATHY (CCRH)

The Central Council for Research in Homoeopathy (CCRH) functions as the primary research body within the Ministry of AYUSH, Government of India, dedicated to conducting, coordinating, advancing, disseminating, and advocating scientific research in Homoeopathy.

Head quarter of CCRH is situated in New Delhi, which oversees a network of 26 institutes/units spread across India to facilitate multi-centric research activities.

Its responsibilities encompass formulating and executing research programs/projects, collaborating with esteemed national and international institutes for evidence-based research in both fundamental and applied aspects of Homoeopathy, overseeing extramural research endeavors, and disseminating research findings through various channels such as monographs, journals, newsletters, informational materials, seminars, and workshops. Embracing contemporary scientific standards, the research conducted aims to translate into practical applications, benefiting both the profession and the public.

The Governing Body provides policy formulation, direction, and overall guidance to the Council. Chaired by the Honorable Minister of AYUSH,

Government of India, the Governing Body exercises general control over the Council's activities.

Development of CCRH

The Government of India established a Central Council for Research in Indian Medicines and Homoeopathy (CCRIMH) in 1969 as an autonomous body under the Ministry of Health and Family Welfare. The Central Council for Research in Homoeopathy (CCRH) was formally constituted on 30th March, 1978, as an autonomous organization and registered under the Societies Registration Act XXI, 1860. CCRH is fully funded and regulated by by the Ministry of AYUSH.

Objectives of CCRH

Following are the constitutional objectives of CCRH:

"... Main Objectives

1. To formulate the aims and patterns of research on scientific lines in Homoeopathy
2. To initiate, develop, undertake and coordinate scientific research in fundamental and applied aspects of Homoeopathy
3. To exchange information with other institutions, associations and societies interested in the objectives similar to those of the Council
4. To collaborate research studies with other Institutes of Excellence towards promotion of Homoeopathy
5. To propagate research findings through monographs, journals, newsletters, I.E.&C. materials, seminars/workshops and develop audio-visual aids for dissemination of information to the profession and public.

Other Objectives

6. To finance enquiries and researches for the furtherance of objects of the Central Council.
7. To issue appeals and make applications for money and funds in furtherance of the objects of the Central Council and to accept for the aforesaid purpose gifts, donations and subscriptions of cash and securities and of any property whether movable or immovable.
8. To borrow or raise monies with or without security or on security mortgage charge, hypothecation or pledge of all or any of the immovable or movable properties belonging to the Central Council or in any other manner whatever.
9. To invest and deal with the funds and monies of the Central Council or entrusted to the Central Council not immediately required in such

manner as may from time to time be determined by the Governing Body of the Central Council.

10. To permit the funds of the Central Council to be held by the Government of India.
11. To acquire and hold, whether temporarily or permanently any movable or immovable properly necessary or convenient for the furtherance of the objects of the Central Council.
12. To sell, lease, mortgage and exchange, and otherwise transfer any of the properties movable or immovable of the Central Council provided prior approval of the Central Government is obtained for the transfer of immovable property.
13. To purchase, construct, maintain and alter any buildings or works necessary or convenient for the purpose of the Central Council.
14. To undertake and accept the management of any endowment or trust fund for donation, the undertaking or acceptance whereof may seem desirable.
15. To offer prizes and grant of scholarships, including travelling scholarships in furtherance of the objects of the Central Council.
16. To create administrative, technical and ministerial and other posts under the Society and to make appointments thereto in accordance with the rules and regulations of the Society.
17. To establish a provident fund and/or pension fund for the benefit of the Central Council's employees and/or their family members.
18. To do all such other lawful things either alone or in conjunction with others as the Central Council may consider necessary or as being incidental or conducive to the attainment of the above objects."

Name of the CCRH National Institutes

1. Dr. D.P. Rastogi Central Research Institute (H), Noida
2. National Homoeopathy Research Institute in Mental Health, Kottayam

Name of the CCRH Regional Institutes

1. Regional Research Institute (H), Gudivada
2. Regional Research Institute (H), Guwahati
3. Regional Research Institute (H), Puri
4. Regional Research Institute (H), Imphal
5. Regional Research Institute (H), Jaipur
6. Dr. Anjali Chatterjee Regional Research Institute (H), Kolkata
7. Regional Research Institute (H), Shimla

8. Regional Research Institute (H), Mumbai
9. Regional Research Institute (H), Agartala
10. Dr. Abhin Chandra Homoeopathic Medical College And Hospital, Bhubaneswar

5.8 THE CENTRAL COUNCIL FOR RESEARCH IN UNANI MEDICINE (CCRUM)

The Central Council for Research in Unani Medicine (CCRUM) was established in 1978 as an autonomous institute. Presently, it acts as an autonomous institute under Ministry of AYUSH. CCRUM acts as the apex government organization for research in Unani Medicine and responsible in conducting scientific research in the following field of Unani Medicne:

1. Clinical research
2. Standardization of drugs
3. Survey and cultivation of medicinal plant
4. Revival and translation of Unani medicine text
5. Information, Education and Communication

Objectives of CCRUM

CCRUM was established on 30th March 1978 under the Societies Registration Act, 1860; and effective from 0th January 1979. The main objectives of the Council are as follows as per the memorandum by laws:"..

- Formulation of aims and patterns of research on scientific lines in Unani Medicine
- To undertake research or any other programmes in Unani Medicine
- Prosecution of and assistance in research and propagation of knowledge and experimental measures generally in connection with the causation, mode of spread and prevention of diseases
- To initiate, aid, develop and coordinate scientific research on different aspects, fundamental and applied, of Unani Medicine, and to promote and assist institutions of research for the study of diseases, their prevention, causation and remedy
- To finance enquiries and researches for the furtherance of the objectives of the Council
- To exchange information with other institutions, associations and societies interested in the objectives similar to those of the Council, especially in the

observation and study of diseases in the East in general, and in India in particular

- To prepare, print, publish and exhibit any papers, posters, pamphlets, periodicals and books for furtherance of the objectives of the Council and to contribute to such literature
- was established on 30th March 1978 under the Societies Registration Act, 1860; however, it started functioning from 10thJanuary 1979. The main objectives of the Council are as follows:
- Formulation of aims and patterns of research on scientific lines in Unani Medicine
- To undertake research or any other programmes in Unani Medicine
- Prosecution of and assistance in research and propagation of knowledge and experimental measures generally in connection with the causation, mode of spread and prevention of diseases
- To initiate, aid, develop and coordinate scientific research on different aspects, fundamental and applied, of Unani Medicine, and to promote and assist institutions of research for the study of diseases, their prevention, causation and remedy
- To finance enquiries and researches for the furtherance of the objectives of the Council
- To exchange information with other institutions, associations and societies interested in the objectives similar to those of the Council, especially in the observation and study of diseases in the East in general, and in India in particular
- To prepare, print, publish and exhibit any papers, posters, pamphlets, periodicals and books for furtherance of the objectives of the Council and to contribute to such literature. …"

Objective Type Questions

Serial Number	Question	Module Number
1	Full form of TKDL is ______________________________	5
2	TKDL is an initiative of ______________ and ______________________	5
3	In TKDL, traditional knowledge from the existing literature existing in local languages such as Sanskrit, Urdu, Arabic, Persian and Tamil is converted into digitized format, and is available in five international languages including English, German, Spanish, French and __________	5
4	Full form of TKRC is ________________	5
5	In 1995, two expatriate Indians at the University of Mississippi Medical Centre (Suman K. Das and Hari Har P. Cohly) were granted a US patent (no.5, 401,504) on use of ____________ in ________________.	5
6	In February, 2023 TKDL Access Agreement with Eurasian Patent Office. (True/False)	5
7	The Ministry of AYUSH was established on 9th November 2014 to promote the optimal development and dissemination of AYUSH systems of health care. (True/False)	5
8	Full form of CCRYN is ______________________________.	5

Serial Number	Question	Module Number
9	____ _______in relation to goods, means an indication which identifies such goods as agricultural goods, natural goods or manufactured goods as originating, or manufactured in the territory of a country, or a region or locality in that territory, where a given quality, reputation or other characteristic of such goods is essentially attributable to its geographical origin and in case where such goods are manufactured goods one of the activities of either the production or of processing or preparation of the goods concerned takes place in such territory, region or locality, as the case may be.	5
10	Full form of TRIPS is	4
11	The word "Yoga" is derived from the Sanskrit root yuj which means ___________	2
12	Asthanga (8 limbs) yoga denotes yama (abstinences), niyama (observances), asana (yoga postures), pranayama (breath control), pratyahara (withdrawal of the senses), dharana (concentration), dhyana (meditation) and ____ a. samadhi (absorption) b . mukti (liberation) c. tyaga (renunciation)	2
13	Rule 134 of Drug and Cosmetics rule 1945 defines schedule T (True/False)	4
14	A ___________________________________in the context of medicinal plants is a cultivation programme designed to ensure optimal yield in terms of both quality and quantity of any crop intended for health purposes.	4
15	_______________________is the science and activities relating to the detection, assessment, understanding and prevention of adverse effects or any other possible drug-related problems.	4
16	Decoction of Herbs are used in Aristha formulation. (True/false)	2

Serial Number	Question	Module Number
17	Which herbal therapy acts on the odorant receptors (ORs), which are individually expressed at the ciliary surface of olfactory sensory neurons (OSNs) located in the olfactory epithelium (OE)?	2
18	Benedict Lust is Known as the father of modern-day________________________.	2
19	In India, revival of Naturopathy took place with the translation of Germany's Louis Kuhne's book ''New Science of Healing''. The translation was done in the Telugu language by Shri D. Venkat Chelapati Sharma in 1894. Afterward, it was translated into Hindi and Urdu languages in 1904 by Shri Shroti Kishan Swaroop. (True/false)	2
20	____________ diet focuses on cleaning the body and thus, elements of food that a. Eliminative b. soothing c. constructive	2
21	Calorie restriction (CR) or intermittent fasting regimes profoundly affect both gross and cellular physiology. (False/true)	2
22	Acupressure works on the specific reflex points located along the energy lines that run through the body (called meridians). (true/false)	2
23	According to Traditional Chinese medicine, human body is composed of ______________ meridian lines a.12 b.13 c.14 d.15	2
24	As per Traditional Chinese medicine, "health" is a balance of yang and__________	2
25	*Woodfordia fruticosa* is the source of __________________ in aristha preparation.	3
26	Sodhana and Marana are the purification steps associated with which Formulation? a) Asava b) Aristha c) Bhasma d) Churna	

Serial Number	Question	Module Number
27	Kasaya refers ________________ in Ayurveda.	3
28	In aristha formulation , drugs specified in the formula in solution undergoes a process of fermentation which is happened due to presence of adhered yeasts present on the surface of ______________________	
29	Yasad Bhasma denotes chemically ______________ .	3
30	Huboob And Aqras are ________________ formulation	3
31	Mention the condition of accelerated stability study.	3
32	In Ayurvedic medicine 'Kasaya' means a) Decoction b) Maceration c) Formulation d) Soxhlation	3
33	Which of the following preparation has self-generated alcohol? a) Aristha b) Kasaya c) Churna d) Gutika	3
34	_______ is a semi-solid preparation of drugs, prepared with addition of jaggery, sugar or sugar-candy and boiled with prescribed drug juice or decoction. a) Lehya b) Churna c) Gutika d) Utensils	3
35	Small cakes (chakrikas) are made to prepare _____	3

36	Burning pit of Bhasma is known as__________	3
37	Ilaj-bil-Yad is Surgery . True/False	1
38	Ayurveda is type ________herbal medicine as per WHO . a.2 b. 4 c. 1 d. 3	1
39	Rene-Maurice Gattefosse, a French cosmetic chemist coined the term__________	2
40	Which of the following is a fundamental principle of Naturopathy? a) Disease is caused by external factors such as bacteria or viruses b) The body has an inherent ability to heal itself c) drugs are the most effective treatment for all diseases d) Surgery is the preferred treatment for most diseases	2
41	Which of the following natural therapies is commonly used in Naturopathy? a) Acupuncture b) Chemotherapy c) Radiation therapy d) Surgery	2
42	________ is considered as father of Yoga	2
43	According to Yoga, Pingala is example of _______	2
44	In Ayurveda, which of the following is not a component of Tridosha ? a) Vata b) Pitta c) Purisha d) Kapha	
45	Salakya chikitsa means____ a) ENT b) Gynecology c) Pediatrics d) Surgery	2

Serial Number	Question	Module Number
46	The Ministry of AYUSH was formed on 9th November,_____ a) 2014 b) 2017 c) 2019 d) 2020	5
47	According to Geographical Indications Of Goods (Registration and Protection) Rules, 2002, coffee, tea, cocoa belongs to class ______ product.	5
48	Hakim Ajmal Khan is the father figure of which ISM?	1
49	Ilaj-bil-Dava is Surgery. True/False	1
50	What are 4 humours in Unani?	1
51	Full form of CCRH __________	5
52	Kayachikitsa means in Ayurveda	1
53	Homeopathy Central Council Act, was passed in ___________	5
54	Give one example of sarcodes.	1
55	The Raja Yoga is alternatively known as _____ yoga a) Saranga b) Astanga c) Panchanga d) Ida	2
56	What is Gunapadam in Siddha medicine? a) A classification system for raw drugs b) A purification process for metals c) A dosage form for herbal medicines d) A diagnostic tool for determining Mizaj	3

Serial Number	Question	Module Number
57	Which system of medicine follows the principle of "Like cures Like"? a) Ayurveda b) Siddha c) Unani d) Homoeopathy	1
58	Which system of medicine believes in the concept of Tri-dosha? a) Ayurveda b) Siddha c) Unani d) Homoeopathy	1
59	What are the different streams of Yoga? a) Hatha, Raja, Karma, Bhakti, Jnana, and Tantra b) Power, Vinyasa, Bikram, Iyengar, and Kundalini c) Tai Chi, Qi Gong, and Pilates d) None of the above	1
60	What is Pranayama in Yoga? a) Breathing exercises that help to regulate the flow of vital energy in the body b) Physical postures that help to stretch and strengthen the body c) Meditation techniques d) Chanting mantras	2
61	What are carrier oils used for in Aromatherapy? a) to dilute essential oils for topical use b) to enhance the fragrance of essential oils c) to promote relaxation and reduce stress d) none of the above	2

Serial Number	Question	Module Number
62	What are the parameters that are evaluated in Stability Studies? a) physical, chemical, and microbiological parameters b) efficacy and safety c) pharmacological properties d) none of the above	2
63	Which of the following is a liquid dosage form? a) Aristha b) Churna c) Gutika d) Bhasma	2
64	What is CCRS? a) Central Council for Research in Ayurvedic Sciences b) Central Council for Research in Siddha c) Central Council for Research in Homoeopathy d) None of the above	5
65	Which of the following is the process of making Asava and Arishta? a. Fermentation b. distillation c. evaporation	2
66	Give one example of imponderabilia_________	3
67	Which of the following is an example of Asana? a) Saranga b) Astanga c) Panchanga d) Bajrasana	2
68	Under IMCC Act, _______________ [THE INDIAN MEDICINE CENTRAL COUNCIL ACT]registered Vaidyas, Siddhas and Hakeems who prepare medicines on their own to dispense to their patients and not selling such drugs in the market are exempted from the purview of G.M.P. a. 1970 b.1945 c. 1980 d.1999	4

Serial Number	Question	Module Number
69	Minimum manufacturing space required for Anjana/Pisti is ___________ sq. ft.	4
70	Minimum manufacturing space required for Habb (Pills) and tablets.is ___________ sq. ft.	4
71	__________________________is a wide-ranging concept covering all matters that individually or collectively influence the quality of a product. It is the totality of the arrangements made with the object of ensuring that pharmaceutical products are of the quality required for their intended use. Quality assurance therefore incorporates GMP and other factors, including those outside the scope of this guide such as product design and development	4
72	Full form of NMPB_______________	4
73	____________________is a quality system concerned with the organisational process and the conditions under which non-clinical health and environmental safety studies are planned, performed, monitored, recorded, archived and reported.	4
74	Pharmacovigilance is the science and activities relating to the detection, assessment, understanding and prevention of _____________or any other possible drug-related problems.	4
75	_____________ is an ancient methodology of treatment that uses the visible spectrum of electromagnetic radiation to cure diseases.	2

ANSWERS

Question	Answer	Question	Answer
1	Traditional Knowledge Digital Library	22	True
2	Council of Scientific and Industrial and Ministry of Ayush	23	a
3	Japanese	24	Yin
4	Traditional Knowledge Resource Classification	25	Yeast for fermentation
5	Turmeric, wound healing	26	c
6	True	27	Decoction
7	True	28	Dhataki Pushpa
8	Central Council for Research in Yoga & Naturopathy	29	Zinc oxide
9	Geographical Indication	30	Unani
10	Trade-Related Aspects of Intellectual Property Rights	31	40°C/75% RH for the duration of the six-month accelerated study
11	To join	32	a
12	a	33	a
13	False	34	a
14	Good Agricultural Practice	35	Bhasma
15	Pharmacovigilance	36	Puta
16	True	37	True
17	Aromatherapy	38	a
18	Aromatherapy	39	Aromatherapy
19	True	40	b
20	a	41	a
21	True	42	Maharshi Patanjali

Question	Answer	Question	Answer
43	Nadi	61	a
44	c	62	a
45	a	63	a
46	a	64	b
47	30	65	a
48	Unani	66	X ray
49	False	67	d
50	dam (blood), balgham (phlegm), safra (yellow bile), and sawda (black bile)	68	a
51	Central Council for Research in Homoeopathy	69	100
52	General Medicine	70	100
53	19th December, 1973	71	Quality assurance
54	Thyroidinum	72	National Medicinal Plant board
55	b	73	GLP
56	a	74	Adverse effect
57	d	75	Chromotherapy
58	a		
59	a		
60	a		

SHORT ANSWER TYPE QUESTIONS

Serial Number	Question	Module Number
1	Mention the characteristic and standardization parameters for Bhasma.	3
2	How are asava and aristha standardized?	3
3	What is aromatherapy? Explain basic principle of aromatherapy	2

Serial Number	Question	Module Number
4	Explain the different types of yoga practices for health and wellness.	2
5	What are the philosophies associated with naturopathy. Mention 7 principles of naturopathy.	2
6	What are the different sources of medicine in homoeopathy. Give examples. What is mother tincture?	2
7	What is traditional medicine? Classify Herbal Medicine according to WHO with example.	1
8	Define Category 1 herbal medicines. Give example.	1
9	What is Herbal medicine in systems?	1
10	Explain the basic principles of Ayurveda	1
11	Explain Rasa, Guna, Virya, Vipaka & Prabhava in the context of Ayurveda.	1
12	What is Panchakarma?	1
13	List the different treatments in Ayurveda	1
14	Explain the steps of Bhasma preparation.	3
15	Mention the ideal characteristics of Bhasma.	3
16	Give 2 examples of Bhasma.	3
17	Explain the method of preparation of Lehya.	3
18	Define Siddha system of medicine. How it was evolved?	1
19	Explain Hippocrates 4 humour concept.	1
20	What is Acupuncture?	2
21	Explain the basic concept of Acupuncture.	2
22	Explain the rasapanchaka (panchasheel) in Ayurveda	1
23	What is Kayachikitsa ?	1
24	Explain different prevention, diagnosis and treatment in Unani system of medicine.	1

Serial Number	Question	Module Number
25	What is Gutika?	3
26	Explain the preparation, characteristic and storage of Gutika formulation.	3
27	Explain chromo therapy and fasting therapy.	2
28	What is Acupressure? Explain the basic concept of Acupressure.	3
29	Define the term naturopathy. Who is regarded as father of modern naturopathy? How naturopathy become as Indian system of medicine?	2
30	What is the safety concern associated with aromatherapy?	2
31	What are the standardization parameters for lehya, avaleha and Churna formulation?	3

LONG ANSWER TYPE QUESTIONS

Serial Number	Question	Module Number
1	Define Yoga. Explain the salient features of Yoga. List the types of yoga. Explain principle of Raja yoga and Japa yoga.	2
2	Define naturopathy. List the salient features of naturopathy. Explain the methodology, benefits and application of magnet Therapy.	2
3	What is Panchamahavutasiddhanta? Explain the panchakarma process in Ayurveda. Explain the Gunapadam Marunthiyal. List some Siddha formulations.	1
4	Mention the major Challenges in monitoring the safety of herbal medicines Regulation. Explain the benefits of GAP. Explain health and hygiene, documentation and records as per the schedule T.	4
5	What is Unani System of Medicine? Explain the Al -Umoor -Al Tabiyah of Unani Medicine. List some Unani formulation. Explain Law of proving and principle of minima.	1

Serial Number	Question	Module Number
6	What is AYUSH? Define Homoeopathy. How Homoeopathy became an integral part of the Indian Health System? Explain principle of individualization and Principle of similia in Homoeopathy.	1
7	Define Sarcodes, nosodes and imponderabilia with examples How are Homoeopathic medicines standardized? Explain the different categories of raw material standardization procedure in Homoeopathy.	3
8	What is Schedule T? List the major functions of Schedule T. Explain the major requirement of factory premises according to schedule T. List the recommended machinery, equipment and minimum manufacturing premises required for the manufacture of various categories of ayurvedic formulation as per the schedule T.	4
9	What is TKDL? Explain the major steps of GAP. Define GI. Explain different steps of GI registration process in India.	5
10	Compare Aristha and Asava. Mention the steps of Aristha Preparation schematically. What precautions to be taken in Asava preparation. List the essential properties of Asava and Aristha.	3
11	Explain the Marana and Jarana process in Bhasma formulation. List the characteristic features of Bhasma formulation. Explain General method of preparation of churna formulation.	3

Serial Number	Question	Module Number
12	Define aromatherapy. Explain the basic MOA of Aromatherapy. List the different essential oils used in Aromatherapy with their pharmacological and other benefits.	2
13	What is mud therapy? Why monitoring of safety of Herbal Medicine is challenging? Who are the major sources of report on adverse effects of Herbal Medicine? How adverse event of herbal drug case reports are assessed?	2, 3
14	Define Pharmacovigilance. Why Pharmacovigilance is essential in Herbal Medicine How data collection is done Pharmacovigilance centre? List some toxicity and adverse health effects of some common herbal medicine	4
15	Explain the significance of TKDL. "Traditional Knowledge Digital Library - A tool for prevention of misappropriations of traditional knowledge" .....Justify it List and explain some examples of Biopiracy. Explain the steps and requirement for Preparation of documents for new drug application and export registration.	5

Bibliography

1. Ali B, Al-Wabel NA, Shams S, Ahamad A, Khan SA, Anwar F. Essential oils used in aromatherapy: A systemic review. Asian Pacific Journal of Tropical Biomedicine. 2015;5(8):601–11.
2. Anonymous. Guidelines Series-I General Guidelines for Drug Development of Ayurvedic Formulations Central Council for Research in Ayurvedic Sciences Ministry of AYUSH, Government of India New Delhi [Internet]. [cited 2024 Mar 20]. Available from: http://www.ccras.nic.in/sites/default/files/viewpdf/Publication/CCRAS_Guideline%20of%20Drug%20Development.pdf
3. Anonymous. Good Agricultural Practices for Medicinal Plants. New Delhi: National Medicinal Plant Board Department of AYUSH Ministry of Health and Family Welfare, Government of India; 2009.
4. Anonymous. Unani System of Medicine: The Science of Health and Healing. New Delhi: Department of AYUSH, Ministry of Health and Family Welfare, Govt. of India; 2013.
5. Anonymous. Geographical indications: An Introduction. WIPO; 2013.
6. Anonymous. National Formulary of Unani Medicine. Government of India Ministry of Health & Family Welfare Department of Ayurveda, Yoga & Naturopathy, Unani, Siddha and Homoeopathy (Ayush) New Delhi; 2007.
7. Anonymous. The ayurvedic pharmacopoeia of India. Part 2, Formulations. New Delhi: Govt. Of India, Ministry of Health and Family Welfare, Dept. Of Ayurveda, Yoga & Naturopathy, Unani, Siddha, And Homoeopathy; 2007.
8. Anonymous. The Ayurvedic Formulary of India. [New Delhi]: Government of India, Ministry of Health and Family Planning, Department of Health; 1978.
9. Anonymous. GOVERNMENT OF INDIA MINISTRY OF HEALTH AND FAMILY WELFARE (Department of Health) THE DRUGS AND COSMETICS ACT AND RULES THE DRUGS AND COSMETICS

ACT, 1940 (23 OF 1940) THE DRUGS AND COSMETICS RULES, 1945 [Internet]. 2016 [cited 2024 Mar 22]. Available from: https://cdsco.gov.in/opencms/export/sites/CDSCO_WEB/Pdf-documents/acts_rules/2016DrugsandCosmeticsAct1940Rules1945.pdf

10. Anonymous. 21 June International Day of Yoga Common Yoga Protocol [Internet]. New Delhi: Director Morarji Desai National Institute of Yoga, Ministry of AYUSH, Govt. of India; [cited 2024 Mar 20]. Available from: https://yoga.ayush.gov.in/public/assets/front/pdf/CYPEnglishLeaflet.pdf

11. Anonymous. The ayurvedic pharmacopoeia of India. Part 1. New Delhi: Government of India, Ministry of Health and Family Welfare, Dept. Of Ism & H; 1999.

12. Anonymous. Key technical issues of herbal medicines with reference to interaction with other medicines. World Health Organization; 2021.

13. Anonymous. Research in Siddha System of Medicine the Science of Holistic Health [Internet]. Central council for Research in siddha ministry of Ayush, Government of India; [cited 2024 Mar 20]. Available from: https://siddhacouncil.com/downloads/ccrs-ebook.pdf

14. AYUSH [Internet]. ayush.gov.in. [cited 2024 Mar 22]. Available from: https://ayush.gov.in/index.html#

15. Azeemi STY, Raza M. A Critical Analysis of Chromotherapy and Its Scientific Evolution. Evidence-Based Complementary and Alternative Medicine. 2005;2(4):481–8.

16. CSIR celebrates 20 years of India's Traditional Knowledge Digital Library, the first of its kind globally [Internet]. pib.gov.in. 2021 [cited 2024 Mar 20]. Available from:

    https://pib.gov.in/PressReleasePage.aspx?PRID=1693143

17. CCRAS | Ministry of AYUSH (Govt. of India) | [Internet]. www.ccras.nic.in. [cited 2024 Mar 22]. Available from: http://www.ccras.nic.in/

18. Central Council for Research in Siddha [Internet]. https://siddhacouncil.com. [cited 2024 Mar 22]. Available from: https://siddhacouncil.com/ccrs/home/

19. Connolly P. A Student's Guide to the History and Philosophy of Yoga (Revised Edition). Equinox Publishing Ltd.; 2014.

20. CCRH [Internet]. www.ccrhindia.nic.in. [cited 2024 Mar 22]. Available from: https://www.ccrhindia.nic.in/

21. Farrar AJ, Farrar FC. Clinical Aromatherapy. Nursing Clinics of North America. 2020;55(4):489–504.

22. Fredriksson M. India's Traditional Knowledge Digital Library and the Politics of Patent Classifications. Law Crit. 2021;34(1):1–19.

23. Fung TKH, Lau BWM, Ngai SPC, Tsang HWH. Therapeutic Effect and Mechanisms of Essential Oils in Mood Disorders: Interaction between the Nervous and Respiratory Systems. Int J Mol Sci. 2021;22(9).

24. Good Laboratory Practice (GLP) - OECD [Internet]. www.oecd.org. [cited 2024 Mar 22]. Available from: https://www.oecd.org/chemicalsafety/testing/good-laboratory-practiceglp.htm#:~:text=The%20OECD%20Principles%20of%20Good

25. Government of India Ministry of Ayurveda, Yoga & Naturopathy, Unani, Siddha and Homoeopathy (Ayush) Lok Sabha Starred Question No.256 To Be Answered On 12 Th March, 2021 Quality of Ayurvedic Medicines †*256. Shri Ajay Bhatt [Internet]. [cited 2024 Mar 22]. Available from: https://sansad.in/getFile/loksabhaquestions/annex/175/AS256.pdf?source=pqals

26. Gunapadam [Internet]. National Institute of Siddha. 2021 [cited 2024 Mar 22]. Available from: https://nischennai.org/main/gunapadam/

27. Home- Central Council for Research in Unani Medicine Ministry of AYUSH, Government of India [Internet]. ccrum.res.in. [cited 2024 Mar 22]. Available from: https://ccrum.res.in/

28. Krishnananda S. A Textbook of Yoga. Rishikesh: Sivananda Ashram; 1991.

29. Kayne SB. Homoeopathic Pharmacy: Theory and Practice. Philadelphia: Elsevier's Health Sciences; 2006.

30. Lloyd I, Steel A, Wardle J, editors. Naturopathy Practice, Effectiveness, Economics & Safety. Toronto: World Naturopathic Federation; 2021.

31. Major Milestones [Internet]. www.tkdl.res.in. [cited 2024 Mar 20]. Available from: https://www.tkdl.res.in/tkdl/langdefault/common/milestones.asp?GL=Eng

32. Mehta P, Dhapte V, Kadam S, Dhapte V. Contemporary acupressure therapy: Adroit cure for painless recovery of therapeutic ailments. Journal of Traditional and Complementary Medicine. 2017;7(2):251–63.

33. MOU signed between Ministry of AYUSH and Council of Scientific and Industrial Research [Internet]. pib.gov.in. 2019 [cited 2024 Mar 22]. Available from: https://pib.gov.in/PressReleasePage.aspx?PRID=1570951

34. Production [Internet]. www.who.int. [cited 2024 Mar 22]. Available from: https://www.who.int/teams/health-product-and-policy-standards/standards-and-specifications/norms-and-standards-for-pharmaceuticals/guidelines/production#:~:text=WHO%20good%20manufacturing%20practices

35. Pathak N, Agarwal S. AYUSH Exports: Regulatory Opportunities and Challenges in Key Markets. New Delhi: RIS; 2023.

36. Samal J. Role of AYUSH workforce, therapeutics, and principles in health care delivery with special reference to National Rural Health Mission. Ayu. 2015;36(1):5.

37. State Wise Registration Details Of G.I Applications. [cited 2024 Mar 20]; Available from:https://ipindia.gov.in/writereaddata/Portal/Images/pdf/State_wise_Registered_Geographical_Indications.pdf

38. Traditional Knowledge Resource Classification (TKRC) [Internet]. www.tkdl.res.in. [cited 2024 Mar 20]. Available from: https://www.tkdl.res.in/tkdl/langdefault/common/TKRC.asp?GL=Eng

39. World Health Organization. Safety issues in the preparation of homeopathic medicines. Geneva: World Health Organization; 2009.

40. World Health Organization. WHO guidelines on safety monitoring of herbal medicines in pharmacovigilance systems. Geneva: World Health Organization; 2004.

41. World Health Organization. Quality assurance of pharmaceuticals. Vol. 2 : a compendium of guidelines and related materials : Good manufacturing practices and inspection. Geneva: World Health Organization; 2007.

42. Zhang Y, Pan Y, Matsunami H, Zhuang H. Live-cell Measurement of Odorant Receptor Activation Using a Real-time cAMP Assay. J Vis Exp. 2017;128(e55831).

Index

www.ingramcontent.com/pod-product-compliance
Lightning Source LLC
Chambersburg PA
CBHW071223230926
51849CB00001B/19
* 9 7 8 9 3 4 8 7 3 4 8 7 7 *